Many Happy Returns,
17 march 1989
Steve & Norma.

EDINBURGH

EDINBURGH

*edited by Owen Dudley Edwards
and Graham Richardson*

CANONGATE
Edinburgh
1983

First published in 1983
by Canongate Publishing Ltd
17 Jeffrey Street, Edinburgh

© Preface, Notes, Selection and Translation, Owen Dudley Edwards and
Graham Richardson

ISBN 86241 049 5

For permission to reprint the poems, stories, extracts and letters,
acknowledgement is made to the following: for the letter from the late J. M.
Barrie from *I Can Remember Robert Louis Stevenson*, to Samuel French and the
estate of J. M. Barrie; for the extract from *Two Worlds* by David Daiches, to
David Higham Associates Ltd.; for the extract from *The Prime of Miss Jean Brodie*
by Muriel Spark, to David Higham Associates Ltd.; for *Talking with Five
Thousand People in Edinburgh* by the late Hugh MacDiarmid from *Poetry Scotland
No. 2*, to Michael Grieve; for *Poem to Eimhir* from *Dàin do Eimhir* by Sorley
Maclean, to William Maclellan and the author; for *King and Queen o the Fowr
Airts* by the late Sydney Goodsir Smith from *So Late into the Night*, to Mrs
Goodsir Smith; for *A Trifle Unnecessary* by the late Moray McLaren from *A
Dinner with the Dead*, to his estate; for a press conference with the late Sir
Thomas Beecham reported in the *Scotsman*, 1949, to the *Scotsman*; for *Edinburgh
Spring* by Norman MacCaig from *Riding Lights*, to the Hogarth Press Ltd.; for an
article in the *New Statesman*, 1967, by Tom Nairn, to the author; for *59x: A True
Tale* by Robert Nye, first published in the *Scotsman*, 1974, to the author; for
Betrayal in Morninside by Donald Campbell from *Akros, Poems 1971*, to the
author. Apologies are tendered in advance to any copyright holders who could
not be traced.

Typeset in 12pt Bembo by Witwell Ltd., Liverpool
Printed by Redwood Burn Ltd., Trowbridge
Bound by Butler & Tanner Ltd., London and Frome

Contents

Where a piece selected enjoys no universally recognised title, or has been excerpted from a longer work, we have taken the liberty of attempting to provide one. Such titles are marked with an asterisk.

Preface

THERE IS LITTLE POINT in defining Edinburgh, since we have a group of persons hereafter presented who are much better (or, as in the case of the great McGonagall, worse) qualified to do it. In any case it is hardly a matter of definition, but one of perspective and impression. Edinburgh is particularly distinguished for the entirely new landscapes thrown before the walker at every turn of the corner. One of the editors sees from his doorstep a perfect fall of classical houses towards the sea, the other sees from his kitchen window a mingling of mountain, stream and golf-course. What we have sought to do here is to give that sense in which everyone's Edinburgh has involved the turning of a different corner, the excitement of a new discovery.

Certainly, Edinburgh is typical of much of the rest of humanity, notably in the failure of its successive rulers to make the most of the environment or of the cultural possibilities: and nostalgists who despair of the present may find comfort in Ruskin and Hugh MacDiarmid fighting earlier phases of the same wars. It is unusual in its problem of definition. It was comparatively late in becoming a capital. St Andrews, Perth, and Dunfermline all have prior claims in the ecclesiastical and constitutional history of Scotland, and Glasgow, the late arrival, towered into industrial and merchant predominance over it from the late eighteenth and nineteenth centuries. It lacks a hinterland comparable to Aberdeen, whose university serves a geographical area from the Shetlands to Fife and westward to the farthest Hebrides.

But it possesses its own excitement in having been so long the focal point for competing cultures, sometimes with very striking consequences such as the great Scottish Enlightenment exhibited. The evidence for this complex of influences vanishes into antiquity. It may seem unjust to the memory of John Major that he is represented here by two pieces of mythology from the earliest parts of his great history, a work far in advance of his time particularly in the use of comparative technique, but at once he establishes the symbol of the multiplicity of traditions and the confluence of divergent cultures. Edinburgh's international heritage may even be older than itself, so to speak.

We necessarily had to choose our perspectives in presenting it in somewhat arbitrary fashion. Hector Boece's account of the stag and the king is supported by an austere charter, but, save to the eye of love, fascination tends to flag after forty or fifty of these, and hence we have left it to Robert the Bruce (or rather his more civil servants) to do this work. Froissart brings to life rapidly the sense of Edinburgh as a developing point of crisis in the rivalries between England, France, Scotland and elsewhere. It was then still a capital only by being the royal residence most of the time. In fact its importance increased as the English threat mounted, and it bore much of the brunt of military attack. Of this we have said relatively little, although glancing reference to the heritage of Edinburgh's southern invaders finds mention as late as Cobbett. But in the early eighteenth century its invaders were from the north, in the army of the dispossessed Jacobites, and the cultural life of the city was torn between old and new, painfully and productively. In this volume the child's rhyme about the spirit-vision of Jacobitism – 'As I went by the Luckenbooths' – captures the charm but increasing irrelevance and even blasphemy of the Jacobite temptation. Scott's *Waverley* makes great literature of the question, for Edinburgh and for Scotland as a whole; so, too, does Stevenson's *Kidnapped*: perhaps the truest symbolic moment in literature about Edinburgh is the very end of that book, as David Balfour turns with a grief he cannot fully comprehend from the departing Allan Breck (a grief much more for Allan's culture than for Allan himself, whom he expects shortly to meet again), and finds himself at the doorway of the British Linen Bank.

Many Edinburgh intellectuals such as the historian William Robertson, the novelist Compton Mackenzie and the children's writer R.M. Ballantyne, seemed to flourish best on subjects other than their city. Others, such as Bruce Marshall, are not easily represented by extracts, although in his case there are splendid simple sentences such as his tribute to the financial world of the city as mentioned in the Paris-based novel *The Bank Audit*: 'chartered accountants in Edinburgh, Sir Eric sometimes thought, must be like pretty prostitutes in Paris: a good one waiting under every other lamp-post.' The best work is often constructed so as to defy satisfactory selection. This can be true even of a book of loosely connected short stories, such as George MacDonald Fraser's *The General Danced at Dawn*, or a brilliantly creative work of literary criticism such as G.K. Chesterton's *Robert Louis Stevenson*, both of which include splendid but, we felt, inextricable, Edinburgh passages.

Time dictates some forms of selection. The recent past in

Edinburgh, and its peculiar role in the rise of Scottish nationalism, needs a little time for its classical documents to be established: in voting terms the city remained obdurately Unionist, in speech and journalism it swung powerfully towards devolution. The extracts here which do represent this phenomenon are, interestingly, strongly critical of Edinburgh: Hugh MacDiarmid's poem, Tom Nairn's critique of the Festival. Significantly, both of them saw changes so much so that Nairn would not wish his article included without a word as to the revolutionary alteration in the relationship of Edinburgh culture to the people, achieved since the 'sixties by the Festival Fringe. On the 'official' Festival itself, John Drummond's Directorship (1979–83) firmly followed MacDiarmid's demand and brought the people and the Festival into more and more significant interaction. The growth of Scottish theatre in the 1970s and the part Edinburgh did – and didn't – play in it will have to await some little time to gain its anthologist.

Indeed the best pieces to be written on such events may lie far in the future. In thinking of the famous events of Edinburgh history we have sometimes chosen writings close in time to the events, such as Sinclair on the '15 or Elcho on the '45, prejudiced participants, or a figure more remote in distance but memorable in genius and alert in sympathy, such as Clarendon on Montrose. But over three centuries lie between Arthur Conan Doyle and the first subject printed from him here. Sometimes the hour did not produce the man, and sometimes the man was inappropriate. We found in the *Book of the Old Edinburgh Club* (volume 27) a diary by a student named Kincaid on Edinburgh in 1688–89, and here, it seemed, we could gain precisely the unusual and striking perspective we sought on so major an event in the city's history. Certainly young Kincaid was needing a little diversion such as the Glorious Revolution. His days seemed to be passed in getting up at five in the morning (in the depressingly exemplary fashion of students in those days) and thinking (rather than reading) about 'chymie', but having little to fill his pages save noting what he was supposedly studying or recording his sister's epileptic fits. Unfortunately when the Glorious Revolution arrived, it found itself crowded into backstage: he had discovered 'the glove', and began to fill pages and pages of his journal discussing the best form of stance, the problems of pressing, and all the rest of that arcane religion so dear to its votaries and to readers of P.G. Wodehouse. Wodehouse, in fact, would have been delighted with Kincaid: devotion to 'the glove' and oblivion to the rise and fall of kingships accords perfectly with his concept of the stuff of which the Scot are truly made. It is moving to imagine Kincaid wondering if the Union would result in better supplies of golf-balls, and fearing the tumults of the '15 might put him off his game, and, had he survived so long, being exceptionally irritated during the Porteous Riot when the noise of the cheers at the hanging of the City Guard captain caused him to sink a putt into the rough while attempting a match by moonlight.

We would, certainly, have liked to put in something on the Porteous Riot, when the mob so strikingly avenged the loss of its members by Porteous's orders to his men to fire, a riot the more interesting because mob action only took place after sentence of death on Porteous had been pronounced and execution then deferred and likely to be quashed. And the prime literary account is that in the opening chapters of Scott's *The Heart of Midlothian*. But three of its long chapters have to be included, and it seems preferable to send readers to the work, rather than allow it to swamp the rest of the cast here. Andrew Lang's account of the strange case of Captain Green takes a problem less well known and, if it deals with it less artistically, it offers a touch of mystery as well as piracy, the economic warfare leading to the Union and the avarice and ruthlessness of the relations of the Scottish as well as the English capital in its dealing with the wider world. On the other hand, we firmly rejected any question of certain other writers and pieces: Christopher North, alias Professor John Wilson, we decided on reading and reflection to be a sadistic and poisonous old fraud, unfit for the company of our contributors, including McGonagall. As opposed to this, Fred Urquhart's 'The Poor Sisters' we excluded because it was rather too good: it is a brilliant and savage short story which would be violently distasteful to many readers of this anthology. We approved of the sentiments of Dunbar's attack on the city merchants, of course, but it seemed somewhat depressingly repetitious (probably arising from its roots in some form of curse). We were vastly entertained at Oliver Goldsmith's laying down the law on the comparative quality of university education in Edinburgh as opposed to the rest of the world, which for sheer impudence from one of the worst students ever to have graced the Old College deserves its own prize; but in fact the passage is mostly padding, hack-work, and only inferentially relevant to Edinburgh. Benjamin Rush has had to do duty for a vast congerie of foreign students who had delighted in, or been infuriated by, the city, whether in their attendance at its University or at its Fringe: the list has stretched from Oliver Wendell Holmes, Senior, to Dr Julius Nyerere, and probably a very fine anthology on the wider world's view of Edinburgh could be achieved on its own. Alas, chauvanistic governmental sanctions against foreign students are likely to reduce such sources of new life-blood to Edinburgh to a thinner and thinner stream.

As to the visitors from England, we have chosen them very much on their interest. It is pleasant but not enthralling to notice that Charlotte Brontë found Edinburgh more agreeable than London, but neither was of any consequence in her life in comparison to Yorkshire. It is interesting to know where Thackerey went when lecturing here, but, as it turns out, not what he said about it. On the other hand the fact that Tennyson and Wilde wrote a love poem and a love letter, respectively, while here, does seem worth recording: if the city saw the birth of two works of art, then they deserve remembering in the context of the city, even if both works are chiefly concerned to regret the writer's presence in the city. Edinburgh has often been at its most inspiring when it has most repelled: in which it is not alone.

Where a piece selected enjoys no universally recognised title, or has been excerpted from a longer work, we have taken the liberty of attempting to provide one that intimates the style and content of the piece to the reader. Such titles are denoted by an asterisk in the table of contents. As with the piece itself, the simplicity and clarity of the title of David Hume's *My Own Life* provided an ideal towards which we could only strive.

Similarly, the collection has been arranged chronologically, the dates assigned being those when the event in each case happened in Edinburgh. Occasionally this has been slightly varied: the main events in Stevenson's *The Bodysnatcher* supposedly take place just before the public discovery of the Burke and Hare murders, but we have put Scott's factual account before Stevenson's fiction in order to place the reader on a firm footing. Again, Fergusson's poem *Caller Oysters* was written before his salute to Dr. Johnson, but the latter follows naturally from Boswell and hence the Doctor comes before the Oysters. Some ascriptions of date have to be highly problematical. Dickens' *Story of the Bagman's Uncle*, for instance, is supposedly narrated to Mr Pickwick in the early 1830s. The Bagman himself is old, but his uncle as described in the story is spry enough, which implies a date about the time of the Bagman's own birth, when the uncle would have been in his prime, to wit about seventy years before. Transport from Edinburgh to London was still as practical by sea as by land at that time, and no fear of hostile craft is implied, so that it would be soon after 1763. The uncle later finds himself in an earlier time still, but that is not the key date; although in another story leaping time, Conan Doyle's *The Silver Mirror*, we have of course dated from the spectral incident as that is the Edinburgh event.

In our quest for material for inclusion and footnote information, as well as for assistance in allied problems of time arising from the book, we must express our gratitude to George Shepperson, Leila Dudley Edwards, Michael Grieve, Norman MacCaig, Roger Mullin, Rollo Clery-Fox, Michael Foot, B.C. Ransom, John MacInnes, Maurice Fleming, Colin Nicolson, Graham Sutton, Frank Bechhofer, Julian Russell, Ray Footman, Leslie Macfarlane, David Campbell, Alan Boyd, David Williamson, Conor Cruise O'Brien, Trevor Royle, Sorley Maclean, Ian Campbell, Rhodri Jeffreys-Jones, Geoffrey Carnall, R.L.C. Lorimer and K.A. Fowler. Donald Rutherford has been a most helpful and stimulating resource. Rosemary Gentleman, Colin Affleck, Roger Savage and Jamie Donald went to much trouble to place invaluable material in our possession, and some of the happiest choices are due to them. Jean Bechhofer placed her unrivalled knowledge of folk culture at our disposal, and to her we owe both the choice and textual provenance of our old songs. Kenneth Fielding drew on his mastery of Carlyle to supply us with the most appropriate items for inclusion, and we join the great forest of scholars who owe so much to his care and wisdom. Elizabeth Balbirnie Lee encouraged (and fed) us during the ordeal. The proofs were disposed of with the generous assistance of Leile, Sara and Michael Dudley Edwards. To Bonnie Dudley Edwards our obligations are irreparable if necessarily divergent. And Stephanie Wolfe Murray, our publisher, has been a fount of inspiration and haven of restoration from first to last: it is a delight to have worked under her banner. Librarians have always been essential allies in our work, especially the staffs of Edinburgh University Library, the National Library of Scotland, the Edinburgh Central Library, and the Erskine Medical Library. We are also indebted to the Students' Association of Edinburgh University and to Mrs Catherine Clephane.

Edinburgh, Winter-Spring 1983

ODE
GCR

for
George and Isabel

Robert Louis Stevenson
Introductory

From Edinburgh. Picturesque Notes *which originally appeared in 1878. Stevenson (1850–1894) had a highly-developed geographical rather than historical sense of the past. The tensions of his native Edinburgh erupt not only in his Scottish novels such as* Kidnapped *(1886),* Catriona *(1893) and* Weir of Hermiston *(uncompleted: 1896) but also though not explicitly in works set elsewhere, such as* Treasure Island *(1883) and* The Strange Case of Dr Jekyll and Mr Hyde *(1886). After journeys in Europe and North America he went to the South Seas for his rapidly declining health in 1888, and died there.*

THE ANCIENT AND FAMOUS metropolis of the North sits overlooking a windy estuary from the slope and summit of three hills. No situation could be more commanding for the head city of a kingdom; none better chosen for noble prospects. From her tall precipice and terraced gardens she looks far and wide on the sea and broad champaigns. To the east you may catch at sunset the spark of the May lighthouse, where the Firth expands into the German Ocean; and away to the west, over all the carse of Stirling and you can see the first snows upon Ben Ledi.

But Edinburgh pays cruelly for her high seat in one of the vilest climates under heaven. She is liable to be beaten upon by all the winds that blow, to be drenched with rain, to be buried in cold sea fogs out of the east, and powdered with the snow as it comes flying southward from the Highland hills. The weather is raw and boisterous in winter, shifty and ungenial in summer, and a downright meteorological purgatory in the spring. The delicate die early, and I, as a survivor, among bleak winds and plumping rain, have been sometimes tempted to envy them their fate. For all who love shelter and the blessings of the sun, who hate dark weather and perpetual tilting against squalls, there could scarcely be found a more unhomely and harassing place of residence. Many such aspire angrily after that Somewhere-else of the imagination, where all troubles are supposed to end. They lean over the great bridge which joins the New Town with the Old—that windiest spot, or high altar, in this northern temple of the winds—and watch the trains smoking out from under them and vanishing into the tunnel on a voyage to brighter skies. Happy the passengers who shake off the dust of Edinburgh, and have heard for the last time the cry of the east wind among her chimney-tops! And yet the place establishes an interest in people's hearts; go where they will they find no city of the same distinction; go where they will, they take a pride in their old home.

Venice, it has been said, differs from all other cities in the sentiment which she inspires. The rest may have admirers; she only, a famous fair one, counts lovers in her train. And indeed, even by her kindest friends, Edinburgh is not considered in a similar sense. These like her for many reasons, not any one of which is satisfactory in itself. They like her whimsically, if you will, and somewhat as a virtuoso dotes upon his cabinet. Her attraction is romantic in the narrowest meaning of the term. Beautiful as she is, she is not so much beautiful as interesting. She is pre-eminently Gothic, and all the more so since she has set herself off with some Greek airs, and erected classic temples on her crags. In a word, and above all, she is a curiosity. The Palace of Holyrood has been left aside in the growth of Edinburgh, and stands grey and silent in a workman's quarter and among breweries and gas-works. It is a house of many memories. Great people of yore, kings and queens, buffoons and grave ambassadors, played their stately farce for centuries in Holyrood. Wars have been plotted, dancing has lasted deep into the night, murder has been done in its chambers. There Prince Charlie held his phantom levées, and in a very gallant manner represented a fallen dynasty for some hours. Now, all these things of clay are mingled with the dust, the king's crown itself is shown for sixpence to the vulgar; but the stone palace has outlived these changes. For fifty weeks together, it is no more than a show for tourists and a museum of old furniture; but on the fifty-first, behold the palace reawakened and mimicking its past. The Lord Commissioner, a kind of stage sovereign, sits among stage courtiers; a coach and six and clattering escort come and go before the gate; at night, the windows are lighted up, and its near neighbours, the workmen, may dance in their own houses to the palace music. And in this the palace is typical. There is a spark among the embers; from time to time the old volcano smokes. Edinburgh has but partly abdicated, and still wears, in parody, her metropolitan trappings. Half a capital and half a country town, the whole city leads a double existence; it has long trances of the one and flashes of the other; like the king of the Black Isles, it is half alive and half a monumental marble. There are armed men and cannon in the citadel overhead; you may see the troops marshalled on the high parade; and at night after the early winter evenfall, and in the morning before the laggard winter dawn, the wind carries abroad over Edinburgh the

17

sound of drums and bugles. Grave judges sit bewigged in what was once the scene of imperial deliberations. Close by in the High Street perhaps the trumpets may sound about the stroke of noon; and you see a troop of citizens in tawdry masquerade; tabard above, heather-mixture trouser below, and the men themselves trudging in the mud among unsympathetic bystanders. The grooms of a well-appointed circus tread the streets with a better presence. And yet these are the Heralds and Pursuivants of Scotland, who are about to proclaim a new law of the United Kingdom before two score boys, and thieves, and hackney-coachmen. Meanwhile, every hour the bell of the University rings out over the hum of the streets, and every hour a double tide of students, coming and going, fills the deep archways. And lastly, one night in the spring-time—or say one morning rather, at the peep of day—late folk may hear the voice of many men singing a psalm in unison from a church on one side of the old High Street; and a little after, or perhaps a little before, the sound of many men singing a psalm in unison from another church on the opposite side of the way. There will be something in the words about the dew of Hermon, and how goodly it is to see brethren dwelling together in unity. And the late folk will tell themselves that all this singing denotes the conclusion of two yearly ecclesiastical parliaments—the parliaments of Churches which are brothers in many admirable virtues, but not specially like brothers in this particular of a tolerant and peaceful life.

Again, meditative people will find a charm in a certain consonancy between the aspect of the city and its odd and stirring history. Few places, if any, offer a more barbaric display of contrasts to the eye. In the very midst stands one of the most satisfactory crags in nature—a Bass Rock upon dry land, rooted in a garden, shaken by passing trains, carrying a crown of battlements and turrets, and describing its warlike shadow over the liveliest and brightest thoroughfare of the new town. From their smoky beehives, ten stories high, the unwashed look down upon the open squares and gardens of the wealthy; and gay people sunning themselves along Princes Street, with its mile of commercial palaces all beflagged upon some great occasion, see, across a gardened valley set with statues, where the washings of the old town flutter in the breeze at its high windows. And then, upon all sides, what a clashing of architecture! In this one valley, where the life of the town goes most busily forward, there may be seen, shown one above and behind another by the accidents of the ground, buildings in almost every style upon the globe. Egyptian and Greek temples, Venetian palaces and Gothic spires, are huddled one over another in a most admired disorder; while, above all, the brute mass of the Castle and the summit of Arthur's Seat look down upon these imitations with a becoming dignity, as the works of Nature may look down upon the monuments of Art. But Nature is a more indiscriminate patroness than we imagine, and in no way frightened of a strong effect. The birds roost as willingly among the Corinthian capitals as in the crannies of the crag; the same atmosphere and daylight clothe the eternal rock and yesterday's imitation portico; and as the soft northern sunshine throws out everything into a glorified distinctness—or easterly mists, coming up with the blue evening, fuse all these incongruous features into one, and the lamps begin to glitter along the street, and faint lights to burn in the high windows across the valley—the feeling grows upon you that this also is a piece of nature in the most intimate sense; that this profusion of eccentricities, this dream in masonry and living rock, is not a drop-scene in a theatre, but a city in the world of every-day reality, connected by railway and telegraph-wire with all the capitals of Europe, and inhabited by citizens of the familiar type, who keep ledgers, and attend church, and have sold their immortal portion to a daily paper. By all the canons of romance, the place demands to be half deserted and leaning towards decay; birds we might admit in profusion, the play of the sun and winds, and a few gypsies encamped in the chief thoroughfare; but these citizens, with their cabs and tramways, their trains and posters, are altogether out of key. Chartered tourists, they make free with historic localities, and rear their young among the most picturesque sites with a grand human indifference. To see them thronging by, in their neat clothes and conscious moral rectitude, and with a little air of possession that verges on the absurd, is not the least striking feature of the place.[1]

And the story of the town is as eccentric as its appearance. For centuries it was a capital thatched with heather, and more than once, in the evil days of English invasion, it has gone up in flame to heaven, a beacon to ships at sea. It was the jousting-ground of jealous nobles, not only on Greenside or by the King's Stables, where set tournaments were fought to the sound of trumpets and under the authority of the royal presence, but in every alley where there was room to cross swords, and in the main street, where popular tumult under the the Blue Blanket alternated with the brawls of outlandish clansmen and retainers. Down in the palace John Knox reproved his queen in the accents of modern democracy. In the town, in one of those little shops plastered like so many swallows' nests among the buttresses of the old Cathedral, that familiar autocrat, James VI., would gladly share a bottle of wine with George Heriot the goldsmith. Up on the Pentland Hills, that so quietly look down on the Castle with the city lying in waves around it, those mad and dismal fanatics, the Sweet Singers, haggard from long exposure on the moors, sat day and night with 'tearful psalms' to see Edinburgh consumed with fire from heaven, like another Sodom and Gomorrah. There, in the Grass-market, stiff-necked, covenanting heroes offered up the often un-necessary, but not less honourable, sacrifice of their lives, and bade eloquent farewell to sun, moon, and stars, and earthly friendships, or died silent to the roll of drums. Down by yon outlet rode Grahame of Claverhouse and his thirty dragoons, with the town beating to arms behind their horses' tails—a sorry handful thus riding for their lives, but with a man at the head who was to return in a different temper, make a dash that staggered Scotland to the heart, and die happily in the thick of fight. There Aikenhead was hanged for a piece of boyish incredulity; there, a few years afterwards, David Hume ruined Philo-sophy and Faith, an undisturbed and well-reputed citizen; and thither in yet a few years more, Burns came from the plough-tail, as to an academy of gilt unbelief and artificial letters. There, when the great exodus was made across the valley, and the New Town began to spread abroad its draughty parallelograms and rear its long frontage on the opposing hill, there was such a flitting, such a change of domicile and dweller, as was never excelled in the history of cities: the cobbler succeeded the earl; the beggar ensconced himself by the judge's chimney; what had been a palace was used as a pauper refuge; and great mansions were so parcelled out among the least and lowest in society, that the hearthstone of the old proprietor was thought large enough to be partitioned off into a bedroom by the new.

[1] These sentences have, I hear, given offence in my native town, and a proportionable pleasure to our rivals of Glasgow. I confess the news caused me both pain and merriment. May I remark, as a balm for wounded fellow-townsmen, that there is nothing deadly in my accusations? Small blame to them if they keep ledgers: 'tis an excellent business habit. Church-going is not, that ever I heard, a subject of reproach; decency of linen is a mark of prosperous affairs, and conscious moral rectitude one of the tokens of good living. It is not their fault if the city calls for something more specious by way of inhabitants. A man in a frock-coat looks out of place upon an Alp or Pyramid, although he has the virtues of a Peabody and the talents of a Bentham. And let them console themselves—they do as well as anybody else; the population of (let us say) Chicago would cut quite as rueful a figure on the same romantic stage. To the Glasgow people I would say only one word, but that is of gold: *I have not yet written a book about Glasgow.*

John Major
The Naming of Edinburgh
1st, 6th Centuries A.D.
Arthur
Early 6th Century

John Major, or Mair (1469–1550), styled himself 'by name indeed a Scot, but by profession a Theologian', studied in Cambridge and Paris, and taught at the Sorbonne, at Glasgow and at St Andrews where he was Provost of St Salvator's College, 1533–50. In 1521 he published his History of Greater Britain, both England and Scotland from whose translation by Archibald Constable (Edinburgh, 1892) these extracts from Book I, Chapter xiii, and Book II, Chapter vi, are taken.

The Naming of Edinburgh

. . . In the time of the emperor Claudius, a mighty war began between the confederated Scots and Picts on the one hand, and the Britons on the other—a war which lasted without a break for one hundred and fifty-four years. According to our chroniclers, the Romans were aiming, with the help of the Britons, at making the Scots and Picts tributaries to them; which when these peoples came to understand, they made a fierce attack upon the Romans and the Britons, sparing neither sex, and levelling with the ground some fair cities of the Britons—Agned for one, which, when it had been rebuilt by Heth, the king of the Picts, came to be called Hethburg, and to-day is known to all men as Edinburgh, the royal seat in Scotland . .

Arthur

. . . what is certain is this: that Arthur, youth as he was, was declared king of the Britons. But his natural endowment was of the noblest; he was fair and beautiful to look on, of a most chivalrous spirit, and none was more ambitious of warlike renown. The Saxons he drove from the island, the Scots and Picts likewise (if we are to credit British chroniclers) he brought under subjection and compelled to obedience. At Edinburgh, in Scotland, was Arthur's kingly seat, and to this day that spot near Edinburgh bears his name . . .

Hector Boece
The Hart and Holyrood
1128

Hector Boece, or Boethius (1465?–1536), was born in Dundee, educated there and at the Sorbonne were he taught, and aided William Elphinstone in founding the University of Aberdeen whose first Principal he was. This passage from the twelfth book of his Chroniklis of Scotland (1527) in the translation by John Bellenden was printed in 1536; it was the second work on Scotland of its kind after that of John Major, to which historians rank it much inferior, but the present extract is at least supported by King David I's charter to the Abbey at Holyrood which is more substantial evidence than lay at Major's disposal for the passages on Heth and Arthur.

EFTIR DEITH OF ALEXANDER THE FIRST, his brothir David come out of Ingland, and wes crounit at Scone, the yeir of God, MCXXIV yeris; and did gret justice, efter his coronation, in all partis of his realme. He had na weris during the time of King Hary; and wes sa pietuous, that he sat daylie in jugement, to caus his pure commonis to have justice: and causit the actionis of his noblis to be decidit be his othir jugis. He gart ilk juge redres the skaithis that come to the party be his wrang sentence: throw quhilk, he decorit his realm with mony nobil actis, and ejeckit the vennomus custome of riotus cheir, quhilk wes inducit afore be Inglismen, quhen thay com with Quene Margaret; for the samin wes noisum to al gud maneris, makand his pepil tender and effeminat.

In the fourt yeir of his regne, this nobill prince come to visie the madin Castell of Edinburgh. At this time, all the boundis of Scotland wer ful of woddis, lesouris, and medois; for the cuntre wes more gevin to store of bestiall, than any productioun of cornis: and about this castell wes ane gret forest, full of haris, hindis, toddish, and siclike maner of beistis. Now wes the Rude Day cumin, callit the Exaltation of the Croce; and, becaus the samin wes ane hie solempne day, the king past to his contemplation. Eftir that the messis wer done with maist solempnite and reverence, comperit afore him, mony young and insolent baronis of Scotland, richt desirus to haif sum pleseir and solace, be chace of hundis in the said forest. At this time, wes with the king ane man of singulare and devoit life, namit Alkwine, Channon

22

eftir the ordour of Sanct Augustine; quhilk wes lang time confessoure, afore, to King David in Ingland, the time that he wes Erle of Huntingtoun and Northumbirland. This religious man dissuadit the king, be mony reasonis, to pas to this huntis; and allegit the day wes so solempne, be reverence of the haly croce, that he suld gif him erar, for that day, to contemplation, than ony othir exercition. Nochtheles, his dissuasionsis litill avalit; for the king wes finalie so provokit, be inoportune solicitatioun of his baronis, that he past, nochtwithstanding the solempnite of this day, to his hountis. At last, quhen he wes cumin throw the vail that lyis to the gret eist fra the said castell, quhare now lyis the Cannogait; the staill past throw the wod with sic noyis and din of rachis and bugillis, that all the bestis wer rasit fra thair dennis. Now wes the king cumin to the fute of the crag, and all his noblis severit, heir and thair, fra him, at thair game and solace; quhen suddanlie apperit to his sicht, the farest hart that evir wes sene afore with levand creatour. The noyis and din of this hart, rinnand, as apperit, with auful and braid tindis, maid the kingis hors so effrayit, that na renyeis micht hald him; bot ran, perforce, ouir mire and mossis, away with the king. Nochtheles, the hart followit so fast, that he dang baith the king and his hors to the ground. Than the king kest abak his handis betwix the tindis of this hart, to haif savit him fra the strak thairof; and the haly croce slaid, incontinent, in his handis. The hart fled away with gret violence, and evanist in the same place quhare now springis the Rude Well. The pepill, richt affrayitly, returnit to him out of all partis of the wod, to comfort him efter his trubill; and fell on kneis, devotly adoring the haly croce: for it was not cumin but sum hevinly providencc, as weill apperis; for thair is na man can schaw of quhat mater it is of, metal or tre. Sone efter, the king returnit to his castel; and in the nicht following, he was admonist, be ane vision in his sleip, to big ane abbay of channonis regular in the same place quhare he gat the croce. Als sone as he was awalkinnit, he schew his vision to Alkewine, his confessour; and he na thing suspendit his gud mind, bot erar inflammit him with maist fervent devotion thairto. The king, incontinent, send his traist servandis in France and Flanderis, and brocht richt crafty masonis to big this abbay; syne dedicat it in the honour of this haly croce.

Robert the Bruce
The City Confirmed
1329

Robert de Bruce (1274–1329), grandson of the homonymous and unsuccessful claimant on the Scottish crown after the death of Alexander III and his heir, first paid homage to Edward I of England in the latter's attempt to rule Scotland but later led the patriotic forces despite many years of ill-fortune. Crowned king in 1306, recognized as such by the Scottish clergy in 1310, he defeated Edward II at Bannockburn in 1314, was accepted by the Pope, 1323, and concluded the treaty of Edinburgh and Northampton with Edward III, 1328, after which he granted Edinburgh this charter. (The earlier charter of Alexander, to which it refers, has been lost.) His forces had taken Edinburgh Castle from the English three months before Bannockburn.

ROBERT, by the grace of God King of Scots, to all good men of all his land, greeting. Know that we have given, granted, and to feuferm let, and by this our present charter confirmed, to the Burgesses of our Burgh of Edinburgh, our foresaid Burgh of Edinburgh, together with the Port of Leith, mills, and others their pertinents. To have and to hold to the said Burgesses and their successors, of us and our heirs, freely, quietly, fully, and honourably by all their right meiths and marches, with all the commodities, liberties, and easements which justly pertained to the said Burgh in the time of King Alexander, our predecessor last deceased, of good memory: Paying therefor the said Burgesses and their successors to us and our heirs, yearly, fifty-two merks sterling, at the terms of Whitsunday and Martinmas in winter, by equal portions. In witness whereof we have commanded our seal to be affixed to our present charter. Witnesses, Walter of Twynham our chancellor; Thomas Ranulph, Earl of Moray, Lord of Annandale and Man, our nephew; James Lord of Douglas; Gilbert of Hay our constable; Robert de Keth our marischall of Scotland, and Adam More, knights. At Cardros the twenty-eighth day of May, in the twenty-fourth year of our reign.

Froissart
The Year of the French
1385

The Chroniques of Jean Froissart (ca. 1337–ca. 1410) were the work of a protégé of Edward III's Queen, Philippa of Hainault; he visited Scotland not long after his first arrival in England in 1361. On his return to England in 1395 he was welcomed by Richard II whose wars against Scotland, then ruled by Robert II, form the background to this extract. The lively Penguin version maintains Froissart's continued popularity today, but does not include the present passage, which is taken from the translation by John Bourchier, Lord Berners, commanded by Henry VIII and published in 1523–25, one of the first major works printed in England. For the sake of clarity the letters 'v' and 'u' are restored to their current usage in English spelling, and occasional abbreviations are written in full, but otherwise it follows Berners' standards of spelling and typography.

... NOWE ... let us shewe howe the admyrall of Fraunce toke lande in the realme of Scotlande, and what chere they had made to them at their firste lodyinge.

The french army that went in scotlande had wynde at will; it was in the monethe of Maye, when the waters be peaseable and meke, and the ayre softe and swete. First they costed Flanders, Holande, zelande, and Frise, and at last aproched to the sight of Scotlande; but are they aryved, ther fell an harde adventure to a yonge knyght of Fraunce, a proper man of armes, called sir Aubert Dangyers: the knyght was yong and of haute courage, and to shewe his strength and ligthnesse of body, he lepte up clene armed on the walle of the shyppe, and in the lightynge his fete slypped, and so fell over the borde into the see, so that he coulde not be holpen, for incontynent he sanke downe, bycause of the weight of his harnes, and also the ship sayled ever forthe. Of this knightes adventure all the barownes and knyghtes were sore dyspleased, but there was no remedy: and so longe they sayled, that they arryved at Edenborowe, the chiefe towne in Scotlande, and wher as the kyng in tyme of peace moost commenly laye. And as soone as the erle Duglas and the Erle Morette knewe of their comynge, they went to the havyn and mette with them, and receyved them swetely, sayeng, howe they were right welcome into that countrey: and the barons of Scotlande knewe ryght well sir Geffray de Charney, for he had been the some before, two monethes in their company: sir Geffray acquaynted them with the Admyrall, and the other knyghtes of Fraunce; as at the tyme the kynge of Scottes was not there, for he was in the wylde Scottyshe; but it was shewed these knyghtes, howe the kyng wold be there shortly; wherwith they were well content, and so were lodged there about in the vyllages; for Edenborough, thoughe the kynge kept there his chefe resydence, and that it is Parys in Scotlande, yet it is not lyke Tourney or Valencennes, for in all the towne there is not four thousande [a slip for "four hundred"] houses; therfor it behoved these lordes and knyghtes to be lodged about in vyllages, as at Donser, Melyne, Cassell, Donbare, aluest, and suche other. Anone tydynges sprange about in Scotlande, that a great nombre of men of armes of Fraunce were come into their countre: some therat did murmure and grudge, and sayde, who the devyll hath sent for them? What do they here? Cannot we maynteyne our warre with Englande well ynoughe withoute their helpe? We shall do no good as longe as they be with us. Let it be shewed unto them, that they may retourne agayne, and that we be stronge ynough in Scotlande to maynteyne our warre without theym; and therfore we wyll none of their company. They understande not us nor we them; therfore we cannot speke toguyder: they wyll anone ryffle and eate up all that ever we have in this countrey: they shall do us more dispytes and domages than thoughe the Englysshemen shulde fyght with us; for thoughe the Englysshemen brinne our houses, we care lytell therfore; we shall make them agayne chepe ynough; we are but thre dayes to make them agayne, if we maye geate foure or fyve stakes, and bowes to cover them.

Thus the scottes sayde in Scotlande, at the comynge of the frenchmen thyder, for they dyde sette nothynge by them, but hated them in their courage and dissamed theym in their language as moche as they myght, lyke rude people without honoure, as they be. All thynges consydered, it was to great an armye of so many noblemen to come into Scotlande, and knewe no reason why; a twentie or thirttie knyghtes of Fraunce had been better than all that nombre of fyve hundred or a thousande; and the cause why is this:

In Scotlande ye shall fynde no man lyghtlye of honoure nor gentylnesse; they be lyke wylde and savage people; they wyll be with no man acquaynted, and are greatly envyous with the honoure or prosyte of any other man, and they dought ever to lese that they have, for it is a poore countre; and whan the Englysshemen maketh any roode or voyage into the countre, as they have done often before this tyme, if they thynke to lyve, they muste cause their provysion and vitayle to folowe theym at their backe, for they shall fynde nothyng in that countrey but with moche payne; nor they shall fynde none yron to showe their horses, nor leddar to make harnesse, sadelles, or bridelles; for all suche thynges come to them redy made out of Flaunders; and when that provision sayleth, there is none to gette in the countrey. Whan the barownes and knyghtes of Fraunce who were wonte to fynde fayre hostryes, halles hanged, and goodly castelles, and softe beddes to reste in, sawe themselfe in that necessite, they began to smyle, and said to the admyrall, Sir, what pleasure hath brought us hyder? we never knewe what povertie ment tyll nowe: we fynde nowe the olde sayenge of our fathers and mothers true, whanne they wolde saye, Go your waye, and ye lyve long, ye shall fynde harde and poore beddes, whiche nowe we fynde; therfore lette us go oure voyage that we be come for; lette us ryde into Englande; the long taryenge here in Scotlande is to us nother honourable nor profytable. The admyrall apeased them as well as he myght, and sayde, Sirs, it behoveth us to suffre a lytell, and to speke fayre, sithe we be in this daunger; he have a great longe waye yet to passe, and by Englande we can not retourne; therfore lette us take in gres that we fynde; we can not be alwayes at Paris or Dygeon, at Beautie or at Chalons: it behoveth them that wyll lyve in this worlde, thynkynge to have honoure, to suffre somtyme as well povertie as welth. . . .

27

Sir Walter Scott
The Eve of Flodden
1513

Marmion (1808)–of which this forms Canto V, verse 30–was the second of the great narrative poems by Scott (1771–1832), who was also novelist, lawyer, antiquary, folklorist, historical editor and Tory politician. Although concerned with the frightful defeat of Scotland at Flodden in 1513, when James IV perished with the flower of the country, its focus of attention is the courageous but cruel and corrupt English knight Marmion. The realism lying behind the romantic narrative in Scott was here, as elsewhere, too strong for many of his critics including Byron. In this passage, Marmion is being conducted by Scottish nobles on a diplomatic mission to James IV.

Still on the spot Lord Marmion stay'd,
For fairer scene he ne'er survey'd.
  When stated with the martial show
  That peopled all the plain below,
  The wandering eye could o'er it go,
  And mark the distant city glow
    With gloomy splendour red;
  For on the smoke-wreaths, huge and slow,
  That round her sable turrets flow,
    The morning beams were shed,
  And tinged them with a lustre proud,
  Like that which streaks a thunder-cloud.
Such dusky grandeur clothed the height,
Where the huge Castle holds its state,
    And all the steep slope down,
Whose ridgy back heaves to the sky,
Piled deep and massy, close and high,
    Mine own romantic town!

But northward far, with purer blaze,
On Ochil mountains fell the rays,
And as each heathy top they kissed,
It gleam'd a purple amethyst.
Yonder the shores of Fife you saw;
Here Preston-Bay and Berwick-Law:

And, broad between them roll'd,
The gallant Frith the eye might note,
Whose islands on its bosom float,
    Like emeralds chased in gold.
Fitz-Eustace' heart felt closely pent:
As if to give his rapture vent,
The spur he to his charger lent,
    And raised his bridle hand,
And, making demi-volte in air,
Cried, "Where's the coward that would not dare
    To fight for such a land!"
The Lindesay smiled his joy see;
Nor Marmion's frown repress'd his glee.

John Knox
The Reformation: Iconoclasm
1556

The History of the Reformation of Religioun within the realme of Scotland by John Knox (1505–1572), whence this extract is taken, is a vivid account of the growth of Protestantism in Scotland with much emphasis on the part played in it by the author; it was first printed in 1584. Knox was an orator of extraordinary power who played a great part in bringing to Scotland the doctrines of Calvin, whom he met in Geneva in 1554. Knox had begun preaching the reformed religion in Scotland in 1547, and on his return after 1558 inspired much of the popular character of the religious revolt in Edinburgh, having his first and very plain-spoken confrontation with the newly-returned Mary I, Queen of Scots, in 1561. He issued the Book of Common Order, enshrining the new service, in 1564, and won confirmation for reformation from the Scottish Parliament in 1567. He was appointed minister in Edinburgh where he died.

AND SO THE DAY of summons being discharged, began the brethren universally to be further encouraged. But yet could the Bishops in no sort be quiet; for Saint Giles Day approaching, they gave charge to the Provost, Bailies and Council of Edinburgh either to get again the old Saint Giles, or else upon their expenses to make a new image. The Council answered "That to them the charge appeared very unjust; for they understood that God in some places had commanded idols and images to be destroyed; but where he had commanded images to be set up they had not been read; and desired the Bishop to find a warrant for his commandment." Whereat the Bishop offended, admonished under pain of cursing; which they prevented by a formal appellation; appealing from him, as from a partial and corrupt judge, unto the Pope's holiness and so greater things shortly following, that passed into oblivion. Yet would not the priests and friars cease to have that great solemnity and manifest abomination which they accustomably had upon St Giles day, to with, they would have that idol borne, and therefore was all preparation duly made. A marmoset idol was borrowed from the Grey Friars (a silver piece of James Carmichael was laid in pledge). It was fast fixed with iron nails upon a barrow, called their fertar. There assembled priests, friars, canons and rotten Papists, with tabors and trumpets, banners and bagpipes and who was there to lead the ring, but the Queen Regent herself with all her shavelings, for honour of that feast. West goes about it, and comes down the High Street and down to Canon Cross. The Queen Regent dined that day in Sandy Carpentyne's house, betwix the Bass, and so when the idol returned back again, she left it, and passed into her dinner. The hearts of the brethren were wondrously inflamed and, seeing such abomination so mainifestly maintained, were decreed to be revenged. They were divided into several companies, whereof not one knew of another. There were some temporiseres that day (amongst whom David Forest, called the General, was one) who, fearing the chance to be done as it fell, laboured to stay the brethren. But that could not be; for immediately after that the Queen was entered in the lodging, some of those that were of the enterprise due nigh to the idol, as willing to help to bear him, and getting the fertour upon their shoulders, began to shoulder, thinking that thereby the idol should have fallen. But that was prevented by iron nails, as we have said; and so, begun one to cry "Down with the idol, down with it"; and so without delay it was pulled down. Some brag made the priests' patrons at the first; but when they saw the feebleness of their god (for they took him by the heels, and dadding his head to the calsay, left Dagon without head or hands, and said "Fie upon thee, thou Young Saint Files, thy father would have tarried four such"); this considered (we say) the priests and friars fled faster than they did at Pinkie Cleuch. There might have been seen so sudden a fray as seldom has been seen amongst that sort of men within this realm; for down goes the crosses, off goes the surplice, round caps corner with the crowns. The Grey Friars gaped, the Black Friars blew, the priests panted and fled: and happy was he that first got at the house; for such a sudden fray never came amongst the generation of Antichrist within this realm before. By chance there lay upon the stair a merry Englishman, and seeing the discomfiture to be without blood, thought he would add some merriness to the matter, and so cried he over a stair and said, "Fie upon you, whoresons, why have ye broken order! Down the street ye passed in array and with great mirth. Why fly ye villains now, without order? Turn and strike everyone a stroke for the honour of his god. Fie, cowards, fie, ye shall never be judged worthy of your wages again!" But exhortations were then unprofitable; for after that Bell had broken his neck, there was no comfort to his confused army.

Arthur Conan Doyle
The Silver Mirror
1566

The Edinburgh-born Sir Arthur Conan Doyle (1859–1930) was the elder son of the artist Charles Altamont Doyle, who as an official of the Board of Works in Edinburgh played an important part in the restoration of Holyrood Palace. The accountant and the financier in this story are clearly based on Rufus Isaacs, Q.C. (later Marquess of Reading), and Whitaker Wright, the swindler: Isaacs's cross-examination of Wright in 1904 revealed an outstanding mastery of highly complex financial intricacies behind which Wright vainly sought to shelter. The physical descriptions accord perfectly with those of the protagonists. The Silver Mirror was first published in the Strand *magazine in August, 1908.*

JAN. 3.—This affair of White and Wotherspoon's accounts proves to be a gigantic task. There are twenty thick ledgers to be examined and checked. Who would be a junior partner? However, it is the first big bit of business which has been left entirely in my hands. I must justify it. But it has to be finished so that the lawyers may have the result in time for the trial. Johnson said this morning that I should have to get the last figure out before the twentieth of the month. Good Lord! Well, have at it, and if human brain and nerve can stand the strain, I'll win out at the other side. It means office-work from ten to five, and then a second sitting from about eight to one in the morning. There's drama in an accountant's life. When I find myself in the still early hours, while all the world sleeps, hunting through column after column for those missing figures which will turn a respected alderman into a felon, I understand that it is not such a prosaic profession after all.

On Monday I came on the first trace of defalcation. No heavy game hunter ever got a finer thrill when first he caught sight of the trail of his quarry. But I look at the twenty ledgers and think of the jungle through which I have to follow him before I get my kill. Hard work—but rare sport, too, in a way! I saw the fat fellow once at a City dinner, his red face glowing above a white napkin. He looked at the little pale man at the end of the table. He would have been pale, too, if he could have seen the task that would be mine.

Jan. 6.—What perfect nonsense it is for doctors to prescribe rest when rest is out of the question! Asses! They might as well shout to a man who has a pack of wolves at his heels that what he wants is absolute quiet. My figures must be out by a certain date; unless they are so, I shall lose the chance of my lifetime, so how on earth am I to rest? I'll take a week or so after the trial.

Perhaps I was myself a fool to go to the doctor at all. But I get nervous and highly strung when I sit alone at my work at night. It's not a pain—only a sort of fullness of the head with an occasional mist over the eyes. I thought perhaps some bromide, or chloral, or something of the kind might do me good. But stop work? It's absurd to ask such a thing. It's like a long-distance race. You feel queer at first and your heart thumps and your lungs pant, but if you have only the pluck to keep on, you get your second wind. I'll stick to my work and wait for my second wind. If it never comes—all the same, I'll stick to my work. Two ledgers are done, and I am well on in the third. The rascal has covered his tracks well, but I pick them up for all that.

Jan. 9.—I had not meant to go to the doctor again. And yet I have had to. "Straining my nerves, risking a complete breakdown, even endangering my sanity." That's a nice sentence to have fired off at one. Well, I'll stand the strain and I'll take the risk, and so long as I can sit in my chair and move a pen I'll follow the old sinner's slot.

By the way, I may as well set down here the queer experience which drove me this second time to the doctor. I'll keep an exact record of my symptoms and sensations, because they are interesting in themselves—"a curious psycho-physiological study," says the doctor—and also because I am perfectly certain that when I am through with them they will all seem blurred and unreal, like some queer dream betwixt sleeping and waking. So now, while they are fresh, I will just make a note of them if only as a change of thought after the endless figures.

There's an old silver-framed mirror in my room. It was given me by a friend who had a taste of antiquities, and he, as I happen to know, picked it up at a sale and had no notion where it came from. It's a large thing—three feet across and two feet high—and it leans at the back of a side-table on my left as I write. The frame is flat, about three inches across, and very old; far too old for hall-marks or other methods of determining its age. The glass part projects, with a bevelled edge, and has the magnificent reflecting power which is only, as it seems to me, to be found in very old mirrors. There's a feeling of perspective when you look into it such as no modern glass can ever give.

The mirror is so situated that as I sit at the table I can usually see nothing in it but the reflection of the red window curtains. But a queer thing happened last night. I had been working for some hours, very much against the grain, with continual bouts of that mistiness of which I had complained. Again and again I had to stop and clear my eyes. Well, on one of these occasions I chanced to look at the mirror. It had the oddest appearance. The red curtains which should have been reflected in it were no longer there, but the glass seemed to be clouded and steamy, not on the surface, which glittered like steel, but deep down in the very grain of it. This opacity, when I stared hard at it, appeared to slowly rotate this way and that, until it was a thick, white cloud swirling in heavy wreaths. So real and solid was it, and so reasonable was I, that I remember turning, with the idea that the curtains were on fire. But everything was deadly still in the room—no sound save the ticking of the clock, no movement save the slow gyration of that strange woolly cloud deep in the heart of the old mirror.

Then, as I looked, the mist, or smoke, or cloud, or whatever one may call it, seemed to coalesce and solidify at two points quite close together, and I was aware, with a thrill of interest rather than a fear, that these were two eyes looking out into the room. A vague outline of a head I could see—a woman's by the hair, but this was very shadowy. Only the eyes were quite distinct; such eyes—dark, luminous, filled with some passionate emotion, fury or horror, I could not say which. Never have I seen eyes which were so full of intense, vivid life. They were not fixed upon me, but stared out into the room. Then as I sat erect, passed my hand over my brow, and made a strong conscious effort to pull myself together, the dim head faded into the general opacity, the mirror slowly cleared, and there were the red curtains once again.

A sceptic would say, no doubt, that I had dropped asleep over my figures, and that my experience was a dream. As a matter of fact, I was never more vividly awake in my life. I was able to argue about it even as I looked at it, and to tell myself that it was a subjective impression—a chimera of the nerves—begotten by worry and insomnia. But why this particular shape? And who is the woman, and what is the dreadful emotion which I read in those wonderful eyes? They come between me and my work. For the first time I have done less than the daily tally which I had marked out. Perhaps that is why I have had no abnormal sensations to-night. To-morrow I must wake up, come what may.

Jan. 11.—All well, and good progress with my work. I wind the net, coil after coil, round that bulky body. But the last smile may remain with him if my own nerves break over it. The mirror would seem to be a sort of barometer which marks my brain pressure. Each night I have observed that it had clouded before I reached the end of my task.

Dr. Sinclair (who is, it seems, a bit of a psychologist) was so interested in my account that he came round this evening to have a look at the mirror. I had observed that something was scribbled in crabbed old characters upon the metal work at the back. He examined this with a lens, but could make nothing of it. "Sanc. X. Pal." was his final reading of it, but that did not bring us any further. He advised me to put it away into another room; but, after all, whatever I may see in it is, by his own account, only a sympton. It is in the cause that the danger lies. The twenty ledgers—not the silver mirror—should be packed away if I could only do it. I'm at the eighth now, so I progress.

Jan. 13.—Perhaps it would have been wiser after all if I had packed away the mirror. I had an extraordinary experience with it last night. And yet I find it so interesting, so fascinating, that even now I will keep it in its place. What on earth is the meaning of it all?

I suppose it was about one in the morning, and I was closing my books preparatory to staggering off to bed, when I saw her there in front of me. The stage of mistiness and development must have passed unobserved, and there she was in all her beauty and passion and distress, as clear-cut as if she were really in the flesh before me. The figure was small, but very distinct—so much so that every feature, and every detail of dress, are stamped in my memory. She is seated on the extreme left of the mirror. A sort of shadowy figure crouches down beside her—I can dimly discern that it is a man—and then behind them is cloud, in which I see figures—figures which move. It is not a mere picture upon which I look. It is a scene in life, an actual episode. She crouches and quivers. The man beside her cowers down. The vague figures make abrupt movements and gestures. All my fears were swallowed up in my interest. It was maddening to see so much and not to see more.

But I can at least describe the woman to the smallest point. She is very beautiful and quite young—not more than five-and-twenty, I should judge. Her hair is of a very rich brown, with a warm chestnut shade fining into gold at the edges. A little flat-pointed cap comes to an angle in front and is made of lace edged with pearls. The forehead is high, too high perhaps for perfect beauty; but one would not have it otherwise, as it gives a touch of power and strength to what would otherwise be a softly feminine face. The brows are most delicately curved over heavy eyelids, and then come those wonderful eyes—so

35

large, so dark, so full of overmastering emotion, of rage and horror, contending with a pride of self-control which holds her from sheer frenzy! The cheeks are pale, the lips white with agony, the chin and throat most exquisitely rounded. The figure sits and leans forward in the chair, straining and rigid, cataleptic with horror. The dress is black velvet, a jewel gleams like a flame in the breast, and a golden crucifix smoulders in the shadow of a fold. This is the lady whose image still lives in the old silver mirror. What dire deed could it be which has left its impress there, so that now, in another age, if the spirit of a man be but worn down to it, he may be conscious of its presence?

One other detail: On the left side of the skirt of the black dress was, as I thought at first, a shapeless bunch of white ribbon. Then, as I looked more intently or as the vision defined itself more clearly, I perceived what it was. It was the hand of a man, clenched and knotted in agony, which held on with a convulsive grasp to the fold of the dress. The rest of the crouching figure was a mere vague outline, but that strenuous hand shone clear on the dark background, with a sinister suggestion of tragedy in its frantic clutch. The man is frightened—horribly frightened. That I can clearly discern. What has terrified him so? Why does he grip the woman's dress? The answer lies amongst those moving figures in the background. They have brought danger both to him and to her. The interest of the thing fascinated me. I thought no more of its relation to my own nerves. I stared and stared as if in a theatre. But I could get no further. The mist thinned. There were tumultuous movements in which all the figures were vaguely concerned. Then the mirror was clear once more.

The doctor says I must drop work for a day, and I can afford to do so, for I have made good progress lately. It is quite evident that the visions depend entirely upon my own nervous state, for I sat in front of the mirror for an hour to-night, with no result whatever. My soothing day has chased them away. I wonder whether I shall ever penetrate what they all mean? I examined the mirror this evening under a good light, and besides the mysterious inscription "Sanc. X. Pal.," I was able to discern some signs of heraldic marks, very faintly visible upon the silver. They must be very ancient, as they are almost obliterated. So far as I could make out, they were three spear-heads, two above and one below. I will show them to the doctor when he calls to-morrow.

Jan. 14.—Feel perfectly well again, and I intend that nothing else shall stop me until my task is finished. The doctor was shown the marks on the mirror and agreed that they were armorial bearings. He is deeply interested in all that I have told him, and cross-questioned me closely on the details. It amuses me to notice how he is torn in two by conflicting desires—the one that his patient should lose his symptoms, the other that the medium—for so he regards me—should solve this mystery of the past. He advised continued rest, but did not oppose me too violently when I declared that such a thing was out of the question until the ten remaining ledgers have been checked.

Jan. 17.—For three nights I have had no experiences—my day of rest has borne fruit. Only a quarter of my task is left, but I must make a forced march, for the lawyers are clamouring for their material. I will give them enough and to spare. I have him fast on a hundred counts. When they realise what a slippery, cunning rascal he is, I should gain some credit from the case. False trading accounts, false balance-sheets, dividends drawn from capital, losses written down as profits, suppression of working expenses, manipulation of petty cash—it is a fine record!

Jan. 18.—Headaches, nervous twitches, mistiness, fullness of the temples—all the premonitions of trouble, and the trouble came sure enough. And yet my real sorrow is not so much that the vision should come as that it should cease before all is revealed.

But I saw more to-night. The crouching man was as visible as the lady whose gown he clutched. He is a little swarthy fellow, with a black, pointed beard. He has a loose gown of damask trimmed with fur. The prevailing tints of his dress are red. What a fright the fellow is in, to be sure! He cowers and shivers and glares back over his shoulder. There is a small knife in his other hand, but he is far too tremulous and cowed to use it. Fierce faces, bearded and dark, shape themselves out of the mist. There is one terrible creature, a skeleton of a man, with hollow cheeks and eyes sunk in his head. He also has a knife in his hand. On the right of the woman stands a tallman, very young, with flaxen hair, his face sullen and dour. The beautiful woman looks up at him in appeal. So does the man on the ground. This youth seems to be the arbiter of their fate. The crouching man draws closer and hides himself in the woman's skirts. The tall youth bends and tries to drag her away from him. So much I saw last night before the mirror cleared. Shall I never know what it leads to and whence it comes? It is not a mere imagination, of that I am very sure. Somewhere, some time, this scene has been acted, and this old mirror has reflected it. But when—where?

Jan. 20.—My work draws to a close, and it is time. I feel a tenseness within my brain, a sense of intolerable strain, which warns me that something must give. I have worked myself to the limit. But to-night should be the last night. With a supreme effort I should finish the final ledger and complete the case before I rise from my chair. I will do it. I will.

Feb. 7.—I did. My God, what an experience! I hardly know if I am strong enough yet to set it down.

Let me explain in the first instance that I am writing this in Dr. Sinclair's private hospital some three weeks after the last entry in my diary. On the night of January 20 my nervous system finally gave way, and I remembered nothing afterwards until I found myself, three days ago, in the home of rest. And I can rest with a good conscience. My work was done before I went under. My figures are in the solicitor's hands. The hunt is over.

And now I must describe that last night. I had sworn to finish my work, and so intently did I stick to it, though my head was bursting, that I would never look up until the last column had been added. And yet it was fine self-restraint, for all the time I knew that wonderful things were happening in the mirror. Every nerve in my body told me so. If I looked there was an end of my work. So I did not look up till all was finished. Then, when at last with throbbing temples I threw down my pen and raised my eyes, what a sight was there!

The mirror in its silver frame was like a stage, brilliantly lit, in which a drama was in progress. There was no mist now. The oppression of my nerves had wrought this amazing clarity. Every feature, every movement, was as clear-cut as in life. To think that I, a tired accountant, the most prosaic of mankind, with the account-books of a swindling bankrupt before me, would be chosen of all the human race to look upon such a scene!

It was the same scene and the same figures, but the drama had advanced a stage. The tall young man was holding the woman in his arms. She strained away from him and looked up at him with loathing in her face. They had torn the crouching man away from his hold upon the skirt of her dress. A dozen of them were round him—savage men, bearded men. They hacked at him with knives. All seemed to strike him together. Their arms rose and fell. The blood did not flow from him—it squirted. His red dress was dabbled in it. He threw himself this way and that, purple upon crimson, like an over-ripe plum. Still they hacked, and still the jets shot from him. It was horrible-horrible! They dragged him kicking to the door. The woman looked over her shoulder at him and her mouth gaped. I heard nothing, but I knew that she was screaming. And then whether it was this nerve-racking vision before me, or whether, my task finished, all the overwork of the past weeks came in one crushing weight upon me, the room danced round me, the floor seemed to sink away beneath my feet, and I remembered no more. In the early morning my land-lady found me stretched senseless before the silver mirror, but I knew nothing myself until three days ago I awoke in the deep peace of the doctor's nursing home.

Feb. 9.—Only to-day have I told Dr. Sinclair my full experience. He had not allowed me to speak of such matters before. He listened with an absorbed interest. "You don't identify this with any well-known scene in history?" he asked, with suspicion in his eyes. I assured him that I knew nothing of history. "Have you no idea whence that mirror came and to whom it once belonged?" he continued. "Have you?" I asked, for he spoke with meaning. "It's incredible," said he, "and yet how else can one explain it? The scenes which you described before suggested it, but now it has gone beyond all range of coincidence. I will bring you some notes in the evening."

Later.—He has just left me. Let me set down his words as closely as I can recall them. He began by laying several musty volumes upon my bed.

"These you can consult at your leisure," said he. "I have some notes here which you can confirm. There is not a doubt that what you have seen is the murder of Rizzio by the Scottish nobles in the presence of Mary, which occurred in March 1566. Your description of the woman is accurate. The high forehead and heavy eyelids combined with great beauty could hardly apply to two women. The tall young man was her husband, Darnley. Rizzio, says the chronicle, 'was dressed in a loose dressing-gown of furred damask, with hose of russet velvet.' With one hand he clutched Mary's gown, with the other he held a dagger. Your fierce, hollow-eyed man was Ruthven, who was new-risen from a bed of sickness. Every detail is exact."

"But why to me?" I asked, in bewilderment. "Why of all the human race to me?"

"Because you were in the fit mental state to receive the impression. Because you chanced to own the mirror which gave the impression."

"The mirror! You think, then, that it was Mary's mirror—that it stood in the room where the deed was done?"

"I am convinced that it was Mary's mirror. She had been Queen of France. Her personal property would be stamped with the Royal arms. What you took to be three spear-heads was really the lilies of France."

"And the inscription?"

" 'Sanc. X. Pal.' You can expand it into Sanctæ Crucis Palatium.

Someone has made a note upon the mirror as to whence it came. It was the Palace of the Holy Cross."

"Holyrood!" I cried.

"Exactly. Your mirror came from Holyrood. You have had one very singular experience, and have escaped. I trust that you will never put yourself into the way of having such another."

Old Song
Mary Hamilton
Circa 1566

The part played in the murder of Rizzio (or Riccio) by Mary's husband Henry Lord Darnley deepened the rupture between husband and wife, and Protestant legend hinted Mary's complicity in Darnley's murder the following year: the charge is probably false. There was an infanticide at her Court at Holyrood of which Knox, anxious to associate Mary's Catholicism with licentiousness, was to make much in his History: the Queen had a French lady-in-waiting named Marie who killed her child fathered by the Queen's apothecary, for which both were hanged. Knox also speaks of forcing a marriage between two of the courtiers where pregnancy had ensued. The real Mary Hamilton, however, was a Scots lady-in-waiting to the Czarina of Russia during the reign of Peter the Great in the early eighteenth century, and, supposedly, murdered her natural child. This was discovered and Peter, lifting its severed head, kissed it on the lips. (This presumably implied his paternity: on the other hand he certainly killed his own legitimate son, so that tenderness of feeling is not the strongest of clues to admission of fatherhood in his case.) A Scots version of Mary Hamilton's story appeared some years later and was imposed on the tragedy of Mary Queen of Scots and Darnley, giving the Queen a further motive to kill him.

THERE lived a knight into the North,
    And he had daughters three:
The ane of them was a barber's wife,
    The other a gay ladie;

And the youngest o'them to Scotland is gane
    The Queen's Mary to be;
And for a' that they could say or do,
    Forbidden she wouldna be.

The prince's bed it was sae saft,
    The spices they were sae fine,
That out of it she could not lye
    While she was scarce fifteen.

She's gane to the garden gay
  To pu' of the savin tree;
But for a' that she could say or do,
  The babie it would not die.

She's rowed it in her handkerchief,
  She threw it in the sea:
Says,—"Sink ye, swim ye, my bonnie babe,
  For ye'll get nae mair of me."

Queen Mary came tripping down the stair,
  Wi' the gold strings in her hair:
"O whare's the little babie," she say,
  "That I heard greet sae sair?"

"O hald your tongue, Queen Mary, my dame,
  Let all those words go free;
It was mysell wi' a fit o' the sair colic,
  I was sick just like to die."

"O hald your tongue, Mary Hamilton,
  Let all those words go free;
O where is the little babie
  That I heard weep by thee?"

"I rowed it in my handkerchief,
  And threw it in the sea;
I bade it sink, I bade it swim,
  It would get nae mair o' me."

"O wae be to thee, Mary Hamilton,
  And all ill deid may you die;
For if you had saved the babie's life,
  It might hae been an honour to thee.

"Busk ye, busk ye, Mary Hamilton,
  O busk ye to be a bride;
For I am going to Edinburgh town
  Your gay wedding to bide."

"You must not put on your robes of black,
    Nor yet your robes of brown;
But you must put on your yellow gold stuffs,
    To shine thro' Edinburgh town."

"I will not put on my robes of black,
    Nor yet my robes of brown;
But I will put on my yellow gold stuffs,
    The shine thro' Edinburgh town."

As she went up the Parliament Close,
    A riding on her horse,
There she saw many a burgess' lady
    Sit greeting at the cross.

"O what means a' this greeting?
    I'm sure it's nae for me;
For I'm come this day to Edinburgh town,
    Weel wedded for to be."

When she gade up the Parliament stair,
    She gied loud lauchters three;
But ere that she had come down again,
    She was condemned to die.

"O little did my mother think,
    The day she prinned my gown,
That I was to come sae far frae hame
    To be hanged in Edinburgh town.

"O what'll my poor father think
    As he comes through the town,
To see the face of his Molly fair
    Hanging on the gallows pin?

"Here's a health to the mariners
    That plough the raging main;
Let neither my mother nor father ken
    But I'm coming hame again.

"Here's a health to the sailors
    That sail upon the sea;
Let neither my mother nor father ken
    That I came here to die.

"Yestreen the Queen had four Maries,
    This night she'll hae but three;
There was Mary Beaton, and Mary Seaton,
    And Mary Carmichael and me."

"O hald your tongue, Mary Hamilton,
    Let all those words go free;
This night ere ye be hanged
    Ye shall gang hame wi' me."

"O hald your tongue, Queen Mary, my dame,
    Let all those words go free;
Since I have come to Edinburgh town,
    It's hanged I shall be;
For it shall ne'er be said that in your court
    I was condemned to die."

Thomas Craufurd
King James his College
1617

Thomas Craufurd (also found as Crawfurd and Crawford) was successively professor of Humanity (Latin Studies) at Edinburgh University, rector of the Edinburgh High School, and from 1640 professor of mathematics at Edinburgh in which post he died in 1662. He had been educated at St Andrews. His History of the University of Edinburgh covers its subject from the foundation in 1584 (and its antecedents from 1580) until 1646, and was evidently in preparation at his death: it was not published until 1808. It is the first history of the University and many of the documents on which it was based have since disappeared.

THIS YEAR IS VERY FAMOUS, in respect of that Royal visite made by King James VI. in his own person, to this his native and ancient kingdom, and the Parliament holden by his Majesty at Edinburgh. As all the parts of the country where his Majesty did come, and all ranks of people improved their abilities to the utmost to do him honour; so the City of Edinburgh was no more in place above the rest of the kingdom, then in zealous demonstration of duety to their Soveraigne, in which the University was not the smallest part. Some monuments remain to this day in print.

The sitting of the Parliament, and other celebrities, forcing the dissipation of the students, the laureation was anticipated; Mr Andrew Young advancing to the maigisteriall degree the 29th, and greatest class that before that day had been known in Scotland, some 46 in number, upon the 29th of June.

The King's Majesty had ane earnest desire to honour the Colledge with his presence, and hearing an publick disputation in Philosophy; but the multitude of busieness distracting him all the time he was at Holyroodhouse, it pleased his Majesty to appoint the Maisters of the Colledge to attend him at Sterling, the 29th day of July, where, in the Royal Chapel, his Majesty, with the flower of the Nobility, and many of the most learned men of both nations, were present a little before five of the o'clock, and continued with much cheerfullness above three hours.

Mr Henry Charteris (then Principal of the Colledge) being naturally averse from publick showes, and Professor of Divinity, moved that Mr John Adamson (then minister of Libberton), should preside in the disputation. Mr James Fairly was chosen to draw and defend the theses; Mr Patrick Sands, (sometime Regent, but at that time attending the Tolbooth), Mr Andrew Young, Mr James Reid, and Mr William King, the other three Regents professing Philosophy for the time, were appoynted to impugne. They divided the theses, each of them chusing three but they insisted only upon such purposes as we conceived would be most acceptable to the King's Majesty and the auditory. The speciall purposes agitate were, first, the theses, That Sheriffs and other inferior Magistrates ought not to be hereditary, oppugned by Mr Sands, with many pretty arguments.

The King was so well pleased with the answers, that, after he himself had pressed some arguments to the contrary, and the defender had directed his answers to Mr Sands, his Majesty turning to the Marques of Hamilton, who was standing behind his chair, and at that time was Heritable Sheriff of Clydsdale, "James, (said he) you see your cause lost, and all that can be said for it clearly satisfied and answered."

Mr Young, who disputed next, insisted upon the Nature of Local Motion, pressing many things by clear testimonies of Aristotle's text. To which, when the defender made his answers, and cleared the purpose, the King said to some English Doctors which were near to him, "These men know Aristotle's mind as well as himself did while he lived."

Mr Reid disputed third, anent the Original of Fountains. The King being much taken with his last argument, notwithstanding the time allotted (three quarters of an houre) was spent, caused him prosecute the purpose. His Majesty himself sometime speaking for the impugner, and sometime for the defender, in good Latin, and with much knowledge of the secrets of Philosophy.

Mr King, who disputed last, had his dissertation, *De Spontaneo et Invito*. In the which, and in all the rest, the King let no argument nor answer passe without taking notice thereof, and speaking to the purpose, with much understanding and good language.

After the disputation, his Majesty went to supper, and, after a very little time, commanded the Maisters of the College of Edinburgh to be brought before him. In their presence, he discoursed very learnedly of all the purposes which had been agitated. Then he fell to speak of the actors. "Methinks (said he) these gentlemen, by their very names, have been destinated for the acts which they have had in hand to-day. Adam was father of all; and very fitly Adamson had the first part of this act. The defender is justly called Fairly: his theses had some fair lies, and he sustained them very fairly, and with many fair lies given to the oppugners. And why should not Mr Sands be the first to enter the sands; but now I clearly see, that all sands are not barren, for certainly he hath shewen a fertile wit. Mr Young is very old in Aristotle. Mr Reid needs not be red with blushing for his acting to-day. Mr King disputed very kingly, and of a kingly purpose, anent the royal supremacy of reason over anger and all passions. I am so well satisfied with this day's exercise, that I will be godfather to the Colledge of Edinburgh, and have it called the Colledge of King James; for after the founding of it had been stopped for sundry years in my minority, so soon as I came to any knowledge, I zealously held hand to it, and caused it be established; and although I see many look upon it with an evil eye, yet I will have them to know, that having given it this name, I have espoused its quarell."

One who stood by, told his Majestie, that there was one of the company of whome he had taken no notice, Mr Henry Charteris, Principal of of the Colledge, (who sate upon the President's right hand), a man of exquisite and universal learning, although not so forward to speak in publick, in so august an assembly. "Well," answered the King, "his name agreeth very well to his nature, for charters contain much matter, yet say nothing, but put great purposes in mens mouths."

These who stood by the King's chair, commended his Majestie's wittie allusions to the actors names; whereupon his Majesty pressed, that the same should be turned in verse, wherein his Majesty both delighted much, and had an singular faculty. Some of these versions, (both in English and Latin verses), were written by such as he and them, and thereafter printed.

One of the English Doctors wondering at his Majesty's readiness and eligancy in the Latin style, "All the world, (said he), knowes that my maister, Mr George Buchanan, was a great maister in that faculty. I follow his pronunciation both of the Latin and Greek, and am sorrie that my people of England doe not the like: For certainly their pronounciation utterly spoils the grace of these two learned languages; but ye see all the University and learned men of Scotland, express the true and native pronounciation of both."

His Majesty continued his discourse anent the purposes of the dispute till ten o'clock at night, and professed, that he was exceedingly satisfied therewith, and promised, that as he had given the Colledge a name, he would also, in time convenient, give to it a

Royall God-bairne gift, (as we say), for enlarging the patrimony thereof.

He took occasion of the purposes ventilate that day, to speak of diverse poynts of philosophy, with much subtilitie and variety of knowledge, to the admiration of the understanding hearers; and being on his return to England, wrote back a letter to the Honourable Council of the Good Town, wherein he both renewed his Royall pleasure for calling the Colledge after his name, King James his Colledge, and his promise of a royall god-bairne gift, which, it is hoped, that his Royall Grandchild King Charles the Second will, in time convenient, royally perform.

Thomas Carlyle
On the Eve of Civil War
1637

Carlyle (1795–1881) had won literary celebrity by his kaleidoscopic The French Revolution *in 1837, and had followed it up by the success of his lectures and essays in subsequent years; he drafted the following passage as an introduction to an account of the half-mythical Jenny Geddes and her supposed attack (by means of a stool thrown at the Bishop's head) on the ritualised church services introduced into Scotland by Charles I in 1637. (Carlyle resented the scholarly 'Dryasdusts' who questioned the story.) It was written in 1843 as part of a projected work on the civil and religious wars under Charles I but was set aside as Carlyle sank deeper into the glorification of Cromwell from the sketch in* On Heroes, Hero-Worship and the Heroic in History *(1841) to* Oliver Cromwell's Letters and Speeches *(1845). It was published in* Historical Sketches *edited by Alexander Carlyle (1898).*

POOR OLD EDINBURGH, it lies there on its hill-face between its Castle and Holyrood, extremely dim to us at this two-centuries' distance; and yet the indisputable fact of it burns for us with a strange illuminativeness; small but unquenchable as the light of stars. Indisputably enough, old Edinburgh is there; poor old Scotland wholly, my old respected Mother! Smoke cloud hangs over old Edinburgh,—for, ever since Æneas Sylvius's time and earlier, the people have had the art, very strange to Æneas, of burning a certain sort of black stones, and Edinburgh with its chimneys is called 'Auld Reekie' by the country people. Smoke-cloud very visible to the imagination: who knows what they are doing under it! Dryasdust with his thousand Tomes is dumb as the Bass Rock, nay, dumber, his Tomes are as the cackle of the thousand flocks of geese that inhabit there, and with deafening noise tell us nothing. The mirror of the Firth with its Inchkeiths, Inchcolms and silent isles, gleams beautiful on us; old Edinburgh rises yonder climbing aloft to its Castle precipice; from the rocks of Pettycur where the Third Alexander broke his neck, from all the Fife heights, from far and wide on every hand, you can see the sky windows of it glitter in the sun, a city set on a hill. But what are they doing there; what are they thinking, saying, meaning there? O Dryasdust!—The gallows stands on the Borough Muir;

visible, one sign of civilisation; and men do plough and reap, and weave cloth and felt bonnets, otherwise they could not live. There are about a million of them, as I guess, actually living in this land; notable in several respects to mankind.

They have a broad Norse speech these people; full of picturesqueness, humour, emphasis, sly, deep meaning. A broad rugged Norse character, equal to other audacities than pirating and sea-kingship; and for the last 1000 years, in spite of Dryasdust's goose-babble, have not been idle. They have tamed the wild bisons into peaceable herds of black-cattle; the wolves are all dead long since; the shaggy forests felled; fields, now green, now red, lie beautiful in the sunshine; huts and stone-and-mortar houses spot for ages this once desert land. Gentle and simple are there, hunters with Lincoln coats and hawk on fist, and flat-soled hodden-grey ploughmen and herdsmen. They have made kings this people, and clothed them long since in bright-dyed silk or velvet with pearls and plumages, with gold and constitutional privileges and adornments. Kings? Nay, they have made Priests of various kinds, and know how to reverence them, and actually worship with them. For they are of deep heart; equal to still deeper than Norse Mythologies, and the gilt Temple of Upsala has for a thousand years lain quite behind them and beneath them. The Nation that can produce a Knox and listen to him is worth something! They have made actual Priests, and will even get High-priests,—though after long circuits I think, and in quite other guise than the Laud simulacra who are not worth naming here. This is the people of Scotland, and Edinburgh is the capital of it; whom this little red-faced man with the querulous voice, small chin and horse-shoe mouth, with the black triangle and white tippets on him, has come to favour with a religion. He, in his black triangle and Four Surplices at Allhallowtide, will do it,—if so please Heaven.

Who knows, or will ever know, what the Edinburgh population were saying while the printing of Laud's Service Book went on? For long it threatened; the Scotch simulacra (of Bishops) were themselves very shy of it, but the little red-faced man whose motto is 'thorough,' drove it on. And so, after various postponements, now on Sunday the 23rd day of July, 1637, the feat is to be done; Edinburgh after generations of abeyance shall again see a day of religion.

James Graham
Marquis of Montrose
His Metrical Prayer
1650

James Graham, first Marquis and fifth Earl of Montrose (1612–1650), soldier and poet, supported the Covenanters who defended the non-ritualistic form of Protestant worship in Scotland against Charles I. Under his leadership they captured Aberdeen and invaded England. But he joined Charles in 1641 when full-scale civil war had broken out in the three kingdoms, drew in heavy support from Highland and Irish Catholic forces, won six battles and summoned a parliament at Glasgow. After defeat at Philiphaugh in 1645 he fled to the continent. On Charles I's death he fruitlessly advised the future Charles II not to accept the Scottish throne from the Covenanters. He returned to Scotland, was defeated and betrayed, and is believed to have scratched this poem with a diamond on the night before he was hanged.

LET them bestow on ev'ry Airth a Limb;
Open all my Veins, that I may swim
To Thee my Saviour, in that Crimson Lake;
Then place my pur-boil'd Head upon a Stake;
Scatter my Ashes, throw them in the Air:
Lord (since Thou know'st where all these Atoms are)
I'm hopeful, once Thou'lt recollect my Dust,
And confident Thou'lt raise me with the Just.

Edward Hyde
Earl of Clarendon
The Death of Montrose
1650

Edward Hyde, first Earl of Clarendon (1609–1674), opposed Charles I at the commencement of the Long Parliament and helped prepare the impeachment of Strafford, but subsequently became the King's ally and adviser, drawing up all his declarations from 1642 to 1645, and opposing concessions to the Scots either by Charles I or his son. As Lord Chancellor under the Restoration he was virtually head of government, but his severe and devout temperament made him unpopular. He was dismissed, and impeached, but saved from the commital by the Lords and fled to France in 1667. The True Narrative of the Rebellion and Civil Wars in England was printed in 1702–04 from a transcript, and in 1826 from the original: recognised as a classic in contemporary history, it provided the financial base for the subsequent expansion of the Oxford University Press.

THE EARL OF MOUNTROSE, a young man of a great spirit and of the most ancient nobility, had been one of the most principal and active covenanters in the beginning of the troubles; but soon after, upon his observation of the unwarrantable prosecution of it, he gave over that party, and his command in that army; and at the king's being in Scotland, after the pacification, 1641, had made full tender of his service to his majesty; and was so much in the jealousy and detestation of the violent party, whereof the earl of Argyle was the head, that there was no cause or room left to doubt his sincerity to the king.

In this state stood the affair in the end of the year 1649: but because of the unfortunate tragedy of that noble person succeeded so soon after, without the intervention of any notable circumstances to interrupt it, we will rather continue the relation of it in this place, than defer it to be resumed in the proper season; which quickly ensued, in the beginning of the next year. The marquis Argyle was vigilant enough, to observe the motion of an enemy that was so formidable to him; and had present information of his arrival in the Highlands, and of the small forces which he had brought with him. The parliament was then sitting at Edinburgh, their messenger being returned to them from Jersey, with an account, 'that the king would treat with their commissioners at Breda'; for whom they were preparing their instructions.

The alarm of Mountrose's being landed startled them all, and gave them no leisure to think of any thing else than of sending forces to hinder the recourse of others to join with him.

So that he had none left, but a company of good officers, and five or six hundred foreigners, Dutch and Germans, who had been acquired with their officers. With these he betook himself to a place of some advantage by the inequality of the ground, and the bushes and small shrubs which filled it: and there they made a defence for some time with notable courage.

But the enemy being so much superior in number, the common soldiers, being all foreigners, after about a hundred of them were killed upon the place, threw down their arms; and the marquis, seeing all lost, threw away his ribbon and George, (for he was a knight of the garter), and found means the change the clothes with a fellow of the country, and so after having gone on foot two or three miles, he got into a house of a gentleman, where he remained concealed about two days: most of the other officers were shortly after taken prisoners, all the country desiring to merit from Argyle by betraying all those into his hands which they believed to be his enemies. And thus, whether by the owner of the house, or any other way, the marquis himself became their prisoner. The strangers who were taken, were set at liberty, and transported themselves into their own countries; and the castle, in which there was a little garrison, presently rendered itself; so that there was no more fear of an enemy in those parts.

The marquis of Mountrose, and the rest of the prisoners were the next day, or soon after, delivered to David Lesley; who was come up with his forces, and had now nothing left to do but to carry them in triumph to Edinburgh; whither notice was quickly sent of their great victory; which was received there with wonderful joy and acclamation. David Lesley treated the marquis with great insolence, and for some days carried him in the same clothes, and habit, in which he was taken; but at last permitted him to buy better. His behaviour was, in the whole time, such as became a great man; his countenance serene and cheerful, as one that was superior to all those reproaches, which they had prepared the people to pour out upon him in all the places through which he was to pass.

When he came to one of the gates of Edinburgh, he was met by some of the magistrates, to whom he was delivered, and by them presently put into a new cart, purposely made, in which there was a high chair, or bench, upon which he sat, that the people might have a full view of him, being bound with a cord drawn over his breast and shoulders, and fastened through holes made in the cart. When he was in this posture, the hangman took off his hat, and rode himself before the cart in his livery, and with his bonnet on; the other officers, who were taken prisoners with him, walking two and two before the cart; the streets and windows being full of people to behold the triumph over a person whose name had made them tremble some few years before, and into whose hands the magistrates of that place had, upon their knees, delivered the keys of the city. In this manner he was carried to the common goal, where he was received and treated as a common malefactor.

That he might not enjoy any ease or quiet during the short remainder of his life, their ministers came presently to insult over him with all the reproaches imaginable; pronounced his damnation; and assured him, 'that the judgement he was the next day to undergo, was but an easy prologue to that which he was to undergo afterwards'. After many such barbarities, they offered to intercede for him to the kirk upon his repentance, and to pray with him; but he too well understood the form of their common prayer, in those cases, to be only the most virulent and insolent imprecations against the persons of those they prayed against, ('Lord, vouchsafe yet to touch the obdurate heart of this proud incorrigible sinner, this wicked, perjured, traitorous, and profane person, who refuses to hearken to the voice of thy kirk', and the like charitable expressions,) and therefore he desired them 'to spare their pains, and to leave him to his devotions'. He told them, 'that they were a miserable, deluded, and deluding people; and would shortly bring that poor nation under the most insupportable servitude ever people had submitted to'. He told them, 'he was prouder to have his head set upon the place it was appointed to be, than he could have been to have his picture hang in the king's bedchamber: that he was so far from being troubled that his four limbs were to be hanged in four cities of the kingdom, that he heartily wished that he had flesh enough to be sent to every city in Christendom, as a testimony of the cause for which he suffered'.

The next day, they executed every part and circumstance of that barbarous sentence, with all the inhumanity imaginable; and he bore it with all the courage and magnanimity, and the greatest piety, that a good Christian could manifest. He magnified the virtue, courage, and religion of the last king, exceedingly commended the justice, and goodness, and understanding of the present king; and prayed, 'that they might not betray him as they had done his father.' When he had ended all he meant to say, and was expecting to expire, they had yet

54

one scene more to act of their tyranny. The hangman brought the book that had been published of his truly heroic actions, whilst he had commanded in that kingdom, which book was tied in a small cord that was put about his neck. The marquis smiled at this new instance of their malice, and thanked them for it; and said, 'he was pleased that it should be there; and was prouder of wearing it, than ever he had been of the garter'; and so renewing some devout ejaculations, he patiently endured the last act of the executioner.

Thus died the gallant marquis of Mountrose, after he had given as great a testimony of loyalty and courage as a subject can do, and per-formed as wonderful actions in several battles, upon as great in-equality of numbers, and as great disadvantages in respect of arms, and other preparations for war, as have been performed in this age. He was a gentleman of a very ancient extraction, many of whose ancestors had exercised the highest charges under the king of that kingdom, and had been allied to the crown itself. He was of very good parts, which were improved by a good education: he had always a great emulation, or rather a great contempt of the marquis of Argyle, (as he was too apt to contemn those he did not love,) who wanted nothing but honesty and courage to be a very extraordinary man, having all other good talents in a very great degree. Mountrose was in his nature fearless of danger, and never declined any enterprise for the difficulty of going through with it, but exceedingly affected those which seemed desperate to other men, and did believe some-what to be in himself which other men were not acquainted with, which made him live more easily towards those who were, or were willing to be, inferior to him, (towards whom he exercised wonder-ful civility and generosity,) than with his superior or equals. He was naturally jealous, and suspected those who did not concur with him in the way, not to mean so well as he. He was not without vanity, but his virtues were much superior, and he well deserved to have his memory preserved, and celebrated amongst the most illustrious persons of the age in which he lived...

Old Song
Waly, Waly
Circa 1670

First printed in 1724 in the poet Allan Ramsay's Tea-Table Miscellany, *and, with music, in 1725 in William Thomson's* Orpheus Caledonius, *this version was temporarily set aside in 1862 when the Edinburgh publisher Robert Chambers substituted in place of the 'less delicate' last line 'And the green grass growing over me', which he said he obtained from 'an old nurse's copy' (possibly an autobiographical description). The old form was restored in the revival of folk scholarship and Child pointed out its relationship to the ballad* Jamie Douglas *of which a variant of this forms part. This fixes the original protagonists as Lady Barbara Erskine, daughter of the Earl of Mar, and James, second Marquis of Douglas (1646?–1700), who deserted her after she had been falsely accused of adultery by his factor, William Lawrie. Lawrie also encompassed Douglas's financial ruin.*

O WALY, waly up the bank,
    And waly, waly, down the brae,
And waly, waly yon burn side,
    Where I and my love wont to gae.

I lean'd my back unto an aik,
    I thought it was a trusty tree;
But first it bow'd, and syne it brak,
    Sae my true love did lightly me!

O waly, waly, but love be bonny,
    A little time while it is new;
But when 'tis auld, it waxeth cauld,
    And fades away like the morning dew.

O wherefore should I busk my head?
    Or wherefore should I kame my hair?
For my true love has me forsook,
    And says he'll never love me mair.

Now Arthur-Seat shall be my bed,
    The sheets shall ne'er be fyl'd by me:
Saint Anton's well shall be my drink,
    Since my true love has forsaken me.

Martinmas wind, when wilt thou blaw,
    And shake the green leaves off the tree?
O gentle death, when wilt thou come?
    For of my life I'm weary.

'Tis not the frost that freezes fell,
    Nor blawing snaw's inclemency;
'Tis not sic cauld that makes me cry,
    But my love's heart grown cauld to me.

When we came in by Glasgow town,
    We were a comely sight to see;
My love was clad in the black velvet,
    And I my sell in cramasie.

But had I wist, before I kiss'd,
    That love had been sae ill to win,
I'd lock'd my heart in a case of gold,
    And pin'd it with a silver pin.

Oh, oh, if my young babe were born,
    And set upon the nurse's knee,
And I my sell were dead and gane!
    For a maid again I'll never be.

Old Song
Within a Mile of Edinburgh
Circa 1670

George Farquhar Graham included this version in his The Songs of Scotland *(1854), noting its obligations to* Twas within a furlong of Edinborough Town, *supposedly by Thomas D'Urfey (1653–1723), a friend of Charles II, but a variant also dates from the late seventeenth century,* Two furlongs from Edinburgh town. *Graham's version employed an air composed by James Hook, father of the wit Theodore Hook. Seasonal harvesting was carried on by Edinburgh labourers in the environs of the city for at least two centuries after this: Burke, Hare and their ladies took a turn at it near Peebles in 1828, following the practice of deserting urban occupations in summer.*

'TWAS within a mile of Edinburgh town,
    In the rosy time of the year;
Sweet flowers bloom'd, and the grass was down,
    And each shepherd woo'd his dear.
        Bonnie Jockie, blythe and gay,
        Kiss'd young Jenny making hay;
The lassie blush'd, and frowning cried, "Na, na, it winna do;
I canna, canna, winna, winna, maunna buckle to."

Young Jockie was a wag that never wad wed,
    Though lang he had followed the lass;
Contented she earn'd and eat her brown bread,
    And merrily turn'd up the grass.
        Bonnie Jockie, blythe and free,
        Won her heart right merrily:
Yet still she blush'd, and frowning cried, "Na, na, it winna do;
I canna, canna, winna, winna, maunna buckle to."

But when he vow'd he wad make her his bride,
   Though his flocks and herds were not few.
She gi'ed him her hand and a kiss beside,
   And vow'd she'd be for ever be true.
      Bonnie Jockie, blythe and free,
      Won her heart right merrily:
At kirk she no more frowning cried, "Na, na, it winna do;
I canna, canna, winna, winna, maunna buckle to."

The Town Council
The Wrath of God
1702

*The city's legislation of 1702 reflects the uneasy religious and political climate in Edinburgh follow-
ing the Revolution of 1688–89 and before the Union of Parliaments. Presbyterianism had been
established as a state religion with the Episcopalians being driven out of St Giles's Cathedral, but
many of the old fiercely anti-establishment heirs of the covenanters were unhappy at the failure to
proscribe their old opponents, under the legal settlement.*

From:

The Acts of the Town Council of Edinburgh etc. for the Suppressing
of VICE and IMMORALITY made since the Happy Revolution,
especially since the Year 1700.
Edinburgh MDCCXLII

ACT anent the Supressing of Immoralities; to be read every Council
Day, after *Whitsunday* and *Martinmas*.

Edinburgh 4th. December 1702.

THE which Day, the Lord Provost, Baillies, Council and Deacons of
Crafts, considering the great Growth of Immoralities of all Sorts,
within this City and Suburbs, and the fearful Rebukes of God by a
dreadful Fire in the *Parliament Close*, *Kirk Heugh* and *Cowgate*, which
happened about Midnight, upon the 3rd. of *February* 1700, and which is
recorded in the Council-Books, with their Christian Sentiments
thereanent, upon the 24th. of *April* thereafter.

As also, remembring that terrible Fire, which happened on the
North-side of the *Lawn Market*, about Mid-day, upon the 28th of
October 1701, wherein several Men and Women, and Children, were
consumed in the Flames, and lost by the Fall of ruinous Walls. And
further considering, that most tremendous and terrible Blowing up
on Gun-Powder in Leith, upon the 3rd. of *July* last, wherein sundry
persons were lost and wonderful ruins made in the Place. And likewise, reflecting on the other Tokens of God's Wrath, lately come

upon us, and what we are more and more threatened with, being moved with the Zeal of God, and the Ties he has laid on us, and that we have taken upon our selves to appear for him in our several Stations, do, in the Lord's Strength, resolve to be more watchful over our Hearts and Ways than formerly; and each of us, in our several Capacities, to reprove Vice, with that due Zeal and Prudence, as we shall have occasion, and to endeavour to promote the vigorous execution of those good laws for Suppressing of Vice, and punishing of the Vicious. And the Council appoints this their solemn Resolution to be recorded and the Clerks to read, or move the reading thereof in the Council, every first Council Day, after *Whitsunday* and *Martinmas* yearly, as a lasting and humbling Memorial of the said three dreadful Fires, and that under the Penalty of twenty Merks *Scots, toties quoties*. And recommends to the Deacons of Crafts, Captain Commandant of the Town Companies, Constables and Merchants of the Merchant Society to more making of the like Resolution, in their respective Incorporations and Societies, and to record the same in their Books.

Extracted,

ADAM WATT

Andrew Lang
The Case of Captain Green
1705

Andrew Lang (1844–1912), Scottish scholar, folklorist and populariser, very much in the tradition of Scott (whose biographer Lockhart's biography he wrote), produced a vast range of works opening up Homeric, French and Scottish culture to countless children, as well as work of critical importance on folklore and its relationship to epic and anthropology. His judgment was vital in the advancement of many younger writers, including Conan Doyle: in turn his Historical Mysteries (1904), of which this is one, show his use of classical detective fiction to aid historical technique. Another essay in that collection discusses the Appin murder so vital to Stevenson's Kidnapped, a mystery whose solution Lang said he knew but might not reveal.

'PLAY ON CAPTAIN GREEN'S WUDDIE,' said the caddy on Leith Links; and his employer struck his ball in the direction of the Captain's gibbet on the sands. Mr. Duncan Forbes of Culloden sighed, and, taking off his hat, bowed in the direction of the unhappy mariner's monument.

One can imagine this little scene repeating itself many a time, long after Captain Thomas Green, his mate, John Madder or Mather, and another of his crew were taken to the sands at Leith on the second Wednesday in April 1705, being April 11, and there hanged within the flood-mark upon a gibbet till they were dead. Mr. Forbes of Culloden, later President of the Court of Session, and, far more than the butcher Cumberland, the victor over the rising of 1745, believed in the innocence of Captain Green, wore mourning for him, attended the funeral at the risk of his own life, and, when the Porteous Riot was discussed in Parliament, rose in his place and attested his conviction that the captain was wrongfully done to death.

Green, like his namesake in the Popish Plot, was condemned for a crime of which he was probably innocent. Nay more, he died for a crime which was not proved to have been committed, though it really may have been committed by persons with whom Green had no connection, while Green may have been guilty of other misdeeds as bad as that for which he was hanged. Like the other Green, executed for the murder of Sir Edmund Berry Godfrey during the

Popish Plot, the captain was the victim of a fit of madness in a nation, that nation being the Scottish. The cause of their fury was not religion—the fever of the Covenant had passed away—but commerce.

'Twere long to tell and sad to trace the origin of the Caledonian frenzy. In 1695 the Scottish Parliament had passed, with the royal assent, an Act granting a patent to a Scottish company dealing with Africa, the Indies, and, incidentally, with the globe at large. The Act committed the occupant of the Scottish throne, William of Orange, to backing the company if attacked by alien power. But it was unlucky that England was then an alien power, and that the Scots Act infringed the patent of the much older English East India Company. Englishmen dared not take shares, finally, in the venture of the Scots; and when the English Board of Trade found out, in 1697, the real purpose of the Scottish company—namely, to set up a factory in Darien and anticipate the advantages dreamed of by France in the case of M. de Lesseps's Panama Canal—'a strange thing happened.' The celebrated philosopher, Mr. John Locke, and the other members of a committee of the English Board of Trade, advised the English Government to plagiarise the Scottish project, and seize the section of the Isthmus of Panama on which the Scots meant to settle. This was not done; but the Dutch Usurper, far from backing the Scots company, bade his colonies hold no sort of intercourse with them. The Scots were starved out of their settlement. The few who remained fled to New York and Jamaica, and there, perishing of hunger, were refused supplies by the English colonial governors. A second Scottish colony succumbed to a Spanish fleet and army, and the company, with a nominal capital of 400,000*l.* and with 220,000*l.* paid up, was bankrupt. Macaulay calculates the loss at about the same as a loss of forty millions would have been to the Scotland of his own day; let us say twenty-two millions.

We remember the excitement in France over the Panama failure. Scotland, in 1700, was even more furious, and that led to the hanging of Captain Green and his men. There were riots; the rioters were imprisoned in the Heart of Midlothian—the Tolbooth—the crowd released them; some of the crowd were feebly sentenced to the pillory, the public pelted them—with white roses; and had the Chevalier de St. George not been a child of twelve, he would have had a fair chance of recovering his throne. The trouble was tided over; William III. died in 1702. Queen Anne came to the Crown. But the bankrupt company was not dead. Its charter was still legal, and, with borrowed money, it sent out vessels to trade with the Indies. The company had a vessel, the 'Annandale,' which was seized in the Thames, at the instance of the East India Company, and condemned for a breach of that company's privileges.

This capture awakened the sleeping fury among my fiery countrymen (1704). An English ship, connected with either the English East India Company or the rival Million Company, put into Leith Road to repair. Here was a chance; for the charter of the Scots company authorised them 'to make reprisals and to seek and take reparation of damage done by sea and land.' On the strength of this clause, which was never meant to apply to Englishmen in Scottish waters, but to foreigners of all kinds on the Spanish Main, the Scottish Admiralty took no steps. But the company had a Celtic secretary, Mr. Roderick Mackenzie, and the English Parliament, in 1695, had summoned Mr. Mackenzie before them, and asked him many questions of an impertinent and disagreeable nature. This outrageous proceeding he resented, for he was no more an English than he was a Japanese subject. The situation of the 'Worcester' in Scottish waters gave Roderick his chance. His chief difficulty, as he informed his directors, was 'to get together a sufficient number of such genteel, pretty fellows as would, of their own free accord, on a sudden advertisement, be willing to accompany me on this adventure' (namely, the capture of the 'Worcester'), 'and whose dress and behaviour would not render them suspected of any uncommon design in going aboard.' A scheme more sudden and daring than the seizure, by a few gentlemen, of a well-armed English vessel had not been executed since the bold Buccleuch forced Carlisle Castle and carried away Kinmont Willie. The day was Saturday, and Mr. Mackenzie sauntered to the Cross in the High Street, and invited genteel and pretty fellows to dine with him in the country. They were given an inkling of what was going forward, and some dropped off, like the less resolute guests in Mr. Stevenson's adventure of the hansom cabs. When they reached Leith, Roderick found himself at the head of eleven persons, of whom 'most be as good gentlemen, and (I must own) much prettier fellows than I pretend to be.' They were of the same sort as Roy, Middleton, Haliburton, and Dunbar, who, fourteen years earlier, being prisoners on the Bass Rock, seized the castle, and, through three long years, held it for King James against the English navy.

The eleven chose Mr. Mackenzie as chief, and, having swords, pistols, 'and some with bayonets, too,' set out. Mackenzie, his servant, and three friends took a boat at Leith, with provision of wine, brandy, sugar, and lime juice; four more came, as a separate party, from Newhaven; the rest first visited an English man-of-war in the

Firth, and then, in a convivial manner, boarded the 'Worcester.' The punch-bowls were produced, liquor was given to the sailors, while the officers of the 'Worcester' drank with the visitors in the cabin. Mackenzie was supposed to be a lord. All was festivity, 'a most compleat scene of a comedy, acted to the life,' when as a Scottish song was being sung, each officer of the 'Worcester' found a pistol at his ear. The carpenter and some of the crew rushed at the loaded blunderbusses that hung in the cabin; but there were shining swords between them and the blunderbusses. By nine at night, on August 12, Mackenzie's followers were masters of the English ship, and the hatches, gunroom, chests, and cabinets were sealed with the official seal of the Scottish African and East India Company. In a day or two the vessel lay without rudder or sails in Bruntisland Harbour, 'as secure as a thief in a mill.' Mackenzie landed eight of the ship's guns and placed them in an old fort commanding the harbour entry, manned them with gunners, and all this while an English man-of-war lay in the Firth!

For a peaceful secretary of a commercial company, with a scratch eleven picked up in the street on a Saturday afternoon, to capture a vessel with a crew of twenty-four, well accustomed to desperate deeds, was 'a sufficient camisado or onfall.' For three or four days and nights Mr. Mackenzie had scarcely an hour's sleep. By the end of August he had commenced an action in the High Court of Admiralty for condemning the 'Worcester' and her cargo, to compensate for the damages sustained by his company through the English seizure of their ship, the 'Annandale'. When Mackenzie sent in his report on September 4, he added that, from 'very odd expressions dropt now and then from some of the ship's crew,' he suspected that Captain Green, of the 'Worcester,' was 'guilty of some very unwarrantable practices.'

The Scottish Privy Council were now formally apprised of the affair, which they cautiously handed over to the Admiralty. The Scottish company had for about three years bewailed the absence of a ship of their own, the 'Speedy Return,' which had never returned at all. Her skipper was a Captain Drummond, who had been very active in the Darien expedition: her surgeon was Mr. Andrew Wilkie, brother of James Wilkie, tailor and burgess of Edinburgh. The pair were most probably descendants of the Wilkie, tailor in the Canongate, who was mixed up in the odd business of Mr. Robert Oliphant, in the Gowrie conspiracy of 1600. Friends of Captain Drummond, Surgeon Wilkie, and others who had disappeared in the 'Speedy Return,' began to wonder whether the crew of the

'Worcester,' in their wanderings, had ever come across news of the missing vessel. One George Haines, of the 'Worcester,' hearing of a Captain Gordon, who was the terror of French privateers, said: 'Our sloop was more terrible upon the coast of Malabar than ever Captain Gordon will be to the French.' Mackenzie asking Haines if he had ever heard of the 'Speedy Return,' the missing ship, Haines replied: 'You need not trouble your head about her, for I believe you won't see her in haste.' He thought that Captain Drummond had turned pirate.

Haines now fell in love with a girl at Bruntisland, aged nineteen, named Anne Seaton, and told her a number of things, which she promised to repeat to Mackenzie, but disappointed him, though she had blabbed to others. It came to be reported that Captain Green had pirated the 'Speedy Return,' and murdered Captain Drummond and his crew. The Privy Council, in January 1705, took the matter up. A seal, or forged copy of the seal, of the Scottish African and East India Company was found on board the 'Worcester,' and her captain and crew were judicially interrogated, after the manner of the French *Juge d'Instruction*.

On March 5, 1705, the Scottish Court of Admiralty began the trial of Green and his men. Charles May, surgeon of the 'Worcester,' and two negroes, Antonio Ferdinando, cook's mate, and Antonio Francisco, captain's man, were ready to give evidence against their comrades. They were accused of attacking, between February and May, 1703, off the coast of Malabar a vessel bearing a red flag, and having English or Scots aboard. They pursued her in their sloop, seized and killed the crew, and stole the goods.

Everyone in Scotland, except resolute Whigs, believed the vessel attacked to have been Captain Drummond's 'Speedy Return.' But there was nothing definite to prove the fact; there was no *corpus delicti*. In fact the case was parallel to that of the Campden mystery, in which three people were hanged for killing old Mr. Harrison, who later turned up in perfect health. In Green's, as in the Campden case, some of the accused confessed their guilt, and yet evidence later obtained tends to prove that Captain Drummond and his ship and crew were all quite safe at the date of the alleged piracy by Captain Green. None the less, it does appear that Captain Green had been pirating some-body, and perhaps he was 'none the waur o' a hanging,' though, as he had an English commission to act against pirates, it was argued that, if he had been fighting at all, it was against pirates that he had been making war. Now Haines's remark that Captain Drummond, as he heard, had turned pirate, looks very like a 'hedge' to be used in case the 'Worcester' was proved to have attacked the 'Speedy Return.'

There was a great deal of preliminary sparring between the advocates as to the propriety of the indictment. The jury of fifteen contained five local skippers. Most of the others were traders. One of them, William Blackwood, was of a family that had been very active in the Darien affair. Captain Green had no better chance with these men than James Stewart of the Glens in face of a jury of Campbells. The first witness, Ferdinando, the black sea cook, deponed that he saw Green's sloop take a ship under English colours, and that Green, his mate, Madder, and others, killed the crew of the captured vessel with hatchets. Ferdinando's coat was part of the spoil, and was said to be of Scottish cloth. Charles May, surgeon of the 'Worcester,' being on shore, heard firing at sea, and, later, dressed a wound, a gunshot he believed, on the arm of the black cook; dressed wounds, also, of two sailors of the 'Worcester,' Mackay and Cuming—Scots obviously, by their names. He found the deck of the 'Worcester,' when he came on board, lumbered with goods and chests. He remarked on this, and Madder, the mate, cursed him, and bade him 'mind his plaister box.' He added that the 'Worcester,' before his eyes, while he stood on shore, was towing another vessel, which, he heard, was sold to a native dealer—Coge Commodo—who told the witness that the 'Worcester' 'had been fighting.' The 'Worcester' sprang a leak, and sailed for five weeks to a place where she was repaired, as if she were anxious to avoid inquiries.

Antonio Francisco, Captain Green's black servant, swore that, being chained and nailed to her forecastle, he heard the 'Worcester' fire six shots. Two days later a quantity of goods was brought on board (captured, it would seem, by the terrible sloop of the 'Worcester'), and Ferdinando then told his witness about the killing of the captured crew, and showed his own wounded arm. Francisco himself lay in chains for two months, and, of course, had a grudge against Captain Green. It was proved that the 'Worcester' had a cipher wherein to communicate with her owners, who used great secrecy; that her cargo consisted of arms, and was of such slight value as not to justify her voyage, unless her real business was piracy. The ship was of 200 tons, twenty guns, thirty-six men, and the value of the cargo was but 1,000l. Really, things do not look very well for the enterprise of Captain Green! There was also found a suspicious letter to one of the crew, Reynolds, from his sister-in-law, advising him to confess, and referring to a letter of his own in which he said that some of the crew 'had basely confessed.' The lady's letter and a copy of Reynolds's, admitted by him to be correct, were before the Court.

Again, James Wilkie, tailor, had tried at Bruntisland to 'pump' Haines about CaptainDrummond; Haines swore profane, but later said that he heard Drummond had turned pirate, and that off the coast of Malabar they had manned their sloop, lest Drummond, whom they believed to be on that coast, should attack them. Other witnesses corroborated Wilkie, and had heard Haines say that it was a wonder the ground did not open and swallow them for the wickedness 'that had been committed during the last voyage on board of that old [I omit a nautical term of endearment] *Bess.*' Some one telling Haines that the mate's uncle had been, 'burned in oil' for trying to burn Dutch ships at Amsterdam, 'the said George Haines did tell the deponent that if what Captain Madder [the mate] had done during his last voyage were known, he deserved as much as his uncle had met with.' Anne Seaton, the girl of Haines's heart, admitted that Haines had told her 'that he knew more of Captain Drummond than he would express at that time,' and she had heard his expressions of remorse. He had blabbed to many witnesses of a precious something hidden aboard the 'Worcester'; to Anne he said that he had now thrown it overboard. We shall see later what this object was. Anne was a reluctant witness. Glen, a goldsmith, had seen a seal of the Scots East India Company in the hands of Madder, the inference being that it was taken from the 'Speedy Return.'

Sir David Dalrymple, for the prosecution, made the most he could of the evidence. The black cook's coat, taken from the captured vessel, 'in my judgment appears to be Scots rugg.' He also thought it a point in favour of the cook's veracity that he was very ill, and forced to lie down in court; in fact, the cook died suddenly on the day when Captain Green was condemned, and the Scots had a high opinion of dying confessions. The white cook, who joined the 'Worcester' after the sea-fight, said that the black cook told him the whole story at that time. Why did the 'Worcester' sail for thirty-five days to repair her leak, which she might have done at Goa or Surat, instead of sailing some 700 leagues for the purpose? The jury found that there was 'one clear witness to robbery, piracy, and murder,' and accumulative corroboration.

The judges ordered fourteen hangings, to begin with those of Green, Madder, and three others on April 4. On March 16, at Edinburgh, Thomas Linsteed made an affidavit that the 'Worcester' left him on shore, on business, about January 1703; that fishing crews reported the fight of the sloop against a vessel unknown; they left before the fight ended; that the Dutch and Portuguese told him how the 'Worcester's' men had sold a prize, and thought but little of it, 'because it is what is ordinary on that coast,' and that the 'Worcester's' people told him to ask them no questions. On March 27 George Haines made a full confession of the murder of a captured crew, he being accessory thereto, at Sacrifice Rock, between Tellicherry and Calicut; and that he himself, after being seized by Mackenzie, threw his journal of the exciting events overboard. Now, in his previous blabbings before the trial, as we have seen, Haines had spoken several times about something on board the 'Worcester' which the Scots would be very glad to lay hands on, thereby indicating this journal of his; and he told Anne Seaton, as she deponed at the trial, that he had thrown the precious something overboard. In his confession of March 27 he explained what the mysterious something was. He also declared (March 28) that the victims of the piracy 'spoke the Scots language.' A sailor named Bruckley also made full confession. These men were reprieved, and doubtless expected to be; but Haines, all the while remorseful, I think, told the truth. The 'Worcester' had been guilty of piracy.

But had she pirated the Scottish ship, the 'Speedy Return,' Captain Drummond? As to that point, on April 5, in England, two of the crew of the 'Worcester,' who must somehow have escaped from Mackenzie's raid, made affidavit that the 'Worcester' fought no ship during her whole voyage. This would be more satisfactory if we knew more of the witnesses. On March 21, at Portsmouth, two other English mariners made affidavit that they had been of the crew of the 'Speedy Return'; that she was captured by pirates, while Captain Drummond and Surgeon Wilkie were on shore, at Maritan in Madagascar; and that these two witnesses 'went on board a Moca ship called the "Defiance," ' escaped from her at the Mauritius, and returned to England in the 'Raper' galley. Of the fate of Drummond and Wilkie, left ashore in Madagascar, they naturally knew nothing. If they spoke truth, Captain Green certainly did not seize the 'Speedy Return,' whatever dark and bloody deeds he may have done off the coast of Malabar.

In England, as Secretary Johnstone, son of the caitiff Covenanter, Waristoun, wrote to Baillie of Jerviswoode, the Whigs made party capital out of the proceedings against Green: they said it was a Jacobite plot. I conceive that few Scottish Whigs, to be sure, marched under Roderick Mackenzie.

In Scotland the Privy Council refused Queen Anne's demand that the execution of Green should be suspended till her pleasure was known, but they did grant a week's respite. On April 10 a mob, partly from the country, gathered in Edinburgh; the Privy Council, between the mob and the Queen, let matters take their course. On

April 11 the mob raged round the meeting-place of the Privy Council, rooms under the Parliament House, and chevied the Chancellor into a narrow close, whence he was hardly rescued. However, learning that Green was to swing after all, the mob withdrew to Leith sands, where they enjoyed the execution of an Englishman. The whole affair hastened the Union of 1707, for it was a clear case of Union or war between the two nations.

As for Drummond, many years later, on the occasion of the Porteous riot, Forbes of Culloden declared in the House of Commons that a few months after Green was hanged letters came from Captain Drummond, of the 'Speedy Return,' 'and from the very ship for whose capture the unfortunate person suffered, informing their friends that they were all safe.' But the 'Speedy Return' was taken by pirates, two of her crew say, off Madagascar, and burned. What was the date of the letters from the 'Speedy Return' to which, long after.-wards, Forbes, and he alone, referred? What was the date of the capture of the 'Speedy Return,' at Maritan, in Madagascar? Without the dates we are no wiser.

Now comes an incidental and subsidiary mystery. In 1729 was published *Madagascar, or Robert Drury's Journal during Fifteen Years' Captivity on the Island, written by Himself, digested into order, and now published at the Request of his Friends.* Drury says, as we shall see, that he, a lad of fifteen, was prisoner in Madagascar from *about* 1703 to 1718, and that there he met Captain Drummond, late of the 'Speedy Return.' If so, Green certainly did not kill Captain Drummond. But Drury's narrative seems to be about as authentic and historical as the so-called *Souvenirs of Madame de Créquy.* In the edition of 1890 of Drury's book, edited by Captain Pasfield Oliver, R.A., author of *Madagascar,* the Captain throws a lurid light on Drury and his volume. Captain Pasfield Oliver first candidly produces what he thinks the best evidence for the genuineness of Drury's story; namely a letter of the Rev. Mr. Hirst, on board H.M.S. 'Lenox,' off Madagascar, 1759. This gentleman praises Drury's book as the best and most authentic, for Drury says that he was wrecked in the 'Degrave,' East Indiaman, and his story 'exactly agrees, as far as it goes, with the journal kept by Mr. John Benbow,' second mate of the 'Degrave.' That journal of Benbow's was burned, in London, in 1714, but several of his friends remembered that it tallied with Drury's narrative. But, as Drury's narrative was certainly 'edited,' probably by Defoe, that master of fiction may easily have known and used Benbow's journal. Otherwise, if Benbow's journal contained the same references to Captain Drummond in Madagascar as Drury gives, then the question is settled: Drummond died in Madagascar after a stormy existence of some eleven years on that island. As to Drury, Captain Pasfield Oliver thinks that his editor, probably Defoe, or an imitator of Defoe, 'faked' the book, partly out of De Flacourt's *Histoire de Madagascar* (1661), and a French authority adds another old French source, Dapper's *Description de l'Afrique*. Drury was himself a pirate, his editor thinks: Defoe picked his brains, or an imitator of Defoe did so, and Defoe, or whoever was the editor, would know the story that Drummond really lost the 'Speedy Return' in Madagascar, and could introduce the Scottish adventurer into Drury's romance.

We can never be absolutely certain that Captain Drummond lost his ship, but lived on as a kind of *condottiere* to a native prince in Madagascar. Between us and complete satisfactory proof a great gulf has been made by fire and water, 'foes of old' as the Greek poet says, which conspired to destroy the journal kept by Haines and the journal kept by Benbow. The former would have told us what piratical adventures Captain Green achieved in the 'Worcester;' the latter, if it spoke of Captain Drummond in Madagascar, would have proved that the captain and the 'Speedy Return' were not among the 'Worcester's' victims. If we could be sure that Benbow's journal corroborated Drury's romance, we could not be sure that the editor of the romance did not borrow the facts from the journal of Benbow, and we do not know that this journal made mention of Captain Drummond, for the only valid testimony as to the captain's appearance in Madagascar is the affidavit of Israel Phippany and Peter Freeland, at Portsmouth, March 31, 1705, and these mariners may have perjured themselves to save the lives of English seamen condemned by the Scots.

Yet, as a patriotic Scot, I have reason for believing in the English affidavit at Portsmouth. The reason is simple, but sufficient. Captain Drummond, if attacked by Captain Green, was the man to defeat that officer, make prize of his ship, and hang at the yardarm the crew which was so easily mastered by Mr. Roderick Mackenzie and eleven pretty fellows. Hence I conclude that the 'Worcester' really had been pirating off the coast of Malabar, but that the ship taken by Captain Green in these waters was not the 'Speedy Return,' but another, unknown. If so, there was no great miscarriage of justice, for the indictment against Captain Green did not accuse him of seizing the 'Speedy Return,' but of piracy, robbery, and murder, though the affair of the 'Speedy Return' was brought in to give local colour. This fact and the national excitement probably turned the scale with the jury, who otherwise would have returned a verdict of 'Not Proven.' That verdict, in fact, would have been fitted to the merits of the case; but 'there was mair tint at Shirramuir' than when Captain Green was hanged. That Green was deeply guilty, I have inferred from the evidence. To Mr. Stephen Ponder I owe corroboration. He cites a passage from Hamilton's *New Account of the East Indies* (1727), chap. 25, which is crucial.

'The unfortunate Captain Green, who was afterwards hanged in Scotland, came on board my ship at sunset, very much overtaken in drink and several of his men in the like condition (at Calicut, February 1703). He wanted to sell Hamilton some arms and ammunition, and told me that they were what was left of a large quantity that he had brought from England, but had been at Madagascar and had disposed of the rest to good advantage among the pirates. I told him that in prudence he ought to keep these as secrets lest he might be brought in trouble about them. He made but little account of my advice, and so departed. About ten in the night his chief mate Mr. Mather came on board of my ship and seemed to be very melancholy... He burst out in tears and told me he was afraid that he was undone, and they had acted such things in their voyage that would certainly bring them to shame and punishment, if they should come to light; and he was assured that such a company of drunkards as their crew was composed of could keep no secret. I told him that I heard at Coiloan (Quilon) that they had not acted prudently nor honestly in relation to some Moors' ships they had visited and plundered *and in sinking a sloop with ten or twelve Europeans in her* off Coiloan. Next day I went ashore and met Captain Green and his supercargo Mr. Callant, who had sailed a voyage from Surat to Sienly with me. Before dinner-time they were both drunk, and Callant told me that he did not doubt of making the greatest voyage that ever was made from England on so small a stock as 500*l*.

'In the evening their surgeon accosted me and asked if I wanted a surgeon. He said he wanted to stay in India, for his life was uneasy on board of his ship, that though the captain was civil enough, yet Mr. Mather had treated him with blows for asking a pertinent question of some wounded men, who were hurt in the engagement with the sloop. I heard too much to be contented with their conduct, and so I shunned their conversation for the little time I staid at Calicut.

'Whether Captain Green and Mr. Mathew had justice impartially in their trial and sentence I know not. I have heard of as great innocents condemned to death as they were.'

The evidence of Hamilton settles the question of the guilt of Green and his crew, as regards some unfortunate vessel, or sloop. Had the 'Speedy Return' a sloop with her?

Robert Burns
The End of the Scottish Parliament
1707

The reputation of Robert Burns (1759–1796) was established with Poems, chiefly in the Scottish Dialect *(Kilmarnock, 1786; Edinburgh, London, 1787), his lyrical mastery and restoration of poetry to its natural surroundings helping to preserve the dying Lallans culture, finding a new vernacular for Gaelic-speakers forced to lose their own language under industrialisation, and successfully challenging the artificiality of prevailing English poetic modes. He followed it up with even greater creative triumphs, including the mock-heroic ballad* Tam o'Shanter *(1790), and outstanding folklore research. His recapture of vanishing songs of the past seemed to enable him to capture some of the spirit of songs already forgotten about far-off events. The present is an example of his Scottish diction in its more classical form. It was composed in 1792 for slow, dirge-like music. The Union came into existence on 1 May 1707, and with it a still unsolved question of Scottish identity.*

Fareweel to a' our Scotish fame,
    Fareweel our ancient glory;
Fareweel even to the Scotish name,
    Sae fam'd in martial story!
Now Sark rins o'er the Solway sands,
    And Tweed rins to the ocean,
To mark whare England's province stands,
    Such a parcel of rogues in a nation!

What force or guile could not subdue,
    Thro' many warlike ages,
Is wrought now by a coward few,
    For hireling traitors' wages.
The English steel we could disdain,
    Secure in valor's station;
But English gold has been our bane,
    Such a parcel of rogues in a nation!

O would, or I had seen the day
   That treason thus could sell us,
My auld grey head had lien in clay,
   Wi' BRUCE and loyal WALLACE!
But pith and power, till my last hour,
   I'll mak this declaration;
We're brought and sold for English gold,
   Such a parcel of rogues in a nation!

The Master of Sinclair

The 'Fifteen
1715

John Sinclair, Master of Sinclair (1683–1750), served under the Duke of Marlborough in Flanders and was sentenced to death for shooting Captain Shaw in 1708, whereupon he fled to Prussia until pardoned in 1712. On the insurrection in Scotland in support of 'James III and VIII' against the House of Hanover, he captured Government stores at Burntisland, failed to distinguish himself at Sheriffmuir, and conceived a venomous distaste for most of his fellow-Jacobites. His acid Memoirs of the Rebellion were not printed until Sir Walter Scott edited and annotated them for the Roxburghe Club in 1828: he himself was pardoned in 1726.

IT WAS BEFORE THIS, that the ſurpriſeing the Caſtle of Edinburgh had failed. I can't be poſitive who laid the ſcheme; but it was projected after the Queen's death, and gone into by ſome younge people about Edinburgh, who had ſcrewd themſelves into the belief that the King was then to land, at which time they were readie to put it in execution. But the hopes of that being over, through impatience to ſhew their diligence, they communicated it to a great many of their friends; and, as it is uſuall, everie new plotter was racking his brain how to improve the firſt ſcheme, to have a ſhare of the honour in caſe ane opportunitie offered, and thereby the meaſures of the whole project were more and more diſconcerted. And thus they continued untill the beginning of Auguſt 1715, that the intention of Lord Mar's goeing to the Highlands was publicklie known; and then thoſe who had been all alonge the principall contrivers of that affair thought there was no time to be loſt in comeing to a finall reſolution about the proper methods, and even in putting them to the tryell, applied themſelves to my Lord Mar, who encouraged it; becauſe, whatever the event might be, it dipt ſo manie who muſt be oblidged to refuge to him. My Lord Drummond, who, amongſt the many good qualities he has inherited of his familie, has that of imagining nothing can be well done except he has the management of it, would undertake the direction of all; and, for that effect, made choice of a little brokne merchant, Charles Forbes, a man according to his own heart, who was to be principall engineer and conductor of that affair. Thomas Arthur, who had formerlie been ane officer in the Caſtle, had, six months before, gained a ſerjeant, and brib'd a ſojer of the guarniſone; the ſerjeant, when he'd have the guard, was to place that ſojer ſentrie at a poſt on the Caſtle wall, which they had agreed on. The ſentrie was to have a clew of ſmall cordes in his pocket, one end of which he was to throw down to thoſe who were to ſurpriſe the Caſtle, who were to tye it to a grapling iron, faſtned at the end of the ſcaladeing ladders, which he was to pull up and fix in the head of the wall or parapet. They propoſed to doe the work with fourſcore or nintie men, whereof ſortie were to be Highlandmen, who were ſent to toun by my Lord Drummond about the time appointed, all by different roads, with orders to obey one Drummond of Bouhadie. Fiftie younge apprentices, advocates' ſervants, writers, and ſome ſervants to thoſe in the Government, were let into the ſecret, to make up the number to be imploy'd in the attack. At laſt, the ſerjeant letting them know the night he could ſerve them, and the time, the Weſt Kirk, a place under the Caſtle wall, was agreed on to be the place of rendezvous, preciſelie at nine of the clock at night, where they were to come armed with piſtells and ſuords. They all mett at the place and hour appointed. Things haveing thus far ſucceeded to their wiſh, they, and it muſt be own'd reaſonablie, haveing brought it ſo great a length, reckoned themſelves ſure of their ſtroak; but the principall thing was ſtill wanting. They had imploy'd a fellow in the Caltone to make the ladders, which Mr Arthur and his brother, Doctor Arthur, were to mount the firſt, becauſe they knew the Caſtle beſt; and had brought the greateſt part of the ladders, with the grapling iron, alonge with them to the Weſt Kirk at the hour appointed; and Charles Forbes had takne it upon him to bring the reſt of the ladders preſiſelie at the came hour, but inſtead of that, ſtay'd till after ten in the citie, drinkeing to good news from the Caſtle, while the others were waiteing impatientlie at the Weſt Kirk; for they had deſigned to begin the attack at ten, which being paſt, and receaveing no neus of Forbes or their ladders, not knowing what to doe, and afraid the ſentre would looſe patience, or be relieved, ſcrambled up the rock, and poſted themſelves at the foot of the wall, with a reſolution, in all events, to ſtay there as longe as they could. And thus they continued till eleven of the clock, when, being out of all patience, and the ſentrie telling he was to be relieved at twelve, they made him pull up the grapling irone, in

76

order to try if the ladders they had could doe; but, as they *ſuſpected*, they found them above a fathome too *ſhort*; and in this *ſituation* did they continue still half an hour after eleven, when the *ſentrie* per-ceaveing the rounds comeing about, called down to them, "God damn you all! you have ruined both *yourſelves* and me! Here comes the round I have been telling you of this hour, I can *ſerve* you no longer." And with that threw down the grapling iron, fired his piece, and called out "Enemie;" upon which everie man *ſhifted* for *himſelf*, the round fireing over the wall after them. And at this time, when the fireing from the wall hapned, Mr Forbes, the ingeneer, had onlie advanced to the back of Bareford's Parks, on the north *ſide* of the North Loch, with the *reſt* of the ladders, and could not been up in time before that *ſentrie* was to be reliev'd.

My Lord *Juſtice*-Clerck, haveing got a hint of the *deſigne*, was the *occaſion* of that rounds goeing about, haveing given the Gourvernour the alarme, and at *ſame* time, with difficultie, got twelve men of the Burgers' Guard from the *Magiſtrats*, of the toun, to goe without the walls, under the command of ane officer, who saw no bodie but two boys, who *ſaid*, they came there by chance, whome he took *priſoners*, together with ane old man, who had fallen from the rock. But all agree, that had the ladders come in time, the *Juſtice*-Clerck's *advertiſement* had come too late; and blamed my Lord Drummond for the *choiſe* of his ingeneer. It was, I may *ſay*, miraculous, that *ſo* many keept the *ſecret*, or rather, that the Gouvernment was not *ſooner* informed by *ſome* indirect way or other; for they were *ſo* far from carrieing on their affairs privately, that a gentleman, who was not concerned, told me that he was in a *houſe* that evening where eighteen of them were drinking, and heard the *hoſteſs ſay*, they were poudering their hair to goe to the attack of the *Caſtle*.

David, Lord Elcho
The 'Forty-five
1745

The attempt of Charles Edward Stuart, son of the exiled James, seemed far more formidable than that of his father in its initial military success and geographical extent, but it never really had the chance of overthrowing the Hanoverians which certainly existed in 1715. David Wemyss, Lord Elcho (1721–1787), was characteristic of the Scottish nobility in coming from a divided family. His great-grandfather had been a Scottish commander, defeated by Montrose in 1644 and 1645, while his grandfather was a commissioner for the Union. He himself visited Britain as a Jacobite agent in 1744 to scout out the possibilities of the rebellion, and during its course he commanded Charles's life-guards. His father James, fourth Earl of Wemyss, died in 1756, but Elcho had been attainted and remained permanently excluded from his title and estates. He died in exile in Paris. This extract is drawn from the narrative of the insurrection which he wrote after its defeat, and which was published in 1907, A Short Account of the Affairs of Scotland in the Years 1744, 1745 and 1746.

AT EIGHT OF THE CLOCK at Night The Prince sent a messauge to the Magistrates of Edinburg to Demand the keys of the Town and to tell them he intended to Enter it either that night or next day, and if their was any resistance made, whoever was found in Arms should be Severely treated; and besides, he Could not answere but if the town was taken by Storm his Soldiers would plunder it. At ten at night, their came four of the town Councill out to the Princes quarters to beg he would give them time to think on his demand. This was a messauge contrived to gain time, for they expected General Copes Army every hour to land at Leith from Aberdeen, and in case he landed time Enough, they intended to wait the Event of a Battle. The Prince, after they had kiss'd his hand, told them that he was going to send of a detachment to Attack the town and lett them defend it at their peril; that if they did the Consequences would be bad, and if they did not he intended no harm to the old Metropolis of his Kingdom. As Soon as they received this answere the Prince order'd Young Lochiel with 800 men to March & attack the town. Their Came out sometime after another deputation of Six Counsellors: Provost Coots was one of them. They Gott the same Answere as the first, and the Prince did not See them. The Coach that they came out in went in at the West port and sett down the Company, and as they were letting out the Coach at the Netherbow Lochiels party who were arrived their rush'd in, seized all the Gaurds of the Town, who made no resistance, and made themselves masters of Edinburgh whihout firing a Shot. They Establish'd Guards at the Gates, Guard house Weigh house, and Parliment house. Notwithstanding of the towns being in this way taken without any Capitulation, the Highlanders did no mischief. The Prince Gott the news of Ednrs being taken the next morning 17 of Sept as he was upon his March and of their having seized 1000 Stand of Arms, which Gave him & his Army a Great deal of joy as they Stood in need of them. When the Army Came near town it was mett by vast Multitudes of people, who by their repeated Shouts & huzzas express'd a great deal of joy to See the Prince. When they Came into the Suburbs the Croud was prodigious and all wishing the Prince prosperity; in Short, nobody doubted but that he would be joined by 10,000 men at Edinburgh if he Could Arm them. The Army took the road to Dediston, Lord Strathallan marching first at the head of the horse, The Prince next on horseback with the Duke of Perth on his right and Lord Elcho on his left, then Lord George Murray on foot at the head of the Colum of Infantry. From Dediston the Army enter'd the Kings park at a breach made in the wall. Lord George halted sometime in the Park, but afterwards march'd the foot to Dediston, and the Prince Continued on horseback always followed by the Croud, who were happy if they could touch his boots or his horse furniture. In the Steepest part of the park Going down to the Abey he was obliged to Alight and walk, but the Mob out of Curiosity, and some out of fondness to touch him or kiss his hand, were like to throw him down, so, as soon as he was down the hill, he mounted his horse and road through St Anes yards into Holyroodhouse Amidst the Cries of 60000 people, who fill'd the Air with the Acclamations of joy. He dismounted in the inner court and went up Stairs into the Gallery, and from thence into the Duke of Hamiltons Apartment, which he Occupied all the time he was at Edinbourgh. The Croud Continued all that night in the outward Court of the Abbey and huzza'd Every time the Prince Appeared at the Window. He was joined Upon his Entring the Abby by the Earl of Kelly, Lord Balmerino, Mr Hepburn of Keith, Mr Lockart younger of Carnwath, Mr Graham younger of Airth, Mr Rollo Younger of Powhouse, Mr Sterling of Craigbarnet, Mr Hamilton of Bangore and Younger of Kilbrackmont, Sir David Murray, and Several other Gentlemen of distinction, but not one of the Mob who were so fond of seeing him Ever ask'd to Enlist in his Service, and when he marched to fight

Cope he had not one of them in his Army. The Princes first orders in Edinburgh were to Cause his Father to be proclaimed and his Manifestos to be read, which was done by the pursuivants in their habits from the Cross by Sound of Trumpet and all the Usual Ceremonies used at a proclamation. There was a paper likewise given about here which had been wrote in the highlands Upon the Princes hearing that the Lords of the regency had put a reward upon his head of 30000pd. This paper offer'd the like sum to any body that would secure the person of the Elector of Hanover (as his Majesty was at the time of the Princes Landing Abroad but Arrived at London soon after). At night their came a Great many Ladies of Fashion, to Kiss his hand, but his behaviour to them was very Cool: he had not been much used to Women Company, and was always embarrassed while he was with them.

Nursery Rhyme
As I went by the Luckenbooths
Circa 1750

This poem for children, collected by Norah and William Montgomerie and included in their Hogarth Book of Scottish Rhymes *(1964) clearly derives from the period subsequent to the 'Forty-five when memories of the romantic royal leader still haunted Scotland. The poem employs the form of Gaelic Jacobite poetry in Scotland and Ireland where a woman, sometimes Ireland, sometimes Scotland or Britain or the cause of Jacobitism, seeks her lost gallant (the exiled Stuart) and hopes for his victorious return: the Irish form,* Aisling, *is customarily a dream-vision. But in this rhyme there is also counterposed the symbol of a new order who in a sense exorcises the spirit-woman, and the reference to France serves to emphasise its alienation from the new Scotland emerging with the 'age of improvement'. France was at war with Britain for much of the period from the 'Forty-five to 1763, by which time the Jacobite cause was hopeless. But Edinburgh remained bitterly hostile to Catholicism; for example, Protestant sentiment induced fierce riots against any grant of civil rights to Catholics when such a proposal was mooted in 1779.*

As I went by the Luckenbooths
    I saw a lady fair
She had long ear-rings in her ears
    And jewels in her hair.
And when she came to our door,
    She spiered at what was ben,
"Oh, have you seen my lost love,
    With his braw Highland men?"

The smile upon her bonnie cheek
    Was sweeter than the bee;
Her voice was like the birds song
    Upon the birken tree.
But when the minister came out
    Her mare began to prance,
Then rode into the sunset
    Beyond the coast of France.

James Hogg
George Dobson's Expedition to Hell
1764

The Private Memoirs and Confessions of a Justified Sinner (1824) by James Hogg (1770–1835) has been recognised in this century as one of the classics of the literature of damnation, its most notable votaries including André Gide. In his own day Hogg, known as the 'Ettrick Shepherd', was presented to his annoyance as an uncouth and eccentric figure notably through dialogue put in his mouth by the literary ruffians of Blackwood's Magazine John Wilson (Christopher North) and John Gibson Lockhart. Scott owed border folk balladry to Hogg's aid, and Hogg's own poems achieved some celebrity, notably Kilmeny. He lived in Edinburgh between 1810 and 1816 and visited it frequently, otherwise working first as shepherd and then, with varying fortunes, as farmer. His The Shepherd's Calendar, Dreams and Apparitions whence this comes, appeared in 1829. It is impossible to date the supposed event exactly; hackney-carriages are first mentioned by Act of Parliament in 1832. Since Hogg clearly wishes to refer to an older time, but not entirely out of living memory, it seems appropriate to place it slightly anterior to Dickens's Bagman's Uncle.

THERE IS NO PHENOMENON in nature less understood, and about which greater nonsense is written, than dreaming. It is a strange thing. For my part, I do not understand it, nor have I any desire to do so; and I firmly believe that no philosopher that ever wrote knows a particle more about it than I do, however elaborate and subtle the theories he may advance concerning it. He knows not even what sleep is, nor can he define its nature, so as that any common mind can comprehend him; and how can he define that ethereal part of it, wherein the soul holds intercourse with the external world?—how, in that state of abstraction, some ideas force themselves upon us, in spite of all our efforts to get rid of them; while others, which we have resolved to bear about with us by night as well as by day, refuse us their fellowship, even at periods when we most require their aid?

No, no; the philosopher knows nothing about either; and if he says he does, I entreat you not to believe him. He does not know what mind is; even his own mind, to which one would think he has the most direct access; far less can he estimate the operations and powers of that of any other intelligent being. He does not even know, with all his subtlety, whether it be a power distinct from his body, or essentially the same, and only incidentally and temporarily endowed with different qualities. He sets himself to discover at what period of his existence the union was established. He is baffled; for consciousness refuses the intelligence, declaring, that she cannot carry him far enough back to ascertain it. He tries to discover the precise moment when it is dissolved, but on this consciousness is altogether silent, and all is darkness and mystery; for the origin, the manner of continuance, and the time and mode of breaking up of the union between soul and body, are in reality undiscoverable by our natural faculties—are not patent, beyond the possibility of mistake: but whosoever can read his Bible, and solve a dream, can do either, without being subjected to any material error.

It is on this ground that I like to contemplate, not the theory of dreams, but the dreams themselves; because they prove to the unlettered and contemplative mind, in a very forcible manner, a distinct existence of the soul, and its lively and rapid intelligence with external nature, as well as with a world of spirits with which it has no acquaintance, when the body is lying dormant, and the same to it as if sleeping in death.

I account nothing of any dream that relates to the actions of the day; the person is not then sound asleep; there is no division between matter and mind, but they are mingled together in a sort of chaos—what a farmer would call compost—fermenting and disturbing one another. I find, that in all these sort of dreams, every calling and occupation of men have their own, relating in some degree to their business; and in the country, at least, their imports are generally understood. Every man's body is a barometer. A thing made up of the elements must be affected by their various changes and convulsions, and so it assuredly is. When I was a shepherd, and all the comforts of my life so much depending on good or ill weather, the first thing I did every morning was strictly to overhaul the dreams of the night, and I found that I could better calculate from them than from the appearance and changes of the sky. I know a keen sportsman, who pretends that his dreams never deceive him. If he dream of angling, or pursuing salmon in deep waters, he is sure of rain; but if fishing on dry ground, or in waters so low that the fish cannot get from him, it forebodes drought; hunting or shooting hares, is snow, and moorfowl, wind, &c. But the most extraordinary professional dream on record is, without all doubt, that well-known one of George Dobson, coach-driver in Edinburgh, which I shall here relate; for though it did not happen in the shepherd's cot, it has often been recited there.

George was part proprietor and driver of a hackney-coach in Edinburgh, when such vehicles were scarce; and one day there comes a gentleman to him whom he knew, and says:—"George, you must drive me and my son here out to a certain place," that he named, somewhere in the vicinity of Edinburgh.—"Sir," says George, "I never heard tell of such a place, and I cannot drive you to it unless you give me very particular directions."

"It is false," returned the gentleman; "there is no man in Scotland who knows the road to that place better than you do. You have never driven on any other road all your life, and I insist on your taking us."

"Very well, sir," says George. "I'll drive you to hell if you have a mind, only you are to direct me on the road."

"Mount and drive on, then," said the other, "and no fear of the road."

George did so, and never in his life did he see his horses go at such a noble rate; they snorted, they pranced, and they flew on; and as the whole road appeared to lie down hill, he deemed that he should soon come to his journey's end. Still he drove on at the same rate, far far down hill,—and so fine an open road he never travelled,—till by degrees it grew so dark that he could not see to drive any further. He called to the gentleman, inquiring what he should do; who answered, that this was the place they were bound to, so he might draw up, dismiss them, and return. He did so, alighted from the dickie, wondered at his foaming horses, and forthwith opened the coach-door, held the rim of his hat with the one hand, and with the other demanded his fare.

"You have driven us in fine style, George," said the elder gentleman, "and deserve to be remembered; but it is needless for us to settle just now, as you must meet us here again tomorrow precisely at twelve o'clock."

"Very well, sir," says George, "there is likewise an old account, you know, and some toll-money;" which indeed there was.

"It shall all be settled to-morrow, George, and moreover, I fear there will be some toll-money to-day."

"I perceived no tolls to-day, your honour," said George.

"But I perceived one, and not very far back neither, which I suspect you will have difficulty in repassing without a regular ticket. What a pity I have no change on me!"

"I never saw it otherwise with your honour," said George, jocularly; "what a pity it is you should always suffer yourself to run short of change!"

"I will give you that which is as good, George," said the gentleman; and he gave him a ticket written with red ink, which the honest coachman could not read. He, however, put it into his sleeve, and inquired of his employer where that same toll was which he had not observed, and how it was that they did not ask toll from him as he came through? The gentlemen replied, by informing George that there was no road out of that domain, and that whoever entered it must either remain in it, or return by the same path; so they never asked any toll till the person's return, when they were at times highly capricious; but that ticket would answer his turn. And he then asked George if he did not perceive a gate, with a number of men in black standing about it.

"Oho! Is yon the spot?" says George; "Then, I assure your honour, yon is no toll-gate, but a private entrance into a great man's mansion; for I do not I know two or three of yon to be gentlemen of the law, whom I have driven often and often; and as good fellows they are too, as any I know—men who never let themselves run short of change. Good day.—Twelve o'clock to-morrow?"

"Yes, twelve o'clock noon, precisely;" and with that, George's employers vanished in the gloom, and left him to wind his way out of that dreary labyrinth the best way he could. He found it no easy matter, for his lamps were not lighted, and he could not see an ell before him—he could not even perceive his horses' ears; and what was worse, there was a rushing sound, like that of a town on fire, all around him, that stunned his senses, so that he could not tell whether his horses were moving or standing still. George was in the greatest distress imaginable, and was glad when he perceived the gate before him, with his two identical friends of the law still standing. George drove boldly up, accosted them by their names, and asked what they were doing there; but they made him no answer, but pointed to the gate and the keeper. George was terrified to look at this latter personage, who now came up and seized his horses by the reins, refusing to let him pass. In order to intoduce himself in some degree to this austere toll-man, George asked him, in a jocular manner, how he came to employ his two eminent friends as assistant gate-keepers?

"Because they are among the last comers," replied the ruffian, churlishly. "You will be an assistant here, to-morrow."

"The devil I will, sir?"

"Yes, the devil you will, sir."

"I'll be d—if I do then—that I will."

"Yes, you'll be d—if you do—that you will."

"Let my horses go in the meantime then, sir, that I may proceed on my journey."

"Nay."

"Nay?—Dare you say nay to me, sir? My name is George Dobson, of the Pleasance, Edinburgh, coach driver, and coach proprietor too; and I'll see the face of the man d—who will say *nay* to me, as long as I can pay my way. I have his Majesty's licence, and I'll go and come as I choose—and that I will. Let go my horses there, and say what is your demand."

"Well, then, I'll let your horses go," said the keeper; "but I'll keep yourself for a pledge." And with that he let go the horses, and seized honest George by the throat, who struggled in vain to disengage himself, and cursed, swore, and threatened, by his own confession, most bloodily. His horses flew off like the wind, so swift, that the coach was flying in the air, and scarcely stotting on the earth once in a quarter of a mile. George was in furious wrath, for he saw that his grand coach and harness would all be broken to pieces, and his gallant pair of horses maimed or destroyed; and how was his family's bread now to be won!—He struggled, swore, threatened, and prayed in vain—the intolerable toll-man was deaf to all remonstrances. He once more appealed to his two genteel acquaintances of the law, reminding them how he had of late driven them to Roslin on a Sunday, along with two ladies, who, he supposed, were their sisters, from their familiarity, when not another coachman in town would engage with them. But the gentlemen, very ungenerously, only shook their heads, and pointed to the gate. George's circumstances now became desperate, and again he asked the hideous toll-man what right he had to detain him, and what were his charges.

"What right have I to detain you, sir, say you? Who are you that make such a demand here? Do you know where you are, sir?"

"No, faith, I do not," returned George; "I wish I did. But I *shall* know, and make you repent your insolence too. My name, I told you, is George Dobson, licensed coach-hirer in Edinburgh, Pleasance; and to get full redress of you for this unlawful interruption, I only desire to know where I am."

"Then, sir, if it can give you so much satisfaction to know where you are," said the keeper, with a malicious grin, "you *shall* know, and you may take instruments by the hands of your two friends there, instituting a legal prosecution. Your redress, you may be assured, will be most ample, when I inform you that you are in Hell, and out of this gate you return no more."

This was rather a damper to George, and he began to perceive that nothing would be gained in such a place by the strong hand, so he addressed the inexorable toll-man, whom he now dreaded more than ever, in the following terms. "But I must go home, at all events, you know, sir, to unyoke my two horses, and put them up, and to inform Chirsty Halliday, my wife, of my engagement. And, bless me! I never recollected till this moment, that I am engaged to be back here to-morrow at twelve o'clock, and see here is a free ticket for my passage this way."

The keeper took the ticket with one hand, but still held George with the other. "Oho! were you in with our honourable friend, Mr R** of L***y?" said he. "He has been on our books for a longe while,—however, this will do, only you must put your name to it likewise; and the engagement is this—You, by this instrument, engage your soul, that you will return here by to-morrow at noon."

"Catch me there, billy!" says George. "I'll engage no such thing, depend on it;— that I will not."

"Then remain where you are," said the keeper, "for there is no other alternative. We like best for people to come here in their own way, in the way of their business;" and with that he flung George backward, heels-over-head down hill, and closed the gate.

George, finding all remonstrance vain, and being desirous once more to see the open day, and breathe the fresh air, and likewise to see Chirsty Halliday, his wife, and set his house and stable in some order, came up again, and in utter desperation, signed the bond, and was suffered to depart. He then bounded away on the track of his horses, with more than ordinary swiftness, in hopes to overtake them; and always now and then uttered a loud wo! in hopes they might hear and obey, though he could not come in sight of them. But George's grief was but beginning, for at a well-known and dangerous spot, where there was a tan-yard on the one hand, and a quarry on the other, he came to his gallant steeds overturned, the coach smashed to pieces, Dawtie with two of her legs broken, and Duncan dead. This was more than the worthy coachman could bear, and many degrees worse than being in hell. There his pride and manly spirit bore him up against the worst of treatment; but here his heart entirely failed him, and he laid himself down, with his face on his two hands, and wept bitterly, bewailing, in the most deplorable terms, his two gallant horses, Dawtie and Duncan.

While lying in this inconsolable state, behold there was one took hold of his shoulder, and shook it; and a well-known voice said to him "Geordie! What is the matter wi' ye, Geordie?" George was provoked beyond measure at the insolence of the question, for he knew the voice to be that of Chirsty Halliday, his wife. "I think you needna ask that, seeing what you see," said George. "O my poor Dawtie,

87

where are a' your jinkings and prancings now, your moopings and your wincings? I'll ne'er be a proud man again—bereaved o' my bonny pair."

"Get up, George; get up, and bestir yourself," said Chirsty Halliday, his wife. "You are wanted directly, to bring in the Lord President to the Parliament House. It is a great storm, and he must be there by nine o'clock.—Get up—rouse yourself, and make ready—his servant is waiting for you."

"Woman, you are demented!" cried George. "How can I go and bring in the Lord President, when my coach is broken in pieces, my poor Dawtie lying with twa of her legs broken, and Duncan dead? And, moreover, I have a previous engagement, for I am obliged to be in hell before twelve o'clock."

Chirsty Halliday now laughed outright, and continued long in a fit of laughter, but George never moved his head from the pillow, but lay and groaned, for, in fact, he was all this while lying snug in his bed; while the tempest without was roaring with great violence, and which circumstance may perhaps account for the rushing and deafening sound which astounded him so much in hell. But so deeply was he impressed with the realities of his dream that he would do nothing but lie and moan, persisting and believing in the truth of all he had seen. His wife now went and informed her neighbours of her husband's plight, and of his singular engagement with Mr R** of L***y at twelve o'clock. She persuaded one friend to harness the horses, and go for the Lord President; but all the rest laughed immoderately at poor coachy's predicament. It was, however, no laughing to him; he never raised his head, and his wife becoming at last uneasy about the frenzied state of his mind, made him repeat every circumstance of his adventure to her, (for he would never believe or admit that it was a dream,) which he did in the terms above narrated; and she perceived, or dreaded, that he was becoming somewhat feverish. She went over and told Dr Wood of her husband's malady, and of his solemn engagement to be in hell at twelve o'clock.

"He maunna keep it, dearie. He maunna keep that engagement at no rate," said Dr Wood. "Set back the clock an hour or twa, to drive him past the time, and I'll ca' in the course of my round. Are ye sure he hasna been drinking hard?" She assured him he had not. "Weel, weel, ye maun tell him that he maunna keep that engagement at no rate. Set back the clock and I'll come and see him. It is a frenzy that maunna be trifled with. Ye maunna laugh at it, dearie,—maunna laugh at it. Maybe a nervish fever, wha kens."

The Doctor and Chirsty left the house together, and as their road lay the same way for a space, she fell a-telling him of the two young lawyers whom George saw standing at the gate of hell, and whom the porter described as two of the last comers. When the Doctor heard this, he staid his hurried stooping pace in one moment, turned full round on the woman, and fixing his eyes on her that gleamed with a deep unstable lustre, he said, "What's that ye were saying, dearie? What's that ye were saying? Repeat it again to me every word." She did so. On which the Doctor held up his hands, as if palsied with astonishment, and uttered some fervent ejaculations. "I'll go with you straight," said he, "before I visit another patient. This is wonderfu'! It is terrible! The young gentlemen are both at rest—both lying corpses at this time!—fine young men—I attended them both—died of the same exterminating disease.—Oh this is wonderful; this is wonderful!"

The Doctor kept Chirsty half running all the way down the High Street and St Mary's Wynd, at such a pace did he walk, never lifting his eyes from the pavement, but always exclaiming now and then, "It is wonderfu'! most wonderfu'!" At length, prompted by woman's natural curiosity, she inquired at the Doctor if he knew anything of their friend Mr R** of L***y? But he shook his head, and replied, "Na, na, dearie,—ken naething about him. He and his son are baith in London,—ken naething bout him; but the tither is awfu'—it is perfectly awfu'!"

When Dr Wood reached his patient, he found him very low, but only a little feverish, so he made all haste to wash his head with vinegar and cold water, and then he covered the crown with a treacle plaster, and made the same application to the soles of his feet, awaiting the issue. George revived a little, when the Doctor tried to cheer him up by joking him about his dream; but on mention of that he groaned, and shook his head. "So you are convinced, dearie, that it is nae dream?" said the Doctor.

"Dear sir, how could it be a dream?" said the patient. "I was there in person, with Mr R** and his son; and see here are the marks of the porter's fingers on my throat." Dr Wood looked, and distinctly, saw two or three red spots on one side of his throat, which confounded him not a little. "I assure you, sir," continued George, "It was no dream, which I know to my sad experience. I have lost my coach and horses, and what more have I?—signed the bond with my own hand, and in person entered into the most solemn and terrible engagement."

"But ye're not to keep it, I tell ye," said Dr Wood. "Ye're to keep it at no rate. It is a sin to enter into a compact wi' the deil, but it is a far greater ane to keep it. Sae let Mr R** and his son bide where they are yonder, for ye sanna stir a foot to bring them out the day."

"Oh, oh! Doctor!" groaned the poor fellow, "this is not a thing to be made a jest o'! I feel that it is an engagement I cannot break. Go I must, and that very shortly. Yes, yes, go I must, and go I shall, though I should borrow David Barclay's pair." With that he turned his face towards the wall, groaned deeply, and fell into a lethargy, while Dr Wood caused them to let him alone, thinking if he would sleep out the appointed time, which was at hand, he would be safe; but all the time he kept feeling his pulse, and by degrees showed symptoms of uneasiness. The wife ran for a clergyman of famed abilities, to pray and converse with her husband, in hopes by that means to bring him to his senses; but after his arrival, George never spoke more, save calling to his horses, as if encouraging them to run with great speed, and thus in imagination driving at full career into hell, he went off in a paroxysm after a terrible struggle, precisely within a few minutes of twelve o'clock.

What made this singular professional dream the more remarkable and unique in all its parts, was not known at the time of George's death. It was a terrible storm on the night of the dream, as has been already mentioned, and during the time of the hurricane, a London smack went down off Wearmouth about three in the morning. Among the sufferers were the Hon. Mr R** of L***y, and his son! George could not know aught of this at break of day, for it was not known in Scotland till the day of his interment; and as little knew he of the deaths of the two young lawyers, who both died of the small-pox the evening before.

Charles Dickens
Story of the Bagman's Uncle
1765

The Englishness of Charles John Huffam Dickens (1812–1870) makes it all the more startling that his first novel, The Posthumous Papers of the Pickwick Club *(1836–37), should have exhibited so accurate a topographical sense of Edinburgh in the following story which is told within the confines of that episodic work. The influence of Hogg will suggest itself to readers of this anthology, and his obvious reflection on Edinburgh at this time will strengthen the case for Fagin and Bill Sikes in his second novel,* Oliver Twist *(1837–39), having some antecedent in Burke and Hare. In fact, Dickens could distinguish himself off his home ground of London and the Home Counties as with Preston in* Hard Times *(1854), America in* Martin Chuzzlewit *(1843), and, in a highly romanticised form, Paris in* A Tale of Two Cities *(1859). The latter work reminds us of his ambition to realise his taste for historical fiction, of which* Barnaby Rudge *(1841) furnishes the most interesting example. Scott was his Master here, as elsewhere: it is significant how essential history is to his view of Edinburgh.*

'MY UNCLE, GENTLEMEN,' said the bagman, 'was one of the merriest, pleasantest, cleverest fellows that ever lived. I wish you had known him, gentlemen. On second thoughts, gentlemen, I *don't* wish you had known him, for if you had, you would have been all, by this time, in the ordinary course of nature, if not dead, at all events so near it, as to have taken to stopping at home and giving up company: which would have deprived me of the inestimable pleasure of addressing you at this moment. Gentlemen, I wish your fathers and mothers had known my uncle. They would have been amazingly fond of him, especially your respectable mothers; I know they would. If any two of his numerous virtues predominated over the many that adorned his character, I should say they were his mixed punch and his after supper song. Excuse my dwelling on these melancholy recollections of departed worth; you won't see a man like my uncle every day in the week.

'I have always considered it a great point in my uncle's character, gentlemen, that he was the intimate friend and companion of Tom Smart, of the great house of Bilson and Slum, Cateaton Street, City. My uncle collected for Tiggin and Welps, but for a long time he went pretty near the same journey as Tom; and the very first night they met, my uncle took a fancy for Tom, and Tom took a fancy for my uncle. They made a bet of a new hat before they had known each other half an hour, who should brew the best quart of punch and drink it the quickest. My uncle was judged to have won the making, but Tom Smart beat him in the drinking by about half a salt-spoon-full. They took another quart a-piece to drink each other's health in, and were staunch friends ever afterwards. There's a destiny in these things, gentlemen; we can't help it.

'In personal appearance, my uncle was a trifle shorter than the middle size; he was a thought stouter too, than the ordinary run of people, and perhaps his face might be a shade redder. He had the jolliest face you ever saw, gentlemen: something like Punch, with a handsomer nose and chin; his eyes were always twinkling and sparkling with good humour; and a smile—not one of your un-meaning wooden grins, but a real, merry, hearty, good-tempered smile—was perpetually on his countenance. He was pitched out of his gig once, and knocked, head first, against a mile-stone. There he lay, stunned, and so cut about the face with some gravel which had been heaped up alongside it, that, to use my uncle's own strong expression, if his mother could have revisited the earth, she wouldn't have known him. Indeed, when I come to think of the matter, gentlemen, I feel pretty sure she wouldn't, for she died when my uncle was two years and seven months old, and I think it's very likely that, even without the gravel, his top-boots would have puzzled the good lady not a little: to say nothing of his jolly red face. However, there he lay, and I have heard my uncle say, many a time, that the man said who picked him up that he was smiling as merrily as if he had tumbled out for a treat, and that after they had bled him, the first faint glimmerings of returning animation, were, his jumping up in bed, bursting out into a loud laugh, kissing the young woman who held the basin, and demanding a mutton chop and a pickled walnut. He was very fond of pickled walnuts, gentlemen. He said he always found that, taken without vinegar, they relished the beer.

'My uncle's great journey was in the fall of the leaf, at which time he collected debts, and took orders, in the north: going from London to Edinburgh, from Edinburgh to Glasgow, from Glasgow back to Edinburgh, and thence to London by the smack. You are to under-stand that his second visit to Edinburgh was for his own pleasure. He used to go back for a week, just to look up his old friends; and what with breakfasting with this one, lunching with that, dining with a third, and supping with another, a pretty tight week he used to make of it. I don't know whether any of you, gentlemen, ever partook of a real substantial hospitable Scotch breakfast, and then went out to a slight lunch of a bushel of oysters, a dozen or so of bottled ale, and a noggin or two of whiskey to close up with. If you ever did, you will agree with me that it requires a pretty strong head to go out to dinner and supper afterwards.

'But, bless your hearts and eye-brows, all this sort of thing was nothing to my uncle! He was so well seasoned, that it was mere child's play. I have heard him say that he could see the Dundee people out, any day, and walk home afterwards without staggering; and yet the Dundee people have as strong heads and as strong punch, gentlemen, as you are likely to meet with, between the poles. I have heard of a Glasgow man and a Dundee man drinking against each other for fifteen hours at a sitting. They were both suffocated, as nearly as could be ascertained, at the same moment, but with this trifling exception, gentlemen, they were not a bit the worse for it.

'One night, within four-and-twenty hours of the time when he had settled to take shipping for London, my uncle supped at the house of a very old friend of his, a Baillie Mac something and four syllables after it, who lived in the old town of Edinburgh. There were the baillie's wife, and the baillie's three daughters, and the baillie's grown-up son, and three or four stout, bushy eye-browed, canny old Scotch fellows, that the baillie had got together to do honour to my uncle, and help to make merry. It was a glorious supper. There were kippered salmon, and Finnan haddocks, and a lamb's head, and a haggis—a celebrated Scotch dish, gentlemen, which my uncle used to say always looked to him, when it came to table, very much like a cupid's stomach—and a great many other things besides, that I forget the names of, but very good things notwithstanding. The lassies were pretty and agreeable; the baillie's wife was one of the best creatures that ever lived; and my uncle was in thoroughly good cue. The consequence of which was, that the young ladies tittered and giggled, and the old lady laughed out loud, and the baillie and the other old fellows roared till they were red in the face, the whole mortal time. I don't quite recollect how many tumblers of whiskey toddy each man drank after supper; but this I know, that about one o'clock in the morning, the baillie's grown-up son became insensible while attempting the first verse of "Willie brewed a peck o' maut;" and he having been, for half an hour before, the only other man visible above the mahogany, it occurred to my uncle that it was almost time to think about going: especially as drinking had set in at seven o'clock, in order that he might get home at a decent hour. But, thinking it might not be quite polite to go just then, my uncle voted himself into the chair, mixed another glass, rose to propose his own health, addressed himself in a neat and complimentary speech, and drank the toast with great enthusiasm. Still nobody woke; so my uncle took a little drop more—neat this time, to prevent the toddy from disagreeing with him—and, laying violent hands on his hat, sallied forth into the street.

'It was a wild gusty night when my uncle closed the baillie's door, and settling his hat firmly on his head, to prevent the wind from taking it, thrust his hands into his pockets, and looking upward, took a short survey of the state of the weather. The clouds were drifting over the moon at their giddiest speed: at one time wholly obscuring her: at another, suffering her to burst forth in full splendour and shed her light on all the objects around: anon, driving over her again, with increased velocity, and shrouding everything in darkness. "Really, this won't do," said my uncle, addressing himself to the weather, as if he felt himself personally offended. "This is not at all the kind of thing for my voyage. It will not do, at any price," said my uncle very impressively. Having repeated this, several times, he recovered his balance with some difficulty—for he was rather giddy with looking up into the sky so long—and walked merrily on.

'The baillie's house was in the Canongate, and my uncle was going to the other end of Leith Walk, rather better than a mile's journey. On either side of him, there shot up against the dark sky, tall gaunt straggling houses, with time-stained fronts, and windows that seemed to have shared the lot of eyes in mortals, and to have grown dim and sunken with age. Six, seven, eight stories high, were the houses; story piled above story, as children build with cards—throwing their dark shadows over the roughly paved road, and making the dark night darker. A few oil lamps were scattered at long distances, but they only served to mark the dirty entrance to some narrow close, or to show where a common stair communicated, by steep and intricate windings, with the various flats above. Glancing at all these things with the air of a man who had seen them too often before, to think them worthy of much notice now, my uncle walked up the middle of the street, with a thumb in each waistcoat pocket, indulging from time to time in various snatches of song, chaunted forth with such good will and spirit, that the quiet honest folk started from their first sleep and lay trembling in bed till the sound died away in the distance; when, satisfying themselves that it was only some drunken ne'er-do-weel finding his way home, they covered themselves up warm and fell asleep again.

'I am particular in describing how my uncle walked up the middle of the street, with his thumbs in his waistcoat pockets, gentlemen, because, as he often used to say (and with great reason too) there is nothing at all extraordinary in this story, unless you distinctly understand at the beginning that he was not by any means of a marvellous or romantic turn.

'Gentlemen, my uncle walked on with his thumbs in his waistcoat pockets, taking the middle of the street to himself, and singing, now a verse of a love song, and then a verse of a drinking one, and when he was tired of both, whistling melodiously, until he reached the North Bridge, which, at this point, connects the old and new towns of Edinburgh. Here he stopped for a minute, to look at the strange irregular clusters of lights piled one above the other, and twinkling afar off so high, that they looked like stars, gleaming from the castle walls on the one side and the Calton Hill on the other, as if they illuminated vertitable castles in the air; while the old picturesque town slept heavily on, in gloom and darkness below: its palace and chapel of Holyrood, guarded day and night, as a friend of my uncle's used to say, by old Arthur's Seat, towering, surly and dark, like some gruff genius, over the ancient city he has watched so long. I say, gentlemen, my uncle stopped here, for a minute, to look about him; and then, paying a compliment to the weather which had a little cleared up, though the moon was sinking, walked on again, as royally as before; keeping the middle of the road with great dignity, and looking as if he would very much like to meet with somebody who would dispute possession of it with him. There was nobody at all disposed to contest the point, as it happened; and so, on he went, with his thumbs in his waistcoat pockets, like a lamb.

'When my uncle reached the end of Leith Walk, he had to cross a pretty large piece of waste ground which separated him from a short street which he had to turn down, to go direct to his lodging. Now, in this piece of waste ground, there was, at that time, an enclosure belonging to some wheelwright who contracted with the Post-office for the purchase of old worn-out mail coaches; and my uncle, being very fond of coaches, old, young, or middle-aged, all at once took it into his head to step out of his road for no other purpose than to peep between the palings at these mails—about a dozen of which, he remembered to have seen, crowded together in a very forlorn and dismantled state, inside. My uncle was a very enthusiastic, emphatic sort of person, gentlemen; so, finding that he could not obtain a good peep between the palings, he got over them, and sitting himself quietly down on an old axletree, began to contemplate the mail coaches with a deal of gravity.

'There might be a dozen of them, or there might be more—my

95

uncle was never quite certain at this point, and being a man of very scrupulous veracity about numbers, didn't like to say—but there they stood, all huddled together in the most desolate condition imaginable. The doors had been torn from their hinges and removed; the linings had been stripped off; only a shred hanging here and there by a rusty nail; the lamps were gone, the poles had long since vanished, the iron-work was rusty, the paint was worn away; the wind whistled through the chinks in the bare wood work; and the rain, which had collected on the roofs, fell, drop by drop, into the insides with a hollow and melancholy sound. They were the decaying skeletons of departed mails, and in that lonely place, at that time of night, they looked chill and dismal.

'My uncle rested his head upon his hands, and thought of the busy bustling people who had rattled about, years before, in the old coaches, and were now as silent and changed; he thought of the numbers of people to whom one of those crazy mouldering vehicles had borne, night after night, for many years, and through all weathers, the anxiously expected intelligence, the eagerly looked-for remittance, the promised assurance of health and safety, the sudden announcement of sickness and death. The merchant, the lover, the wife, the widow, the mother, the schoolboy, the very child who tottered to the door at the postman's knock—how had they all looked forward to the arrival of the old coach. And where were they all now!

'Gentlemen, my uncle used to *say* that he thought all this at the time, but I rather suspect he learnt it out of some book afterwards, for he distinctly stated that he fell into a kind of doze, as he sat on the old axletree looking at the decayed mail coaches, and that he was suddenly awakened by some deep church-bell striking two. Now, my uncle was never a fast thinker, and if he had thought of all these things, I am quite certain it would have taken him till full half-past two o'clock, at the very least. I am, therefore, decidedly of opinion, gentlemen, that my uncle fell into the kind of doze, without having thought about anything at all.

'Be this, as it may, a church bell struck two. My uncle woke, rubbed his eyes, and jumped up in astonishment.

'In one instant after the clock struck two, the whole of this deserted and quiet spot had become a scene of most extraordinary life and animation. The mail coach doors were on their hinges, the lining was replaced, and iron-work was as good as new, the paint was restored, the lamps were alight, cushions and great coats were on every coach box, porters were thrusting parcels into every boot, guards were stowing away letter-bags, hostlers were dashing pails of water against the renovated wheels; numbers of men were rushing about, fixing poles into every coach; passengers arrived, portmanteaus were handed up, horses were put to; in short, it was perfectly clear that every mail there, was to be off directly. Gentlemen, my uncle opened his eyes so wide at all this, that, to the very last moment of his life, he used to wonder how it fell out that he had ever been able to shut'em again.

' "Now then!" said a voice, as my uncle felt a hand on his shoulder, "You're booked for one inside. You'd better get in."

' "*I* booked!" said my uncle, turning round.

' "Yes, certainly."

'My uncle, gentlemen, could say nothing; he was so very much astonished. The queerest thing of all, was, that although there was such a crowd of persons, and although fresh faces were pouring in, every moment, there was no telling where they came from. They seemed to start up, in some strange manner, from the ground, or the air, and disappear in the same way. When a porter had put his luggage in the coach, and received his fare, he turned round and was gone; and before my uncle had well begun to wonder what had become of him, half-a-dozen fresh ones started up, and staggered along under the weight of parcels which seemed big enough to crush them. The passengers were all dressed so oddly too! Large, broad-skirted laced coats with great cuffs and no collars; and wigs, gentlemen,—great formal wigs with a tie behind. My uncle could make nothing of it.

' "Now, *are* you going to get in?" said the person who had addressed my uncle before. He was dressed as a mail guard, with a wig on his head and most enormous cuffs to his coat, and had a lantern in one hand, and a huge blunderbuss in the other, which he was going to stow away in his little arm-chest. "*Are* you going to get in, Jack Martin?" said the guard, holding the lantern to my uncle's face.

' "Hallo!" said my uncle, falling back a step or two. "That's familiar!"

' "It's so on the way-bill," replied the guard.

' "Isn't there a 'Mister' before it?" said my uncle. For he felt, gentlemen, that for a guard he didn't know, to call him Jack Martin, was a liberty which the Post-office wouldn't have sanctioned if they had known it.

' "No, there is not," rejoined the guard coolly.

' "Is the fare paid?" inquired my uncle.

' "Of course it is," rejoined the guard.

'"It is, is it?" said my uncle. "Then here goes! Which coach?"

'"This," said the guard, pointing to an old-fashioned Edinburgh and London Mail, which had the steps down, and the door open. "Stop! Here are the other passengers. Let them get in first."

'As the guard spoke, there all at once appeared, right in front of my uncle, a young gentleman in a powdered wig, and a sky-blue coat trimmed with silver, made very full and broad in the skirts, which were lined with buckram. Tiggin and Welps were in the printed calico and waistcoat piece line, gentlemen, so my uncle knew all the materials at once. He wore knee breeches, and a kind of leggings rolled up over his silk stockings, and shoes with buckles; he had ruffles at his wrists, a three-cornered hat on his head, and a long taper sword by his side. The flaps of his waistcoat came half way down his thighs, and the ends of his cravat reached to his waist. He stalked gravely to the coach-door, pulled off his hat, and held it above his head at arm's length: cocking his little finger in the air at the same time, as some affected people do, when they take a cup of tea. Then he drew his feet together, and made a low grave bow, and then put out his left hand. My uncle was just going to step forward, and shake it heartily, when he perceived that these attentions were directed, not towards him, but to a young lady who just then appeared at the foot of the steps, attired in an old-fashioned green velvet dress with a long waist and stomacher. She had no bonnet on her head, gentlemen, which was muffled in a black silk hood, but she looked round for an instant as she prepared to get into the coach, and such a beautiful face as she disclosed, my uncle had never seen—not even in a picture. She got into the coach, holding up her dress with one hand; and, as my uncle always said with a round oath, when he told the story, he wouldn't have believed it possible that legs and feet could have been brought to such a state of perfection unless he had seen them with his own eyes.

'But, in this one glimpse of the beautiful face, my uncle saw that the young lady cast an imploring look upon him, and that she appeared terrified and distressed. He noticed, too, that the young fellow in the powdered wig, notwithstanding his show of gallantry, which was all very fine and grand, clasped her tight by the wrist when she got in, and followed himself immediately afterwards. An uncommonly ill-looking fellow, in a close brown wig and a plum-coloured suit, wearing a very large sword, and boots up to his hips, belonged to the party; and when he sat himself down next to the young lady, who shrunk into a corner at his approach, my uncle was confirmed in his original impression that something dark and mysterious was going forward, or, as he always said himself, that "there was a screw loose somewhere." It's quite surprising how quickly he made up his mind to help the lady at any peril, if she needed help.

' "Death and lightning!" exclaimed the young gentleman, laying his hand upon his sword as my uncle entered the coach.

' "Blood and thunder!" roared the other gentleman. With this, he whipped his sword out, and made a lunge at my uncle without further ceremony. My uncle had no weapon about him, but with great dexterity he snatched the ill-looking gentleman's three-cornered hat from his head, and, receiving the point of his sword right through the crown, squeezed the sides together, and held it tight.

' "Pink him behind!" cried the ill-looking gentleman to his companion, as he struggled to regain his sword.

' "He had better not," cried my uncle, displaying the heel of one of his shoes, in a threatening manner. "I'll kick his brains out, if he has any, or fracture his skull if he hasn't." Exerting all his strength at this moment, my uncle wrenched the ill-looking man's sword from his grasp, and flung it clean out of the coach-window: upon which the younger gentleman vociferated "Death and lightning!" again, and laid his hand upon the hilt of his sword, in a very fierce manner, but didn't draw it. Perhaps, gentlemen, as my uncle used to say with a smile, perhaps he was afraid of alarming the lady.

' "Now, gentlemen," said my uncle, taking his seat deliberately, "I don't want to have any death, with or without lightning, in a lady's presence, and we have had quite blood and thundering enough for one journey; so, if you please, we'll sit in our places like quiet insides. Here, guard, pick up that gentleman's carving-knife."

'As quickly as my uncle said the words, the guard appeared at the coach-window, with the gentleman's sword in his hand. He held up his lantern, and looked earnestly in my uncle's face, as he handed it in: when, by its light, my uncle saw, to his great surprise, than an immense crowd of mail-coach guards swarmed round the window, every one of whom had his eyes earnestly fixed upon him too. He had never seen such a sea of white faces, red bodies, and earnest eyes, in all his born days.

' "This is the strangest sort of thing I ever had anything to do with," thought my uncle; "allow me to return you your hat, sir."

'The ill-looking gentleman received his three-cornered hat in silence, looked at the hole in the middle with an inquiring air, and finally stuck it on the top of his wig with a solemnity the effect of which was a trifle impaired by his sneezing violently at the moment, and jerking it off again.

' "All right!" cried the guard with the lantern, mounting into his little seat behind. Away they went. My uncle peeped out of the coach-window as they emerged from the yard, and observed that the other mails, with coachmen, guards, horses and passengers, complete, were driving round and round in circles, at a slow trot of about five miles an hour. My uncle burnt with indignation, gentlemen. As a commercial man, he felt that the mail bags were not to be trifled with, and he resolved to memorialise the Post-office on the subject, the very instant he reached London.

'At present, however, his thoughts were occupied with the young lady who sat in the farthest corner of the coach, with her face muffled closely in her hood; the gentleman with the sky-blue coat sitting opposite to her; the other man in the plum-coloured suit, by her side; and both watching her intently. If she so much as rustled the folds of her hood, he could hear the ill-looking man clap his hand upon his sword, and could tell by the other's breathing (it was so dark he couldn't see his face) that he was looking as big as if he were going to devour her at a mouthful. This roused my uncle more and more, and he resolved, come what come might, to see the end of it. He had a great admiration for bright eyes, and sweet faces, and pretty legs and feet; in short, he was fond of the whole sex. It runs in our family, gentlemen—so am I.

'Many were the devices which my uncle practised, to attract the lady's attention, or at all events, to engage the mysterious gentlemen in conversation. They were all in vain; the gentlemen wouldn't talk, and the lady didn't dare. He thrust his head out of the coach-window at intervals, and bawled out to know why they didn't go faster? But he called till he was hoarse; nobody paid the least attention to him. He leant back in the coach, and thought of the beautiful face, and the feet and legs. This answered better; it whiled away the time, and kept him from wondering where he was going, and how it was that he found himself in such an odd situation. Not that this would have worried him much, any way—he was a mighty free and easy, roving, devil-may-care sort of person, was my uncle, gentlemen.

'All of a sudden the coach stopped. "Hallo!" said my uncle, "What's in the wind now?"

'"Alight here," said the guard, letting down the steps.

'"Here!" cried my uncle.

'"Here," rejoined the guard.

'"I'll do nothing of the sort," said my uncle.

'"Very well, then stop where you are," said the guard.

'"I will," said my uncle.

'"Do," said the guard.

'The other passengers had regarded this colloquy with great attention, and, finding that my uncle was determined not to alight, the younger man squeezed past him, to hand the lady out. At this moment, the ill-looking man was inspecting the hole in the crown of his three-cornered hat. As the young lady brushed past, she dropped one of her gloves into my uncle's hand, and softly whispered, with her lips, so close to his face that he felt her warm breath on his nose, the single word "Help!" Gentlemen, my uncle leaped out of the coach at once, with such violence that it rocked on the springs again.

' "Oh! You've thought better of it, have you?" said the guard when he saw my uncle standing on the ground.

'My uncle looked at the guard for a few seconds, in some doubt whether it wouldn't be better to wrench his blunderbuss from him, fire it in the face of the man with the big sword, knock the rest of the company over the head with the stock, snatch up the young lady, and go off in the smoke. On second thoughts, however, he abandoned this plan, as being a shade too melodramatic in the execution, and followed the two mysterious men, who, keeping the lady between them, were now entering an old house in front of which the coach had stopped. They turned into the passage, and my uncle followed.

'Of all the ruinous and desolate places my uncle had ever beheld, this was the most so. It looked as if it had once been a large house of entertainment; but the roof had fallen in, in many places, and the stairs were steep, rugged, and broken. There was a huge fire-place in the room into which they walked, and the chimney was blackened with smoke; but no warm blaze lighted it up now. The white feathery dust of burnt wood was still strewed over the hearth, but the stove was cold, and all was dark and gloomy.

' "Well," said my uncle, as he looked about him, "A mail travelling at the rate of six miles and a half an hour, and stopping for an indefinite time at such a hole as this, is rather an irregular sort of proceeding I fancy. This shall be made known. I'll write to the papers."

'My uncle said this in a pretty loud voice, and in an open unreserved sort of manner, with the view of engaging the two strangers in conversation if he could. But, neither of them took any more notice of him than whispering to each other, and scowling at him as they did so. The lady was at the farther end of the room, and once she ventured to wave her hand, as if beseeching my uncle's assistance.

'At length the two strangers advanced a little, and the conversation began in earnest.

' "You don't know this is a private room; I suppose, fellow?" said the gentleman in sky-blue.

' "No, I do not, fellow," rejoined my uncle. "Only if this is a private room specially ordered for the occasion, I should think the public room must be a *very* comfortable one;" with this my uncle sat himself down in a high-backed chair, and took such an accurate measure of the gentleman, with his eyes, that Tiggin and Welps could have supplied him with printed calico for a suit, and not an inch too much or too little, from that estimate alone.

' "Quit this room," said both the men together, grasping their swords.

' "Eh?" said my uncle, not at all appearing to comprehend the meaning.

' "Quit the room, or you are a dead man," said the ill-looking fellow with the large sword, drawing it at the same time and flourishing it in the air.

' "Down with him!" cried the gentleman in sky-blue, drawing his sword also, and falling back two or three yards. "Down with him!" The lady gave a loud scream.

'Now, my uncle was always remarkable for great boldness, and great presence of mind. All the time that he had appeared so indifferent to what was going on, he had been looking slyly about, for some missile or weapon of defence, and at the very instant when the swords were drawn, he espied, standing in the chimney corner, an old basket-hilted rapier in a rusty scabbard. At one bound, my uncle caught it in his hand, drew it, flourished it gallantly above his head, called aloud to the lady to keep out of the way, hurled the chair at the man in sky-blue, and the scabbard at the man in plum-colour, and taking advantage of the confusion, fell upon them both, pell-mell.

'Gentlemen, there is an old story—none the worse for being true—regarding a fine young Irish gentleman, who being asked if he could play the fiddle, replied he had no doubt he could, but he couldn't exactly say, for certain, because he had never tried. This is not inapplicable to my uncle and his fencing. He had never had a sword in his hand before, except once when he played Richard the Third at a private theatre; upon which occasion it was arranged with Richmond that he was to be run through, from behind, without showing fight at all. But here he was, cutting and slashing with two experienced swordsmen: thrusting and guarding and poking and slicing, and acquitting himself in the most manful and dexterous manner possible, although up to that time he had never been aware that he had the least notion of the science. It only shows how true the old saying is, that a man never knows what he can do, till he tries, gentlemen.

'The noise of the combat was terrific; each of the three combatants swearing like troopers, and their swords clashing with as much noise as if all the knives and steels in Newport market were rattling together, at the same time. When it was at its very height, the lady (to encourage my uncle most probably) withdrew her hood entirely from her face, and disclosed a countenance of such dazzling beauty, that he would have fought against fifty men, to win one smile from it, and die. He had done wonders before, but now he began to powder away like a raving made giant.

'At this very moment, the gentleman in sky-blue turning round, and seeing the young lady with her face uncovered, vented an exclamation of rage and jealousy, and, turning his weapon against the beautiful bosom, pointed a thrust at her heart, which caused my uncle to utter a cry of apprehension that made the building ring. The lady stepped lightly aside, and snatching the young man's sword from his hand, before he had recovered his balance, drove him to the wall, and running it through him, and the panelling, up to the very hilt, pinned him there, hard and fast. It was a splendid example. My uncle, with a loud shout of triumph, and a strength that was irresistible, made his adversary retreat in the same direction, and plunging the old rapier into the very centre of a large red flower in the pattern of his waistcoat, nailed him beside his friend; there they both stood, gentlemen, jerking their arms and legs about, in agony, like the toy-shop figures that are moved by a piece of packthread. My uncle always said, afterwards, that this was one of the surest means he knew of, for disposing of an enemy; but it was liable to one objection on the ground of expense, inasmuch as it involved the loss of a sword for every man disabled.

'"The mail, the mail!" cried the lady, running up to my uncle and throwing her beautiful arms round his neck; "we may yet escape."

'"*May!*" cried my uncle; "why, my dear, there's nobody else to kill, is there?" My uncle was rather disappointed, gentlemen, for he thought a quiet bit of love-making would be agreeable after the slaughtering, if it were only to change the subject.

'"We have not an instant to lose here," said the young lady, "He (pointing to the young gentlemen in sky-blue) is the only son of the powerful Marquess of Filletoville."

'"Well then, my dear, I'm afraid he'll never come to the title," said my uncle, looking coolly at the young gentleman as he stood fixed up against the wall, in the cockchafer fashion I have described. "You have cut off the entail, my love."

'"I have been torn from my home and friends by these villains," said the young lady, her features glowing with indignation. "That wretch would have married me by violence in another hour."

'"Confound his impudence!" said my uncle, bestowing a very contemptuous look on the dying heir of Filletoville.

'"As you may guess from what you have seen," said the young lady, "the party were prepared to murder me if I appealed to any one for assistance. If their accomplices find us here, we are lost. Two minutes hence may be too late. The mail!" With these words, overpowered by her feelings, and the exertion of sticking the young Marquess of Filletoville, she sunk into my uncle's arms. My uncle caught her up, and bore her to the house-door. There stood the mail, with four long-tailed, flowing-maned, black horses, ready harnessed; but no coachman, no guard, no hostler even, at the horses' head.

'Gentlemen, I hope I do no injustice to my uncle's memory, when I express my opinion, that although he was a bachelor, he *had* held some ladies in his arms, before this time; I believe indeed, that he had rather a habit of kissing barmaids; and I know, that in one or two instances, he had been seen by credible witnesses, to hug a landlady in a very perceptible manner. I mention the circumstance, to show what a very uncommon sort of person this beautiful young lady must have been, to have affected my uncle in the way she did; he used to say, that as her long dark hair trailed over his arm, and her beautiful dark eyes fixed themselves upon his face when she recovered, he felt so strange and nervous that his legs trembled beneath him. But, who can look in a sweet soft pair of dark eyes, without feeling queer? *I* can't, gentlemen. I am afraid to look at some eyes I know, and that's the truth of it.

'"You will never leave me," murmured the young lady.

'"Never," said my uncle. And he meant it too.

'"My dear preserver!" exclaimed the young lady. "My dear, kind, brave preserver!"

'"Don't," said my uncle, interrupting her.

'"Why?" inquired the young lady.

'"Because your mouth looks so beautiful when you speak," rejoined my uncle, "that I am afraid I shall be rude enough to kiss it."

'The young lady put up her hand as if to caution my uncle not to do so, and—no, she didn't say anything—she smiled. When you are looking at a pair of the most delicious lips in the world, and see them gently break into a roguish smile—if you are very near them, and nobody else by—you cannot better testify your admiration of their beautiful form and colour than by kissing them at once. My uncle did so, and I honour him for it.

'"Hark!" cried the young lady, starting. "The noise of wheels and horses!"

'"So it is," said my uncle, listening. He had a good ear for wheels, and the trampling of hoofs; but there appeared to be so many horses and carriages rattling towards them, from a distance, that it was impossible to form a guess at their number. The sound was like that of fifty breaks, with six blood cattle in each.

'"We are pursued!" cried the young lady, clasping her hands. "We are pursued. I have no hope but in you!"

'There was such an expression of terror in her beautiful face, that my uncle made up his mind at once. He lifted her into the coach, told her not to be frightened, pressed his lips to hers once more, and then advising her to draw up the window to keep the cold air out, mounted to the box.

'"Stay, love," cried the young lady.

'"What's the matter?" said my uncle, from the coach-box.

'"I want to speak to you," said the young lady; "only a word. Only one word, dearest."

'"Must I get down?" inquired my uncle. The lady made no answer, but she smiled again. Such a smile, gentlemen! It beat the other one, all to nothing. My uncle descended from his perch in a twinkling.

'"What is it, my dear?" said my uncle, looking in at the coach window. The lady happened to bend forward at the same time, and my uncle thought she looked more beautiful than she had done yet. He was very close to her just then, gentlemen, so he really ought to know.

'"What is it, my dear?" said my uncle.

'"Will you never love any one but me; never marry any one beside?" said the young lady.

'My uncle swore a great oath that he never would marry any body else, and the young lady drew in her head, and pulled up the window. He jumped upon the box, squared his elbows, adjusted the ribands, seized the whip which lay on the roof, gave one flick to the off leader, and away went the four long-tailed flowing-maned black horses, at fifteen good English miles an hour, with the old mail coach behind him. Whew! How they tore along!

'The noise behind grew louder. The faster the old mail went, the faster came the pursuers—men, horses, dogs, were leagued in the pursuit. The noise was frightful, but, above all, rose the voice of the young lady, urging my uncle on, and shrieking, "Faster! Faster!"

'They whirled past the dark trees, as feathers would be swept before a hurricane. Houses, gates, churches, haystacks, objects of every kind they shot by, with a velocity and noise like roaring waters suddenly let loose. Still the noise of pursuit grew louder, and still my uncle could hear the young lady wildly screaming, "Faster! Faster!"

'My uncle plied whip and rein, and the horses flew onward till they were white with foam; and yet the noise behind increased; and yet the young lady cried "Faster! Faster!" My uncle gave a loud stamp on the boot in the energy of the moment, and—found that it was grey morning, and he was sitting in the wheelwright's yard, on the box of an old Edinburgh mail, shivering with the cold and wet and stamping his feet to warm them! He got down, and looked eagerly inside for the beautiful young lady. Alas! There was neither door nor seat to the coach. It was a mere shell.

'Of course, my uncle knew very well that there was some mystery in the matter, and that everything had passed exactly as he used to relate it. He remained staunch to the great oath he had sworn to the beautiful young lady; refusing several eligible landladies on her account, and dying a bachelor at last. He always said, what a curious thing it was that he should have found out, by such a mere accident as his clambering over the palings, that the ghosts of mail-coaches and horses, guards, coachmen, and passengers, were in the habit of making journeys regularly every night. He used to add, that he believed he was the only living person who had ever been taken as a passenger on one of these excursions. And I think he was right, gentlemen—at least I never heard of any other.'

'I wonder what these ghosts of mail-coaches carry in their bags,' said the landlord, who had listened to the whole story with profound attention.

'The dead letters, of course,' said the Bagman.

'Oh, ah! To be sure,' rejoined the landlord. 'I never thought of that.'

Benjamin Rush
An American Testimonial
1768

Benjamin Rush (1745–1813), born in Byberry, Pennsylvania and, after preliminary education at the College of New Jersey (now Princeton), educated at Edinburgh University whence he graduated M.D. in 1768, was a signer of the American Declaration of Independence in 1776, as was John Witherspoon (1723–1794), who left Scotland to become President of New Jersey College the year Rush won his doctorate. Both men are associated with the spread of Scottish philosophical, educational and scientific ideas in the United States. Rush held chairs in medical theory and practice at the College of Philadelphia and, after its foundation in 1792, the University of Pennsylvania. His insistence on extensive bleedings as a cure for disease which he believed to be due to spasms in the blood vessels is said to have cost many lives during the yellow fever epidemic in Philadelphia in 1793. George W. Corner published in 1948 The Autobiography of Benjamin Rush *taken in part from the Rush MS* Travels Through Life *whence this extract derives.*

IN MY INTERCOURSE WITH company in Edinburgh I once met David Hume; it was at the table of Sir Alexander Dick. He was civil in his manners and had no affectation of singularity about him. Sir Alexander once referred to him for a fact in the history of England. Mr. Hume could not satisfy him. "Why, said Sir Alexander, you have mentioned it in your history." "That may be (said Mr. Hume), there are many things there which I have forgotten as well as yourself."

I met the celebrated historian Dr. Robertson at the table of Dr. Gregory. He was polite and entertaining in conversation. Before we sat down to dinner Dr. Gregory said grace. Upon recollecting that Dr. Robertson, a clergyman, was present, he asked his pardon for having been his own chaplain. The Doctor told him a Lord of Session had once acted in the same capacity at his table in the presence of his father, who was likewise a clergyman. After he had finished his grace he looked round and saw Mr. Robertson. "Why (said he), I believe the Devil is in me, only think of my saying grace in the presence of a clergyman." "No, my Lord, said my father, it is a sign the Devil is not in you, or you would not have said grace."

I was frequently made happy by the company of the blind poet Dr. Blacklock. He was a man of pleasant manners, and well acquainted with all the common subjects of literary conversation.

It was while I was in Edinburgh that the Revd. Dr. Witherspoon of Paisley in Scotland was elected president of the College of New Jersey. Mr. Richd. Stockton, one of the trustees of the College, who was at the time in London, was appointed to present to the Doctor the minute of his election. This was done in Edinburgh where the Doctor met Mr. Stockton. In consequence of the Doctor's wife's unwillingness to leave her native country he declined the invitation. The summer afterwards I visited the Doctor at Paisley and spent several agreeable days in his family. In the course of our conversation I lamented often in the presence of his wife his not accepting of the charge of the Jersey College, and obviated such of the objections as she had formerly made to crossing the ocean. An account of her change of mind was immediately transmitted to the trustees of the College, who reelected him. The Doctor with his family soon afterwards embarked for America. The College flourished under him for many years. He gave a new turn to education, and spread taste and correctness in literature throughout the United States. It was easy to distinguish his pupils every where when ever they spoke or wrote for the public. He was a man of a great and luminous mind. He seemed to arrive at truth intuitively. He made use of his reasoning powers only to communicate it to others. His works will probably preserve his name to the end of time.

I remained in Edinburgh after the time of my graduating during the summer for the sake of attending a private course of lectures upon the practice of Physic. I made a short excursion during this time to the country seat of the Earl of Leven, to whose family I had been introduced by Mr. Thomas Hogg. Here I beheld noble manners united with a public profession of religion. Order, virtue, innocence and friendship reigned throughout every department of the family. The neighbourhood was composed of his Lordship's tenants, several of whom I visited. They seemed happy. One of them I recollect sat down one evening by invitation in his working dress, and supped with his Lordship's family.

I received from Lord Balgony after I parted with him a gold ring which contained in a small circle about the size of a dime every word and letter of the Lord's Prayer. On the inside of the ring were engraved the day of the month and year on which I left the family seat at Melville.

During my residence in Edinburgh I was often struck in observing the moral order which prevailed among all classes of people. Silence pervaded the streets of that great city after 10 o'clock at night. The churches were filled on Sundays. I never saw a pack of cards in either a public or private house. Dancing supplied the place of silence or insipid conversation in all large evening companies. Swearing was rarely heard in genteel life, and drunkenness was rarely seen among the common people. Instances of fraud were scarcely known among Servants. But integrity descended still lower among the humble ranks of life. I once saw the following advertisement pasted up at the door of the play house, "The gentleman who gave the orange woman a guinea instead of a penny last night is requested to call at the check office for it." This universal morality was not accidental. It was the effect of the parochial instructions of the clergy, who were at that time a regular and conscientious body of men. I have heard with pain that a great change for the worse has taken place in the morals and manners of the inhabitants of that once happy city. Nor was I surprised at it when I heard that the works of several of the most popular writers against Christianity were to be met with in the hands of journeymen mechanics of all descriptions.

Benjamin Franklin
Salvation by Hume
1771

Benjamin Franklin (1706–1790), printer, editor, journalist, scientist, social philosopher, politician and diplomat, was born in Boston and emigrated to Philadelphia in 1723. He won international celebrity initially for his invention of the Franklin stove in 1742 and identification of lightning and electricity in 1752. He went to England as a Pennsylvania Assembly lobbyist in 1757 and visited Scotland first in 1759, becoming closely attached to leaders of the Scottish Enlightenment such as Lord Kames and David Hume (whose religious scepticism cost him a chair at Edinburgh University and clearly amused the pragmatic theist Franklin). He visited Scotland and Ireland in 1771 and grew increasingly alienated from the British rule over the American colonies. On this he grew to differ from his and their friend William Strahan (1715–1785), to whom this letter was written and to whose daughter his joke about his 'wife' alludes (his own wife Deborah remained in Philadelphia): but Strahan sent him a Stilton cheese in 1778 when, having signed the Declaration of Independence, he was the major American diplomat in wooing alliance with France.

Dear Friend,   Edinburgh, Oct. 27. 1771

Thro' Storms and Floods I arrived here on Saturday night, late, and was lodg'd miserably at an Inn; But that excellent Christian David Hume, agreable to the Precepts of the Gospel, has *received the Stranger,* and I now live with him at his House in the new Town most happily. I purpose staying about a Fortnight, and shall be glad to hear from you. I congratulate you on certain political Events that I know give you Pleasure. Let me know how it is with you and yours, how my Wife does, and Sir John Pringle, and our other Friends. With sincerest Esteem I am, my dear Friend, Yours most affectionately

B FRANKLIN

James Boswell
The Johnson Invasion
1773

James Boswell (1740–1795), son of the Scottish judge Alexander Boswell, Lord Auchinleck, studied law at Glasgow under Adam Smith and at Edinburgh. His friendship with Dr Samuel Johnson (1709–1784) began in London in 1763, and became the basis of the most famous biography in human history (1791). This extract comes however from his earlier work, A Journey of a Tour to the Hebrides with Samuel Johnson, LL.D., *published in 1786, a record of an expedition into which he had long sought to draw the ferociously anti-Scottish Johnson. Johnson's own* Journey to the Western Isles of Scotland *appeared in 1785. In all, Johnson spent four days in Edinburgh during August 1773 before heading north and west. The rediscovery of Boswell's personal journals was one of the most exciting and valuable literary finds of this century; it confirms Boswell's reputation as one of the great human observers of his day and the edition of Boswell's writings under the direction of Frederick A. Pottle is exemplary.*

ON SATURDAY THE FOURTEENTH OF AUGUST, 1773, late in the evening, I received a note from him, that he was arrived at Boyd's inn, at the head of the Canongate. I went to him directly. He embraced me cordially; and I exulted in the thought, that I now had him actually in Caledonia. Mr. Scott's amiable manners, and attachment to our *Socrates*, at once united me to him. He told me that, before I came in, the Doctor had unluckily had a bad specimen of Scottish cleanliness. He then drank no fermented liquor. He asked to have his lemonade made sweeter; upon which the waiter, with his greasy fingers, lifted a lump of sugar, and put it into it. The Doctor, in indignation, threw it out of the window. Scott said, he was afraid he would have knocked the waiter down. Mr. Johnson told me, that such another trick was played him at the house of a lady in Paris. He was to do me the honour to lodge under my roof. I regretted sincerely that I had not also a room for Mr. Scott. Mr. Johnson and I walked arm-in-arm up the High-street, to my house in James's court; it was a dusky night; I could not prevent his being assailed by the evening effluvia of Edinburgh. I heard a late baronet, of some distinction in the political world in the beginning of the present reign, observe, that 'walking the streets of Edinburgh at night was pretty perilous, and a good deal odoriferous.' The peril is much abated, by the care which the magistrates have taken to enforce the city laws against throwing foul water from the windows; but, from the structure of the houses in the old town, which consist of many stories in each of which a different family lives, and there being no covered sewers, the odour still continues. A zealous Scotsman would have wished Mr. Johnson to be without one of his five senses upon this occasion. As we marched slowly along, he grumbled in my ear, 'I smell you in the dark.' But he acknowledged that the breadth of the street, and the loftiness of the buildings on each side, made a noble appearance.

My wife had tea ready for him, which it is well known he delighted to drink at all hours, particularly when sitting up late, and of which his able defence against Mr. Jonas Hanway should have obtained him a magnificent reward from the East-India Company. He shewed much complacency upon finding that the mistress of the house was so attentive to his singular habit; and as no man could be more polite when he chose to be so, his address to her was most courteous and engaging; and his conversation soon charmed her into a forgetfulness of his external appearance.

I did not begin to keep a regular full journal till some days after we had set out from Edinburgh; but I have luckily preserved a good many fragments of his *Memorabilia* from his very first evening in Scotland.

We had, a little before this, had a trial for murder, in which the judges had allowed the lapse of twenty years since its commission as a plea in bar, in conformity with the doctrine of prescription in the *civil* law, which Scotland and several other countries in Europe have adopted. He at first disapproved of this; but then he thought there was something in it, if there had been for twenty years a neglect to prosecute a crime which was *known*. He would not allow that a murder, by not being *discovered* for twenty years, should escape punishment. We talked of the ancient trial by duel. He did not think it so absurd as is generally supposed; 'For (said he) it was only allowed when the question was *in equilibrio*, as when one affirmed and another denied; and they had a notion that Providence would interfere in favour of him who was in the right. But as it was found that in a duel, he who was in the right had not a better chance than he who was in the wrong, therefore society instituted the present mode of trial, and gave the advantage to him who was is in the right.'

We sat till near two in the morning, having chatted a good while after my wife left us. She had insisted, that to shew all respects to the Sage, she would give up her own bed-chamber to him, and take a worse. This I cannot but gratefully mention, as one of a thousand obligations which I owe her, since the great obligation of her being pleased to accept of me as her husband.

Sunday, 15th August

Mr. Scott came to breakfast, at which I introduced to Dr. Johnson, and him, my friend Sir William Forbes, now of Pitsligo; a man of whom too much good cannot be said; who, with distinguished abilities and application in his profession of a Banker, is at once a good companion, and a good christian; which I think is saying enough. Yet it is but justice to record, that once, when he was in a dangerous illness, he was watched with the anxious apprehension of a general calamity; day and night his house was beset with affectionate inquiries; and, upon his recovery, *Te deum* was the universal chorus from the *hearts* of his countrymen.

Mr. Johnson was pleased with my daughter Veronica, then a child of about four months old. She had the appearance of listening to him. His motions seemed to her to be intended for her amusement; and when he stopped, she fluttered, and made a little infantine noise, and a kind of signal for him to begin again. She would be held close to him; which was a proof, from simple nature, that his figure was not horrid. Her fondness for him endeared her still more to me, and I declared she should have five hundred pounds of additional fortune.

We talked of the practice of the Law. Sir Williams Forbes said, he thought an honest lawyer should never undertake a cause which he was satisfied was not a just one. 'Sir, (said Mr. Johnson,) a lawyer has no business with the justice or injustice of the cause which he undertakes, unless his client asks his opinion, and then he is bound to give it honestly. The justice or injustice of the cause is to be decided by the judge. Consider, sir; what is the purpose of courts of justice? It is, that every man may have his cause fairly tried, by men appointed to try causes. A lawyer is not to tell what he knows to be a lie: he is not to produce what he knows to be a false deed; but he is not to usurp the province of the jury and of the judge, and determine what shall be the effect of evidence,—what shall be the result of legal argument. As it rarely happens that a man is fit to plead his own cause, lawyers are a class of the community, who, by study and experience, have acquired the art and power of arranging evidence, and of applying to the points at issue what the law has settled. A lawyer is to do for his client all that his client might fairly do for himself, if he could. If, by a superiority of attention, of knowledge, of skill, and a better method of communication, he has the advantage of his adversary, it is an advantage to which he is entitled. There must always be some advantage, on one side or other; and it is better that advantage should be had by talents, than by chance. If lawyers were to undertake no causes till they were sure they were just, a man might be precluded altogether from a trial of his claim, though, were it judicially examined, it might be found a very just claim.'—This was sound practical doctrine, and rationally repressed a too refined scrupulosity of conscience.

Emigration was at this time a common topick of discourse. Dr. Johnson regretted it as hurtful to human happiness: 'For (said he) it spreads mankind, which weakens the defence of a nation, and lessens the comfort of living. Men, thinly scattered, make a shift, but a bad shift, without many things. A smith is ten miles off: they'll do without a nail or a staple. A tailor is far from them: they'll botch their own clothes. It is being concentrated which produces high convenience.'

Sir William Forbes, Mr. Scott, and I, accompanied Mr. Johnson to the chapel, founded by Lord Chief Baron Smith, for the Service of the Church of England. The Reverend Mr. Carre, the senior clergyman, preached from these words, 'Because the Lord reigneth, let the earth be glad.'—I was sorry to think Mr. Johnson did not attend to the sermon, Mr. Carre's low voice not being strong enough to reach his hearing. A selection of Mr. Carre's sermons has, since his death, been published by Sir William Forbes, and the world has acknowledged their uncommon merit. I am well assured Lord Mansfield has pronounced them to be excellent.

Here I obtained a promise from Lord Chief Baron Orde, that he would dine at my house next day. I presented Mr. Johnson to this Lordship, who politely said to him, 'I have not the honour of knowing you; but I hope for it, and to see you at my house. I am to wait on you to-morrow.' This respectable English judge will be long remembered in Scotland, where he built an elegant house, and lived in it magnificently. His own ample fortune, with the addition of his salary, enabled him to be splendidly hospitable. It may be fortunate for an individual amongst ourselves to be Lord Chief Baron; and a most worthy man now has the office; but, in my opinion, it is better for Scotland in general, that some of our publick employments should be filled by gentlemen of distinction from the south side of the Tweed, as we have the benefit of promotion in England. Such an interchange would make a beneficial mixture of manners, and render our union more complete. Lord Chief Baron Orde was on good terms with us all, in a narrow country filled with jarring interests and keen parties; and, though I well knew his opinion to be the same with my own, he kept himself aloof at a very critical period indeed, when the *Douglas cause* shook the sacred security of *birthright* in Scotland to its foundation; a cause, which had it happened before the Union, when there was no appeal to a British House of Lords, would have left the great fortress of honours and of property in ruins.

When we got home, Dr. Johnson desired to see my books. He took down Ogden's Sermons on Prayer, on which I set a very high value, having been much edified by them, and he retired with them to his room. He did not stay long, but soon joined us in the drawing room. I presented to him Mr. Robert Arbuthnot, a relation of the celebrated Dr. Arbuthnot, and a man of literature and taste. To him we were obliged for a previous recommendation, which secured us a very agreeable reception at St. Andrews, and which Dr. Johnson, in his 'Journey,' ascribes to 'some invisible friend.'

Of Dr. Beattie, Mr. Johnson said, 'Sir, he has written like a man conscious of the truth, and feeling his own strength. Treating your adversary with respect, is giving him an advantage to which he is not entitled. The greatest part of men cannot judge of reasoning, and are impressed by character; so that, if you allow your adversary a respectable character, they will think, that though you differ from him, you may be in the wrong. Sir, treating your adversary with respect, is striking soft in a battle. And as to Hume,—a man who has so much conceit as to tell all mankind that they have been bubbled for ages, and he is the wise man who sees better than they,—a man who has so little scrupulosity as to venture to oppose those principles which have been thought necessary to human happiness,—is he to be surprised if another man comes and laughs at him! If he is the great man he thinks himself, all this cannot hurt him; it is like throwing peas against a rock.' He added *something much too rough,* both as to Mr. Hume's head and heart, which I suppress. Violence is, in my opinion, not suitable to the Christian cause. Besides, I always lived on good terms with Mr. Hume, though I have frankly told him, I was not clear that it was right in me to keep company with him. 'But (said I) how much better are you than your books!' He was cheerful, obliging, and instructive; he was charitable to the poor; and many an agreeable hour have I passed with him: I have preserved some entertaining and interesting memoirs of him, particularly when he knew himself to be dying, which I may some time or other communicate to the world. I shall not, however, extol him so very highly as Dr. Adam Smith does, who says, in a letter to Mr. Strahan the Printer (not a confidential letter to his friend, but a letter which is published with all formality): 'Upon the whole, I have always considered him, both in his life-time and since his death, as approaching as nearly to the idea of a perfectly wise and virtuous man as perhaps the nature of human frailty will permit.' Let Dr. Smith consider: Was not Mr. Hume blest with good health, good spirits, good friends, a competent and increasing fortune? And had he not also a perpetual feast of fame? But, as a learned friend has observed to me, 'What trials did he undergo, to prove the perfection of his virtue? Did he ever experience any great instance of adversity?'—When I read this sentence, delivered by my old *Professor of Moral Philosophy*, I could not help exclaiming with the *Psalmist*, 'Surely I have now more understanding than my teachers!'

While we were talking, there came a note to me from Dr. William Robertson.

Dear Sir,
'I have been expecting every day to hear from you, of Dr. Johnson's arrival. Pray, what do you know about his motions? I long to take him by the hand. I write this from the college, where I have only this scrap of paper. Ever yours,

Sunday.

W.R.'

It pleased me to find Dr. Robertson thus eager to meet Dr. Johnson. I was glad I could answer, that he was come: and I begged Dr. Robertson might be with us as soon as he could.

Sir William Forbes, Mr. Scott, Mr. Arbuthnot, and another gentleman dined with us. 'Come, Dr. Johnson, (said I,) it is commonly thought that our veal in Scotland is not good. But here is some which I believe you will like.'—There was no catching him.—*Johnson*. 'Why, sir, what is commonly thought, I should take to be true. *Your* veal may be good; but that will only be an exception to the general opinion; not a proof against it.'

Dr. Robertson, according to the custom of Edinburgh at that time, dined in the interval between the forenoon and afternoon service, which was then later than now; so we had not the pleasure of his company till dinner was over, when he came and drank wine with us. And then began some animated dialogue, of which here follows a pretty full note.

We talked of Mr. Burke.—Dr. Johnson said, he had great variety of knowledge, store of imagery, copiousness of language.—*Robertson*. 'He has wit too.'—*Johnson*, 'No, sir; he never succeeds there. 'Tis low; 'tis conceit. I used to say, Burke never once made a good joke. What I most envy Burke for, is, his being constantly the same. He is never what we call hum-drum; never unwilling to begin to talk, nor in haste to leave off.'—*Boswell*. 'Yet he can listen.'—*Johnson*. 'No; I cannot say he is good at that. So desirous is he to talk, that, if one is speaking at this end of the table, he'll speak to somebody at the other end. Burke, sir, is such a man, that if you met him for the first time in a street where you were stopped by a drove of oxen, and you and he stepped aside to take shelter but for five minutes, he'd talk to you in such a manner, that, when you parted, you would say, this is an extraordinary man. Now, you may be long enough with me, without finding any thing extraordinary.' He said, he believed Burke was intended for the law; but either had not money enough to follow it, or had not diligence enough. He said, he could not understand how a man could apply to one thing, and not to another. *Robertson* said, one man had more judgment, another more imagination.—*Johnson.* 'No, sir; it is only, one man has more mind than another. He may direct it differently; he may, by accident, see the success of one kind of study, and take a desire to excel in it. I am persuaded˙that, had Sir Isaac Newton applied to poetry, he would have made a very fine epick poem. I could as easily apply to law as to tragick poetry.'—*Boswell.* 'Yet, sir, you *did* apply to tragick poetry, not to law.'—*Johnson.* 'Because, sir, I had not money to study law. Sir, the man who has vigour, may walk to the east, just as well as to the west, if he happens to turn his head that way.'—*Boswell.* 'But, sir, 'tis like walking up and down a hill; one man will naturally do the one better than the other. A hare will run up a hill best, from her fore-legs being short; a dog down.'—*Johnson.* 'Nay, sir; that is from mechanical powers. If you make mind mechanical, you may argue in that manner. One mind is a vice, and holds fast; there's a good memory. Another is a file; and he is a disputant, a controversialist. Another is a razor; and he is sarcastical.'—We talked of *Whitefield.* He said, he was at the same college with him, and knew him *before he began to be better than other people* (smiling); that he believed he sincerely meant well, but had a mixture of politicks and ostentation: whereas *Wesley* thought of religion only.—*Robertson* said, Whitefield had strong natural eloquence, which, if cultivated, would have done great things.—*Johnson.* 'Why, sir, I take it, he was at the height of what his abilities could do, and was sensible of it. He had the ordinary advantages of education; but he chose to pursue that oratory which is for the mob.'—*Boswell.* 'He had great effect on the passions.'—*Johnson.* 'Why, sir, I don't think so. He could not represent a succession of pathetick images. He vociferated, and made an impression. *There,* again, was a mind like a hammer.'—Dr. Johnson now said, a certain eminent political friend of ours was wrong, in his maxim of sticking to a certain set of *men* on all occasions. 'I can see that a man may do right to stick to a *party* (said he); that is to say, he is a *Whig,* or he is a *Tory,* and·he thinks one of those parties upon the whole the best, and that, to make it prevail, it

117

must be generally supported, though, in particulars, it may be wrong. He takes its faggot of principles, in which there are fewer rotten sticks than in the other, though some rotten sticks to be sure; and they cannot well be separated. But, to bind one's self to one man, or one set of men, (who may be right to-day and wrong to-morrow,) without any general preference of system, I must disapprove.'

He told us of Cooke, who translated Hesiod, and lived twenty years on a translation of Plautus, for which he was always taking subscriptions; and that he presented Foote to a Club, in the following singular manner: 'This is the nephew of the gentleman who was lately hung in chains for murdering his brother.'

In the evening I introduced to Mr. Johnson two good friends of mine, Mr. William Nairne, Advocate, and Mr. Hamilton of Sundrum, my neighbour in the country, both of whom supped with us. I have preserved nothing of what passed, except that Dr. Johnson displayed another of his heterodox opinions,—a contempt of tragick acting. He said, 'the action of all players in tragedy is bad. It should be a man's study to repress those signs of emotion and passion, as they are called.' He was of a directly contrary opinion to that of Fielding, in his *Tom Jones*; who makes Partridge say, of Garrick, 'why, I could act as well as he myself. I am sure, if I had seen a ghost, I should have looked in the very same manner, and done just as he did.' For, when I asked him, 'Would not you, sir, start as Mr. Garrick does, if you saw a ghost?' He answered, 'I hope not. If I did, I should frighten the ghost.'

Monday, 16th August.

Dr. William Robertson came to breakfast. We talked of *Ogden* on Prayer. Dr. Johnson said, 'The same arguments which are used against GOD's hearing prayer, will serve against his rewarding good, and punishing evil. He has resolved, he has declared, in the former case in the latter.' He had last night looked into Lord Hailes's 'Remarks on the History of Scotland.' Dr. Robertson and I said, it was a pity Lord Hailes did not write greater things. His lordship had not then published his 'Annals of Scotland.'—*Johnson*. 'I remember I was once on a visit at the house of a lady for whom I had a high respect. There was a good deal of company in the room. When they were gone, I said to this lady, "What foolish talking have we had!"—"Yes, (said she,) but while they talked, you said nothing."—I was struck with the reproof. How much better is the man who does any thing that is innocent, than he who does nothing. Besides, I love anecdotes. I fancy mankind may come, in time, to write all aphoristically, except in narrative; grow weary of preparation, and connection, and illustration, and all those arts by which a big book is made.—If a man is to wait till he weaves anecdotes into a system, we may be long in getting them, and get but few, in comparison of what we might get.'

Dr. Robertson said, the notions of Eupham Macallan, a fanatick woman, of whom Lord Hailes gives a sketch, were still prevalent among some of the Presbyterians; and therefore it was right in Lord Hailes, a man of known piety, to undeceive them.

We walked out, that Dr. Johnson might see some of the things which we have to shew at Edinburgh. We went to the Parliament-House, where the Parliament of Scotland sat, and where the *Ordinary Lords* of Session hold their courts; and to the New Session-House adjoining to it, where our Court of Fifteen (the fourteen *Ordinaries*, with the Lord President at their head,) sit as a court of Review. We went to the *Advocates' Library*, of which Dr. Johnson took a cursory view, and then to what is called the *Laigh* (or under) Parliament-House, where the records of Scotland, which has an universal security by register, are deposited, till the great Register Office be finished. I was pleased to behold Dr. Samuel Johnson rolling about in this old magazine of antiquities. There was, by this time, a pretty numerous circle of us attending upon him. Somebody talked of happy moments for composition; and how a man can write at one time, and not at another.—'Nay (said Dr. Johnson) a man may write at any time, if he will set himself *doggedly* to it.'

I here began to indulge *old Scottish* sentiments, and to express a warm regret, that, by our Union with *England*, we were no more;—our independent kingdom was lost.—*Johnson.* 'Sir, never talk of your independency, who could let your Queen remain twenty years in captivity, and then be put to death, without even a pretence of justice, without your ever attempting to rescue her; and such a Queen too! as every man of any gallantry of spirit would have sacrificed his life for.'—Worthy Mr. *James Ker, Keeper of the Records.* 'Half our nation was bribed by English money.'—*Johnson.* 'Sir, that is no defence: that makes you worse.'—Good *Mr. Brown, Keeper of the Advocates Library.* 'We had better say nothing about it.'—*Boswell.* 'You would have been glad, however, to have had us last war, sir, to fight your battles!'—*Johnson.* 'We should have had you for the same price, though there had been no Union, as we might have had Swiss, or other troops. No, no, I shall agree to a separation. You have only to *go home.*'—Just as he had said this, I, to divert the subject, shewed him the signed assurances of the three successive Kings of the Hanover family, to maintain the Presbyterian establishment in Scot-

119

land.—'We'll give you that (said he) into the bargain.'

We next went to the great church of St. Giles, which has lost its original magnificence in the inside, by being divided into four places of Presbyterian worship. 'Come, (said Dr. Johnson jocularly to Principal Robertson,) let me see what was once a church!' We entered that division which was formerly called the *New Church*, and of late the *High Church*, so well known by the eloquence of Dr. Hugh Blair. It is now very elegantly fitted up; but it was then shamefully dirty. Dr. Johnson said nothing at the time; but when we came to the great door of the Royal Infirmary, where, upon a board, was this inscription, *'Clean your feet!'* he turned about slyly, and said, 'There is no occasion for putting this at the doors of your churches!'

We then conducted him down the Post-house stairs, Parliament-close, and made him look up from the Cow-gate to the highest building in Edinburgh, (from which he had just descended,) being thirteen floors or stories from the ground upon the back elevation; the front wall being built upon the edge of the hill, and the back wall rising from the bottom of the hill several stories before it comes to a level with the front wall. We proceeded to the College, with the Principal at our head. Dr. Adam Fergusson, whose 'Essay on the History of Civil Society' gives him a respectable place in the ranks of literature, was with us. As the College buildings are indeed very mean, the Principal said to Dr. Johnson, that he must give them the same epithet that a Jesuit did when shewing a poor college abroad: *'Hæ miseriæ nostræ.'* Dr. Johnson was, however, much pleased with the library, and with the conversation of Dr. James Robertson, Professor of Oriental Languages, the Librarian. We talked of Kennicot's edition of the Hebrew Bible, and hoped it would be quite faithful.—*Johnson.* 'Sir, I know not any crime so great that a man could contrive to commit, as poisoning the sources of eternal truth.'

I pointed out to him where there formerly stood an old wall enclosing part of the college, which I remember bulged out in a threatening manner, and of which there was a common tradition similar to that concerning *Bacon's* Study at Oxford, that it would fall upon some very learned man. It had some time before this been taken down, that the street might be widened, and a more convenient wall built. Dr. Johnson, glad of an opportunity to have a pleasant hit at Scottish learning, said, 'they have been afraid it never would fall.'

We shewed him the Royal Infirmary, for which, and for every other exertion of generous publick spirit in his power, that noble-minded citizen of Edinburgh, George Drummond, will be ever held in honourable remembrance. And we were too proud not to carry him to the Abbey of Holyrood-house, that beautiful piece of architecture, but, alas! that deserted mansion of royalty, which Hamilton of Bangour, in one of his elegant poems, calls

'A virtuous palace, where no monarch dwells.'

I was much entertained while Principal Robertson fluently harangued to Dr. Johnson, upon the spot, concerning scenes of his celebrated History of Scotland. We surveyed that part of the place appropriated to the Duke of Hamilton, as Keeper, in which our beautiful Queen Mary lived, and in which David Rizzio was murdered; and also the State Rooms. Dr. Johnson was a great reciter of all sorts of things serious or comical. I over-heard him repeating here, in a kind of muttering tone, a line of the old ballad, *Johnny Armstrong's Last Good-Night:*

'And ran him through the fair body[1]!'

We returned to my house, where there met him, at dinner, the Duchess of Douglas, Sir Adolphus Oughton, Lord Chief Baron, Sir William Forbes, Principal Robertson, Mr. Cullen, advocate. Before dinner, he told us of a curious conversation between the famous George Faulkner and him. George said that England had drained Ireland of fifty thousand pounds in specie, annually, for fifty years. 'How so, sir! (said Dr. Johnson,) you must have a very great trade?' 'No trade.'—'Very rich mines?' 'No mines.'—'From whence, then, does all this money come?' 'Come! why out of the blood and bowels of the poor people of Ireland!'

He seemed to me to have an unaccountable prejudice against Swift; for I once took the liberty to ask him, if Swift had personally offended him, and he told me, he had not. He said to-day, 'Swift is clear, but he is shallow. In coarse humour, he is inferior to Arbuthnot; in delicate humour, he is inferior to Addison: So he is inferior to his contemporaries; without putting him against the whole world. I doubt if the "Tale of a Tub" was his: it has so much more thinking, more knowledge, more power, more colour, than any of the works which are indisputably his. If it was his, I shall only say, he was *impar sibi.'*

We gave him as good a dinner as we could. Our Scotch muir-fowl, or growse, were then abundant, and quite in season; and, so far as wisdom and wit can be aided by administering agreeable sensations to the palate, my wife took care that our great guest should not be deficient.

Sir Adolphus Oughton, then our Deputy Commander in Chief,

who was not only an excellent officer, but one of the most universal
scholars I ever knew, had learned the Erse language, and expressed
his belief in the authenticity of Ossian's Poetry. Dr. Johnson took the
opposite side of that perplexed question; and I was afraid the dispute
would have run high between them. But Sir Adolphus, who had a
very sweet temper, changed the discourse, grew playful, laughed at
Lord Monboddo's notion of men having tails, and called him a judge *a
posteriori,* which amused Dr. Johnson; and thus hostilities were
prevented. . .

[1] The stanza from which he took this line is,
> 'But then rose up all Edinburgh,
>   'They rose up by thousands three;
> 'A cowardly Scot came John behind,
>   'And ran him through the fair body!'

Robert Fergusson

To Dr Samuel Johnson
1773
Caller Oysters
1772

'O thou, my elder brother in Misfortune', wrote Burns in epitaph on Robert Fergusson (1750–1774), 'By far my elder brother in the Muse'. Fergusson, whose Poems were published in 1773, certainly influenced Burns. His own antecedents were in law; after starting as a student at St Andrews University in 1765 he became a clerk in legal offices. To Dr Samuel Johnson. Food for a new Edition of his Dictionary first appeared in The Weekly Magazine or Edinburgh Amusement on 21 October 1773. Caller Oysters ('caller' is 'fresh') appeared in the issue of 27 August 1777. The epigraph is taken from The Splendid Shilling (1701), a poem of John Philips (1676–1708), in light-hearted imitation of John Milton. Fergusson's sanity was darkened by fears of damnation and finally collapsed after injuries caused by a fall. He was incarcerated in the Edinburgh Bedlam until his premature death.

To Dr Samuel Johnson

Let Wilkes and Churchill rage no more,
   Tho' scarce provision, learning's good;
What can these hungries next explore?
   Even Samuel Johnson loves our food.

Great Pedagogue! whose literarian lore,
With syllable on syllable conjoined,
To transmutate and varify, hast learned
The whole revolving scientific names
That in the alphabetic columns lie,
Far from the knowledge of mortalic shapes:
As we, who never can peroculate
The miracles by thee miraculized,
The Muse, silential long, with mouth apert,
Would give vibration to stagnatic tongue,
And loud encomiate thy puissant name,
Eulogiated from the green decline
Of Thames's banks to Scoticanian shores,
Where Lochlomondian liquids undulize.

To meminate thy name in after times,
The mighty Mayor of each regalian town
Shall consignate thy work to parchment fair,
In roll burgharian, and their tables all
Shall fumigate with fumigation strong:
Scotland, from perpendicularian hills,
Shall emigrate her fair muttonian store,
Which late had there in pedestration walked,
And o'er her airy heights perambulized.

Oh, blackest execrations on thy head,
Edina shameless! Tho' he came within
The bounds of your notation; tho' you knew
His honorific name; you noted not,
But basely suffered him to chariotize
Far from your towers, with smoke that nubilate,
Nor drank one amicitial swelling cup
To welcome him convivial. Bailies all!
With rage inflated, catenations* tear,
Nor ever after be you vinculized,
Since you that sociability denied
To him whose potent Lexiphanian style
Words can prolongate, and inswell his page
With what in others to a line's confined.

Welcome, thou verbal potentate and prince!
To hills and valleys, where emerging oats
From earth assuage our pauperty to bay,
And bless thy name, thy dictionarian skill,
Which there definitive will still remain,
And oft be speculized by taper blue,
While youth studentious turn thy folio page.

Have you, as yet, in per'patetic mood,
Regarded with the texture of the eye
The cave cavernic, where fraternal bard,
Churchill, depicted pauperated swains
With thraldom and bleak want reduced sore;
Where Nature, colourized, so coarsely fades,
And puts her russet par'pharnalia on?

* Catenations, vide *Chains*. JOHNSON.

124

Have you, as yet, the way explorified,
To let lignarian chalice, swelled with oats,
Thy orifice approach? Have you, as yet,
With skin fresh rubified with scarlet spheres,
Applied brimstonic unction to your hide,
To terrify the salamandrian fire,
That from involuntary digits asks
The strong allaceration?—Or can you swill
The usquebalian flames of whisky blue,
In fermentation strong? Have you applied
The kilt aërian to your Anglian thighs,
And with renunciation assignized
Your breeches in Londona to be worn?
Can you, in frigour of Highlandian sky,
On heathy summits take nocturnal rest?
It cannot be:—You may as well desire
An alderman leave plumpuddenian store,
And scratch the tegument from pottage dish,
As bid thy countrymen, and thee, conjoined,
Forsake stomachic joys. Then hie you home,
And be a malcontent, that naked hinds,
On lentiles fed, could make your kingdom quake,
And tremulate Old England libertized!

Caller Oysters

Of a' the waters that can hobble
A fishin yole or salmon coble,
And can reward the fishers trouble,
    Or south or north
There's nane sae spacious and sae noble
    As Firth o' *Forth*.

In her the skate and codlin sail,
The eil fou souple wags her tail,
Wi' herrin, fleuk, and mackarel,
    And whitens dainty:
Their spindle-shanks the labsters trail,
    Wi' partans plenty.

AULD REIKIE'S sons blyth faces wear;
September's merry month is near,
That brings in Neptune's caller cheer,
    New oysters fresh;
The halesomest and nicest gear
    Of fish or flesh.

O! then we needna gie a plack
For dand'ring mountebank or quack,
Wha o' their drogs sae bauldly crack,
    And spred sic notions,
As gar their feckless patient tak
    Their stinkin potions.

Come prie, frail man! for gin thou *art sick*,
The oyster is a rare cathartic,
As ever doctor patient gart lick
    To cure his ails;
Whether you hae the head or heart-ake,
    It ay prevails.

Ye tiplers, open a' your poses,
Ye wha are faush'd wi' plouky noses,
Fling owr your craig sufficient doses,
    You'll thole a hunder,
To fleg awa' your simmer roses,
    And naething under.

Whan big as burns the gutters rin,
Gin ye hae catcht a droukit skin,
To *Luckie Middlemist's* loup in,
    And sit fu snug
Oe'r oysters and a dram o' gin,
    Or haddock lug.

When auld Saunt Giles, at aught o' clock,
Gars merchant lowns their chopies lock,
There we adjourn wi' hearty fock
    To birle our bodles,
And get wharewi' to crack our joke,
    And clear our noddles.

Whan *Phœbus* did his windocks steek,
How aften at that *ingle* cheek
Did I my frosty fingers beek,
    And taste gude fare?
I trow there was nae hame to seek
    Whan steghin there.

While glakit fools, o'er rife o' cash,
Pamper their weyms wi' fousom trash,
I think a chiel may gayly pass;
    He's no ill boden
That gusts his gabb wi' oyster sauce,
    And *hen* weel soden.

At *Musselbrough*, and eke *Newhaven*,
The fisher-wives will get *top livin,*
When *lads* gang out on Sunday's even
    To treat their *joes,*
And tak of fat pandours a prieven,
    Or *mussel brose:*

Than sometimes 'ere they flit their *doup,*
They'll ablins a' their *siller* coup
For liquor clear frae cutty stoup,
    To weet their wizen,
And swallow o'er a dainty soup,
    For fear they gizzen.

A' ye wha canna stand sae sicker,
Whan twice you've toom'd the big-ars'd bicker,
Mix *caller oysters* wi' your liquor,
    And I'm your debtor,
If greedy *priest* or drowthy *vicar*
    Will thole it better.

David Hume
My Own Life
1776

David Hume dated this autobiography 18 April 1776, and died on 29 August of that year. The autobiography was first printed in a letter from Adam Smith to their Scottish-born London publisher William Strahan, in 1777. In 1778 it was published with his History of England, *which Hume produced initially between 1754 and 1761.*

IT IS DIFFICULT for a man to speak long of himself without vanity; therefore I shall be short. It may be thought an instance of vanity that I pretend at all to write my life; but this narrative shall contain little more than the history of my writings; as, indeed, almost all my life has been spent in literary pursuits and occupations. The first success of most of my writings was not such as to be an object of vanity.

I was born the twenty-sixth of April, 1711, old style, at Edinburgh. I was of a good family, both by father and mother: my father's family is a branch of the earl of Home's, or Hume's; and my ancestors had been proprietors of the estate which my brother possesses, for several generations. My mother was daughter of Sir David Falconer, president of the college of justice; the title of Lord Halkerton came by succession to her brother.

My family, however, was not rich; and being myself a younger brother, my patrimony, according to the mode of my country, was of course very slender. My father, who passed for a man of parts, died when I was an infant, leaving me, with an elder brother and sister, under the care of our mother, a woman of singular merit, who, though young and handsome, devoted herself entirely to the rearing and educating of her children. I passed through the ordinary course of education with success, and was seized very early with a passion for literature, which has been the ruling passion of my life, and the great source of my enjoyments. My studious disposition, my sobriety, and my industry, gave my family a notion that the law was a proper profession for me; but I found an insurmountable aversion to every thing but the pursuits of philosophy and general learning; and while they fancied I was poring upon Voet and Vinnius, Cicero and Virgil were the authors which I was secretly devouring.

My very slender fortune, however, being unsuitable to this plan of life, and my health being a little broken by my ardent application, I was tempted, or rather forced, to make a very feeble trial for entering into a more active scene of life. In 1734, I went to Bristol, with some recommendations to several eminent merchants; but in a few months found that scene totally unsuitable to me. I went over to France, with a view of prosecuting my studies in a country retreat; and I there laid that plan of life which I have steadily and successfully pursued. I resolved to make a very rigid frugality supply my deficiency of fortune, to maintain unimpaired my independency, and to regard every object as contemptible, except the improvement of my talents in literature.

During my retreat in France, first at Rheims, but chiefly at La Fleche, in Anjou, I composed my Treatise of Human Nature. After passing three years very agreeably in that country, I came over to London in 1737. In the end of 1738, I published my Treatise, and immediately went down to my mother and my brother, who lived at his country house, and was employing himself very judiciously and successfully in the improvement of his fortune.

Never literary attempt was more unfortunate than my Treatise of Human Nature. It fell dead-born from the press, without reaching such distinction as even to excite a murmur among the zealots. But being naturally of a cheerful and sanguine temper, I very soon recovered the blow, and prosecuted with great ardor my studies in the country. In 1742, I printed at Edinburgh the first part of my Essays. The work was favorably received, and soon made me entirely forget my former disappointment. I continued with my mother and brother in the country, and in that time recovered the knowledge of the Greek language, which I had too much neglected in my early youth.

In 1745, I received a letter from the marquis of Annandale; inviting me to come and live with him in England; I found also that the friends and family of that young nobleman were desirous of putting him under my care and direction, for the state of his mind and health required it. I lived with him a twelve-month. My appointments during that time made a considerable accession to my small fortune. I then received an invitation from General St. Clair to attend him as a secretary to his expedition, which was at first meant against Canada, but ended in an incursion on the coast of France. Next year, to wit, 1747, I received an invitation from the general to attend him in the same station in his military embassy to the courts of Vienna and

Turin. I then wore the uniform of an officer, and was introduced at these courts as aid-de-camp to the general, along with Sir Harry Erskine and Captain Grant, now General Grant. These two years were almost the only interruptions which my studies have received during the course of my life: I passed them agreeably, and in good company; and my appointments, with my frugality, had made me reach a fortune which I called independent, though most of my friends were inclined to smile when I said so: in short, I was now master of near a thousand pounds.

I had always entertained a notion, that my want of success in publishing the Treatise of Human Nature had proceeded more from the manner than the matter, and that I had been guilty of a very usual indiscretion, in going to the press too early. I, therefore, cast the first part of that work anew in the Inquiry concerning Human Understanding, which was published while I was at Turin. But this piece was at first little more successful than the Treatise of Human Nature. On my return from Italy, I had the mortification to find all England in a ferment, on account of Dr. Middleton's Free Inquiry, while my performance was entirely overlooked and neglected. A new edition, which had been published at London, of my Essays, moral and political, met not with a much better reception.

Such is the force of natural temper, that these disappointments made little or no impression on me. I went down, in 1749, and lived two years with my brother at his country house, for my mother was now dead. I there composed the second part of my Essay, which I called Political Discourses, and also my Inquiry concerning the Principles of Morals, which is another part of my Treatise that I cast anew. Meanwhile, my bookseller, A. Millar, informed me, that my former publications (all but the unfortunate Treatise) were beginning to be the subject of conversation; that the sale of them was gradually increasing, and that new editions were demanded. Answers by reverends and right reverends came out two or three in a year; and I found, by Dr. Warburton's railing, that the books were beginning to be esteemed in good company. However, I had fixed a resolution, which I inflexibly maintained, never to reply to any body; and not being very irascible in my temper, I have easily kept myself clear of all literary squabbles. These symptoms of a rising reputation gave me encouragement, as I was ever more disposed to see the favorable than unfavorable side of things; a turn of mind which it is more happy to possess, than to be born to an estate of ten thousand a year.

In 1751, I removed from the country to the town, the true scene for a man of letters. In 1752 were published at Edinburgh, where I then lived, my Political Discourses, the only work of mine that was successful on the first publication. It was well received at home and abroad. In the same year was published, at London, my Inquiry concerning the Principles of Morals; which, in my own opinion, (who ought not to judge on that subject,) is, of all my writings, historical, philosophical, or literary, incomparably the best. It came unnoticed and unobserved into the world.

In 1752, the Faculty of Advocates chose me their librarian, an office from which I received little or no emolument, but which gave me the command of a large library. I then formed the plan of writing the History of England; but being frightened with the notion of continuing a narrative through a period of seventeen hundred years, I commenced with the accession of the house of Stuart, an epoch when, I thought, the misrepresentations of faction began chiefly to take place. I was, I own, sanguine in my expectations of the success of this work. I thought that I was the only historian that had at once neglected present power, interest, and authority, and the cry of popular prejudices; and as the subject was suited to every capacity, I expected proportional applause. But miserable was my disappointment; I was assailed by one cry of reproach, disapprobation, and even detestation; English, Scotch, and Irish, whig and tory, churchman and sectary, freethinker and religionist, patriot and courtier, united in their rage against the man who had presumed to shed a generous tear for the fate of Charles I. and the earl of Strafford; and after the first ebullitions of their fury were over, what was still more mortifying, the book seemed to sink into oblivion. Mr. Millar told me that in a twelvemonth he sold only forty-five copies of it. I scarcely, indeed, heard of one man in the three kingdoms, considerable for rank or letters, that could endure the book. I must only except the primate of England, Dr. Herring, and the primate of Ireland, Dr. Stone, which seem two odd exceptions. These dignified prelates separately sent me messages not to be discouraged.

I was, however, I confess, discouraged; and had not the war been at that time breaking out between France and England, I had certainly retired to some provincial town of the former kingdom, have changed my name, and never more have returned to my native country. But as this scheme was not now practicable, and the subsequent volume was considerably advanced, I resolved to pick up courage and to persevere.

In this interval, I published, at London, my Natural History of Religion, along with some other small pieces. Its public entry was rather obscure, except only that Dr. Hurd wrote a pamphlet against it, with all the illiberal petulance, arrogance, and scurrility, which distinguish the Warburtonian school. This pamphlet gave me some consolation for the otherwise indifferent reception of my performance.

In 1756, two years after the fall of the first volume, was published the second volume of my history, containing the period from the death of Charles I. till the revolution. This performance happened to give less displeasure to the whigs, and was better received. It not only rose itself, but helped to buoy up its unfortunate brother.

But though I had been taught by experience that the whig party were in possession of bestowing all places, both in the state and in Literature, I was so little inclined to yield to their senseless clamor, that in above a hundred alterations, which further study, reading, or reflection engaged me to make in the reigns of the two first Stuarts, I have made all of them invariably to the tory side. It is ridiculous to consider the English constitution before that period as a regular plan of liberty.

In 1759, I published my history of the house of Tudor. The clamor against this performance was almost equal to that against the history of the two first Stuarts. The reign of Elizabeth was particularly obnoxious. But I was now callous against the impressions of public folly, and continued very peaceably and contentedly, in my retreat at Edinburgh, to finish, in two volumes, the more early part of the English history, which I gave to the public in 1761, with tolerable, and but tolerable, success.

But, notwithstanding this variety of winds and seasons, to which my writings had been exposed, they had still been making such advances, that the copy-money given me by the booksellers much exceeded any thing formerly known in England; I was become not only independent, but opulent. I retired to my native country of Scotland, determined never more to set my foot out of it; and retaining the satisfaction of never having preferred a request to one great man, or even making advances of friendship to any of them. As I was now turned of fifty, I thought of passing all the rest of my life in this philosophical manner: when I received, in 1763, an invitation from the earl of Hertford, with whom I was not in the least acquainted, to attend him on his embassy to Paris, with a near prospect of being appointed secretary to the embassy; and, in the mean while, of performing the functions of that office. This offer, however inviting, I at first declined; both because I was reluctant to begin connections with the great, and because I was afraid that the civilities and gay company of Paris would prove disagreeable to a person of my age and humour;

but on his lordship's repeating the invitation, I accepted of it. I have every reason, both of pleasure and interest, to think myself happy in my connections with that nobleman, as well as afterwards with his brother, General Conway.

Those who have not seen the strange effects of modes, will never imagine the reception I met with at Paris, from men and women of all ranks and stations. The more I resiled from their excessive civilities, the more I was loaded with them. There is, however, a real satisfaction in living at Paris, from the great number of sensible, knowing, and polite company with which that city abounds above all places in the universe. I thought once of settling there for life.

I was appointed secretary to the embassy; and, in summer, 1765, Lord Hertford left me, being appointed lord lieutenant of Ireland. I was chargé d'affaires till the arrival of the duke of Richmond, towards the end of the year. In the beginning of 1766, I left Paris, and next summer went to Edinburgh, with the same view as formerly, of burying myself in a philosophical retreat. I returned to that place, not richer, but with much more money, and a much larger income, by means of Lord Hertford's friendship, than I left it; and I was desirous of trying what superfluity could produce, as I had formerly made an experiment of a competency. But in 1767, I received from Mr. Conway an invitation to be under-secretary; and this invitation, both the character of the person, and my connections with Lord Hertford, prevented me from declining. I returned to Edinburgh in 1769, very opulent, (for I possessed a revenue of one thousand pounds a year,) healthy, and though somewhat stricken in years, with the prospect of enjoying long my ease, and of seeing the increase of my reputation.

In spring, 1775, I was struck with a disorder in my bowels, which at first gave me no alarm, but has since, as I apprehend it, become mortal and incurable. I now reckon upon a speedy dissolution. I have suffered very little pain from my disorder; and what is more strange, have, notwithstanding the great decline of my person, never suffered a moment's abatement of my spirits; insomuch, that were I to name a period of my life which I should most choose to pass over again, I might be tempted to point to this later period. I possess the same ardor as ever in study, and the same gayety in company. I consider, besides, that a man of sixty-five, by dying, cuts off only a few years of infirmities; and though I see many symptons of my literary reputation's breaking out at last with additional lustre, I know that I could have but few years to enjoy it. It is difficult to be more detached from life than I am at present.

To conclude historically with my own character: I am, or rather was, (for that is the style I must now use in speaking of myself, which imboldens me the more to speak my sentiments;) I was, I say, a man of mild disposition, of command of temper, of an open, social, and cheerful humour, capable of attachment, but little susceptible of enmity, and of great moderation in all my passions. Even my love of literary fame, my ruling passion, never soured my temper, notwithstanding my frequent disappointments. My company was not unacceptable to the young and careless, as well as to the studious and literary; and as I took a particular pleasure in the company of modest women, I had no reason to be displeased with the reception I met with from them. In a word, though most men, anywise eminent, have found reason to complain of Calumny, I never was touched, or even attacked, by her baleful tooth; and though I wantonly exposed myself to the rage of both civil and religious factions, they seemed to be disarmed in my behalf of their wonted fury. My friends never had occasion to vindicate any one circumstance of my character and conduct; not but that the zealots, we may well suppose, would have been glad to invent and propagate any story to my disadvantage, but they could never find any which they thought would wear the face of probability. I cannot say there is no vanity in making this funeral oration of myself, but I hope it is not a misplaced one; and this is a matter of fact which is easily cleared and ascertained.

John Galt
The Courtesies of the Pulpit
1779

John Galt (1779–1839), was born in Ayrshire and led an itinerant life, combining writing with various, often disastrous, business adventures around the globe, during one of which in 1809 he travelled with Byron from Gibraltar to Malta. Annals of the Parish was begun in 1813 and published in 1821. Its success was immediate, with Scott describing it as excellent and John Stuart Mill later claiming, mistakenly, that he had adopted the word 'utilitarian' from it. Galt was particularly fascinated by the self-absorbed and parochial country cousins confronting the sophistication of Edinburgh, although the main theme of the book is of course Balwhidder's fifty years' ministry (and his three marriages) in the old-fashioned town of 'Dalmailing' where he has so much difficulty in coming to terms with the growing industrial power of its offshoot, 'Cayenneville'. Galt's incisive, ironic, vivid perceptions of Scottish life also appear in his The Provost *and* The Member.

I WAS NAMED in this year for the General Assembly, and Mrs Balwhidder by her continual thrift having made our purse able to stand a shake against the wind, we resolved to go into Edinburgh in a creditable manner. Accordingly, in conjunct with Mrs Dalrymple, the lady of a major of that name, we hired the Irville chaise, and we put up in Glasgow at the Black Boy, where we stayed all night. Next morning, by seven o'clock, we got into the fly-coach for the capital of Scotland, which we reached after a heavy journey about the same hour in the evening. We put up at the public where it stopped till the next day, for really both me and Mrs Balwhidder were worn out with the undertaking, and found a cup of tea a vast refreshment.

Betimes in the morning, having taken our breakfast, we got a caddy to guide us and our wallise to Widow M'Vicar's, at the head of the Covenanters' Close. She was a relation to my first wife, Betty Lanshaw, my own full cousin that was, and we had advised her, by course of post, of our coming and intendment to lodge with her as uncos and strangers. But Mrs McVicar's, at the head of the Covenanters' Close. She was a relation to my first wife, Betty Lanshaw, my own full cousin that was, and we h ad advised her, by course of post, of our coming and intendment to lodge with her as uncos and strangers. But Mrs McVicar kept a cloth shop, and sold plaidings and flannels, beside Yorkshire superfines, and was used to the sudden incoming of strangers, especially visitants, from both the West and the North Highlands, and was withal a gawsy, furthy woman, taking great pleasure in hospitality, and every sort of kindliness and discretion; and she would not allow of such a thing as our being lodgers in her house, but was so cagey to see us, and to have it in her power to be civil to a minister (as she was pleased to say) of such repute, that nothing less would content her but that we must live upon her, and partake of all the best that could be gotten for us within the walls of "the guide town."

When we found ourselves so comfortable, Mrs Balwhidder and me waited on my patron's family that was, the young ladies, and the laird, who had been my pupil, but was now an advocate high in the law. They likewise were kind. In short, everybody in Edinburgh was in the manner wearisome kind, and we could scarcely find time to see the Castle and the palace of Holyrood House, and that more sanctified place where the Maccabeus of the Kirk of Scotland, John Knox, was wont to live.

Upon my introduction to his grace the Commissioner, I was delighted and surprised to find the Lord Eaglesham at the levee. And his lordship was so glad on seeing me that he made me more kenspeckle than I could have wished to have been in his grace's presence; for, owing to the same, I was required to preach before his grace, (upon a jocose recommendation of his lordship), the which gave me great concern, and daunted me so that in the interim I was almost bereft of all peace and studious composure of mind. Fain would I have eschewed the honour that was thus thrust upon me; but both my wife and Mrs McVicar were just lifted out of themselves with the thought.

When the day came, I thought all things in this world were loosened from their hold, and the sure and steadfast earth itself grown coggly beneath my feet, as I mounted the pulpit. With what sincerity I prayed for help that day! And never stood man more in need of it; for through all my prayer the congregation was so watchful and still, (doubtless, to note if my doctrine was orthodox), that the beating of my heart might have been heard to the uttermost corners of the kirk.

I had chosen as my text, from Second Samuel, pointed out that, with our Bible and an orthodox priesthood, we stood in no need of the king's authority, however bound we were, in temporal things, to respect it; and I showed this at some length, crying out, in the words of my text, *Wherefore, then, should thy servant be yet a burden to the king?* In the saying of which, I happened to turn my eyes towards his grace the Commissioner, as he sat on the throne, and I thought his countenance

137

was troubled; which made me add, (that he might not think I meant him any offence), "That the King of the Church was one before whom the great, and the wise, and the good,—all doomed and sentenced convicts,—implore his mercy." "It is true," said I, "that in the days of his tribulation he was wounded for our iniquities, and died to save us; but, at his death, his greatness was proclaimed by the quick and the dead. There was sorrow, and there was wonder, and there was rage, and there was remorse; but there was no shame there: none blushed on that day at the sight but yon glorious luminary." The congregation rose, and looked round, as the sun that I pointed at shone in at the window. I was disconcerted by their movement; and my spirit was spent, so that I could say no more.

When I came down from the pulpit, there was a great pressing in of acquaintance and ministers, who lauded me exceedingly; but I thought it could be only in derision, and therefore I slipped home to Mrs McVicar's as fast as I could.

Mrs McVicar, who was a clever, hearing-all sort of a neighbour, said my sermon was greatly thought of, and that I had surprised everybody; but I was fearful there was something of jocularity at the bottom of this, for she was a flaunty woman, and liked well to give a good-humoured gibe or jeer. However, his grace the Commissioner was very thankful for the discourse, and complimented me on what he called my apostolical earnestness. But he was a courteous man, and I could not trust to him, especially as my Lord Eaglesham had told me in secrecy before,—it's true, it was in his gallanting way,—that, in speaking of the king's servant as I had done, I had rather gone beyond the bounds of modern moderation. Altogether, I found neither pleasure nor profit in what was thought so great an honour, but longed for the privacy of my own narrow pasture and little flock.

It was in this visit to Edinburgh that Mrs Balwhidder bought her silver teapot, and other ornamental articles; but this was not done, as she assured me, in a vain spirit of bravery, (which I could not have abided), but because it was well known that tea draws better in a silver pot, and drinks pleasanter in a china cup, than out of any other kind of cup or teapot.

By the time I got home to the manse, I had been three whole weeks and five days absent, which was more than all my absences together from the time of my placing; and my people were glowing with satisfaction when they saw us driving in a Glasgow chaise through the clachan to the manse...

Sir Walter Scott
The Alternative Court
1780

Scott turned from poems to prose with his anonymous novel Waverley *(1814) which was followed by* Guy Mannering *in 1815. After his time at Edinburgh University he was apprenticed to his father, a writer to the signet, in 1786, and was called to the bar in 1792, was appointed sheriff-depute of Selkirkshire in 1799, and obtained one of the clerkships of the Court of Session in 1806.* Guy Mannering *drew richly on this knowledge of the habits and conduct of leading Edinburgh lawyers, the present extract being taken from Chapter XXXVI and the beginning of Chapter XXXVII. Pleydell is also a very interesting precursor of the detective in fiction, and was to have considerable influence on the detective-work in Poe, Dumas, Dickens and Conan Doyle. Although not regarded as among the very best of Scott's novels,* Guy Mannering *is particularly celebrated for its minor characters—the gypsy Meg Merrilies, the farmer Dandie Dinmont and the amateur theologian Dominie Sampson, in addition to Pleydell himself.*

AS SOON AS THEY ARRIVED in Edinburgh, and were established at the George Inn near Bristo Port, then kept by old Cockburn (I love to be particular), the Colonel desired the waiter to procure him a guide to Mr. Pleydell's, the advocate, for whom he had a letter of introduction from Mr. Mac-Morlan. He then commanded Barnes to have an eye to the Dominie, and walked forth with a chairman, who was to usher him to the man of law.

The period was near the end of the American war. The desire of room, of air, and of decent accommodation, had not as yet made very much progress in the capital of Scotland. Some efforts had been made on the south side of the town towards building houses *within themselves*, as they are emphatically termed; and the New Town on the north, since so much extended, was then just commenced. But the great bulk of the better classes, and particularly those connected with the law, still lived in flats or dungeons of the Old Town. The manners also of some of the veterans of the law had not admitted innovations. One or two eminent lawyers still saw their clients in taverns, as was the general custom fifty years before; and although their habits were already considered as old-fashioned by the younger barristers, yet the custom of mixing wine and revelry with serious business was still maintained by those senior counsellors, who loved the old road, either because it was such, or because they had got too well used to it to travel any other. Among those praisers of the past time, who with ostentatious obstinacy affected the manners of a former generation, was this same Paulus Pleydell, Esq., otherwise a good scholar, an excellent lawyer, and a worthy man.

Under the guidance of his trusty attendant, Colonel Mannering, after threading a dark lane or two, reached the High Street, then clanging with the voices of oyster-women and the bells of piemen; for it had, as his guide assured him, just "chappit eight upon the Tron." It was long since Mannering had been in the street of a crowded metropolis, which, with its noise and clamour, its sounds of trade, of revelry, and of license, its variety of lights, and the eternally changing bustle of its hundred groups, offers, by night especially, a spectacle, which, though composed of the most vulgar materials when they are separately considered, has, when they are combined, a striking and powerful effect on the imagination. The extraordinary height of the houses was marked by lights, which, glimmering ir-regularly along their front, ascended so high among the attics, that they seemed at length to twinkle in the middle sky. This *coup d'œil,* which still subsists in a certain degree, was then more imposing, owing to the uninterrupted range of buildings on each side, which, broken only at the space where the North Bridge joins the main street, formed a superb and uniform Place, extending from the front of the Luckenbooths to the head of the Canongate, and corresponding in breadth and length to the uncommon height of the buildings on either side.

Mannering had not much time to look and to admire. His conduc-tor hurried him across this striking scene, and suddenly dived with him into a very steep paved lane. Turning to the right, they entered a scale staircase, as it is called, the state of which, so far as it could be judged of by one of his senses, annoyed Mannering's delicacy not a little. When they had ascended cautiously to a considerable height, they heard a heavy rap at a door, still two stories above them. The door opened, and immediately ensued the sharp and worrying bark of a dog, the squalling of a woman, the screams of an assaulted cat, and the hoarse voice of a man, who cried in a most imperative tone, "Will ye, Mustard! Will ye? down, sir, down!"

"Lord preserve us!" said the female voice, "an he had worried our cat, Mr. Pleydell would ne'er hae forgi'en me!"

"Aweel, my doo, that cat's no a prin the waur—So he's no in, ye say?"

"Nay, Mr. Pleydell's ne'er in the house on a Saturday at e'en," answered the female voice.

"And the morn's Sabbath too," said the querist; "I dinna ken what will be done."

By this time Mannering appeared, and found a tall, strong countryman, clad in a coat of pepper-and-salt-coloured mixture, with huge metal buttons, a glazed hat and boots, and a large horsewhip beneath his arm, in colloquy with a slipshod damsel, who had in one hand the lock of the door, and in the other, a pail of whiting, or *camstane*, as it is called, mixed with water—a circumstance which indicates Saturday night in Edinburgh.

"So Mr. Pleydell is not at home, my good girl?" said Mannering.

"Ay, sir, he's at hame, but he's no in the house: he's aye out on Saturday at e'en."

"But, my good girl, I am a stranger, and my business express—Will you tell me where I can find him?"

"His honour," said the chairman, "will be at Clerihugh's about this time—hersell could hae tell'd ye that, but she thought you wanted to see his house."

"Well, then, show me to this tavern—I suppose he will see me, as I come on business of some consequence?"

"I dinna ken, sir," said the girl, "he disna like to be disturbed on Saturdays wi' business—but he's aye civil to strangers."

"I'll gang to the tavern too," said our friend Dinmont, "for I am a stranger also, and on business e'en sic like."

"Na", said the handmaiden, "an' he see the gentleman, he'll see the simple body too—but, Lord's sake, dinna say it was me sent ye there!"

"Atweel, I am a simple body, that's true, hinny, but I am no come to steal ony o' his skeel for naething," said the farmer in his honest pride, and strutted away downstairs, followed by Mannering and the cadie. Mannering could not help admiring the determined stride with which the stranger who preceded them divided the press, shouldering from him, by the mere weight and impetus of his motion, both drunk and sober passengers. "He'll be a Teviotdale tup tat ane," said the chairman, "tat's for keeping ta crown o' ta causeway tat gate—he'll no gang far or he'll get somebody to bell ta cat wi' him."

His shrewd augury, however, was not fulfilled. Those who recoiled from the colossal weight of Dinmont, on looking up at his size and strength, apparently judged him too heavy metal to be rashly encountered, and suffered him to pursue his course unchallenged. Following in the wake of this first-rate, Mannering proceeded till the farmer made a pause, and, looking back to the chairman, said, "I'm thinking this will be the close, friend?"

"Ay, ay," replied Donald, "tat's ta close."

Dinmont descended confidently, then turned into a dark alley—then up a dark stair—and then into an open door. While he was whistling shrilly for the waiter, as if he had been one of his collie dogs, Mannering looked around him, and could hardly conceive how a gentleman of a liberal profession, and good society, should choose such a scene for social indulgence. Besides the miserable entrance, the house itself seemed paltry and half ruinous. The passage in which they stood had a window to the close, which admitted a little light during the daytime, and a villainous compound of smells at all times, but more especially towards evening. Corresponding to this window was a borrowed light on the other side of the passage, looking into the kitchen, which had no direct communication with the free air, but received in the daytime, at second hand, such straggling and obscure light as found its way from the lane through the window opposite. At present, the interior of the kitchen was visible by its own huge fires—a sort of Pandemonium, where men and women, half undressed, were busied in baking, broiling, roasting oysters, and preparing devils on the gridiron; the mistress of the place, with her shoes slipshod, and her hair straggling like that of Megæra from under a round-eared cap, toiling, scolding, receiving orders, giving them, and obeying them all at once, seemed the presiding enchantress of that gloomy and fiery region.

Loud and repeated bursts of laughter, from different quarters of the house, proved that her labours were acceptable, and not unrewarded by a generous public. With some difficulty a waiter was prevailed upon to show Colonel Mannering and Dinmont the room where their friend, learned in the law, held his hebdomadal carousals. The scene which it exhibited, and particularly the attitude of the counsellor himself, the principal figure therein, struck his two clients with amazement.

Mr. Pleydell was a lively, sharp-looking gentleman, with a professional shrewdness in his eye, and, generally speaking, a professional formality in his manners. But this, like his three-tailed wig and black coat, he could slip off on a Saturday evening, when surrounded by a party of jolly companions, and disposed for what he called his altitudes. On the present occasion, the revel had lasted since four o'clock, and at length, under the direction of a venerable compotator, who had shared the sports and festivity of three generations, the frolicsome company had begun to practise the ancient and now forgotten pastime of *High Jinks*. This game was played in several different ways. Most frequently the dice were thrown by the company, and those upon whom the lot fell were obliged to assume and maintain, for a time, a certain fictitious character, or to repeat a certain number of fescennine verses in a particular order. If they departed from the characters assigned, or if their memory proved treacherous in the repetition, they incurred forfeits, which were either compounded for by swallowing an additional bumper, or by paying a small sum towards the reckoning. At this sport the jovial company were closely engaged when Mannering entered the room.

Mr. Counsellor Pleydell, such as we have described him, was enthroned, as a monarch, in an elbow-chair, placed on the dining-table, his scratch wig on one side, his head crowned with a bottle-slider, his eye leering with an expression betwixt fun and the effects of wine, while his court around him resounded with such crambo scraps of verse as these:

Where is Gerunto now? and what's become of him?
Gerunto's drowned because he could not swim, &c. &c.

Such, O Themis, were anciently the sports of thy Scottish children! Dinmont was first in the room. He stood aghast a moment,—and then exclaimed, "It's him, sure enough—Deil o' the like o' that ever I saw!"

At the sound of "Mr. Dinmont and Colonel Mannering wanting to speak to you, sir," Pleydell turned his head, and blushed a little when he saw the very genteel figure of the English stranger. He was, however, of the opinion of Falstaff, "Out, ye villains, play out the play!" wisely judging it the better way to appear totally unconcerned. "Where be our guards?" exclaimed this second Justinian; "see ye not a stranger knight from foreign parts arrived at this our court of Holyrood,—with our bold yeoman, Andrew Dinmont, who has succeeded to the keeping of our royal flocks within the forest of Jedwood, where, thanks to our royal care in the administration of justice, they feed as safe as if they were within the bounds of Fife? Where be our heralds, our pursuivants, our Lyon, our Marchmount, our Carrick, and our Snowdown? Let the strangers be placed at our board, and regaled as beseemeth their quality, and this our high holiday—to-morrow we will hear their tidings."

"So please you, my liege, to-morrow's Sunday," said one of the company.

"Sunday, is it? then we will give no offence to the assembly of the kirk—on Monday shall be their audience."

Mannering, who had stood at first uncertain whether to advance or retreat, now resolved to enter for the moment into the whim of the scene, though internally fretting at Mac-Morlan, for sending him to consult with a crack-brained humourist. He therefore advanced with three profound congees, and craved permission to lay his credentials at the feet of the Scottish monarch, in order to be perused at his best leisure. The gravity with which he accommodated himself to the humour of the moment, and the deep and humble inclination with which he at first declined, and then accepted, a seat presented by the master of the ceremonies, procured him three rounds of applause.

"Deil hae me, if they arena a' mad thegither!" said Dinmont, occupying with less ceremony a seat at the bottom of the table, "or else they hae taen Yule before it comes, and are gaun a-guisarding."

A large glass of claret was offered to Mannering, who drank it to the health of the reigning prince. "You are, I presume to guess," said the monarch, "that celebrated Sir Miles Mannering, so renowned in the French wars, and may well pronounce to us if the wines of Gascony lose their flavour in our more northern realm."

Mannering, agreeably flattered by this allusion to the fame of his celebrated ancestor, replied, by professing himself only a distant relation of the preux chevalier, and added, "that in his opinion the wine was superlatively good."

'It's ower cauld for my stamach," said Dinmont, setting down the glass (empty, however).

"We will correct that quality," answered King Paulus, the first of the name; "we have not forgotten that the moist and humid air of our valley of Liddel inclines to stronger potations.—Seneschal, let our faithful yeoman have a cup of brandy; it will be more germain to the matter."

"And now," said Mannering, "since we have unwarily intruded upon your majesty at a moment of mirthful retirement, be pleased to say when you will indulge a stranger with an audience on those affairs of weight which have brought him to your northern capital."

The monarch opened Mac-Morlan's letter, and, running it hastily over, exclaimed, with his natural voice and manner, "Lucy Bertram of Ellangowan, poor dear lassie!"

"A forfeit! a forfeit!" exclaimed a dozen voices; "his majesty has forgot his kingly character."

"Not a whit! not a whit!" replied the king; "I'll be judged by this courteous knight. May not a monarch love a maid of low degree? Is not king Cophetua and the Beggar-maid an adjudged case in point?"

"Professional! professional!—another forfeit," exclaimed the tumultuary nobility.

"Had not our royal predecessors," continued the monarch, exalting his sovereign voice to drown these disaffected clamours, —"Had they not their Jean Logies, their Bessie Carmichaels, their Oliphants, their Sandilands, and their Weirs, and shall it be denied to us even to name a maiden whom we delight to honour? Nay, then, sink state and perish sovereignty! for, like a second Charles V., we will abdicate, and seek in the private shades of life those pleasures which are denied to a throne."

So saying, he flung away his crown, and sprung from his exalted station with more agility than could have been expected from his age, ordered lights and a wash-hand basin and towel, with a cup of green tea, into another room, and made a sign to Mannering to accompany him. In less than two minutes he washed his face and hands, settled his wig in the glass, and, to Mannering's great surprise, looked quite a different man from the childish Bacchanal he had seen a moment before.

"There are folks," he said, "Mr. Mannering, before whom one should take care how they play the fool—because they have either too much malice, or too little wit, as the poet says. The best compliment I can pay Colonel Mannering is to show I am not ashamed to expose myself before him—and truly I think it is a compliment I have not spared to-night on your good-nature.—But what's that great strong fellow wanting?"

Dinmont, who had pushed after Mannering into the room, began with a scrape with his foot and a scratch of his head in unison. "I am Dandie Dinmont, sir, of the Charlieshope—the Liddesdale lad—ye'll mind me?—it was for me ye won yon grand plea."

"What plea, you loggerhead?" said the lawyer, "d'ye think I can remember all the fools that come to plague me?"

"Lord, sir, it was the grand plea about the grazing o' the Langtae Head!" said the farmer.

"Well, curse thee, never mind; give me the memorial and come to me on Monday at ten," replied the learned counsel.

"But sir, I haena got ony distinct memorial."

"No memorial, man?" said Pleydell.

"Na, sir nae memorial," answered Dandie, "for your honour said before, Mr. Pleydell, ye'll mind, that ye liked best to hear us hill-folk tell our ain tale by word o' mouth."

"Beshrew my tongue, that said so!" answered the counsellor, "it will cost my ears a dinning.—Well, say in two words what you've got to say—you see the gentleman waits."

"Ou, sir, if the gentleman likes he may play his ain spring first; it's a' ane to Dandie."

"Now, you looby," said the lawyer, "cannot you conceive that your business can be nothing to Colonel Mannering, but that he may not choose to have these great ears of thine regaled with his matters?"

"Aweel, sir, just as you and he like—so ye see to my business," said Dandie, not a whit disconcerted by the roughness of this reception. "We're at the auld wark o' the marches again, Jock o' Dawston Cleugh and me. Ye see we march on the tap o' Touthop Rigg after we pass the Pomoragrains; for the Pomoragrains, and Slackenspool, and Bloodylaws, they come in there, and they belang to the Peel; but after ye pass Pomoragrains at a muckle great saucer-headed cutlugged stane, that they ca' Charlies Chuckie, there Dawston Cleugh and Charlies-hope they march. Now, I say, the march rins on the tap o' the hill where the wind and water shears; but Jock o' Dawson Cleugh again, he contravenes that, and says, that it hauds down by the auld drove-road that gaes awa by the Knot o' the Gate ower to Keeldar-ward—and that makes an unco difference."

"And what difference does it make, friend?" said Pleydell. "How many sheep will it feed?"

"Ou, no mony," said Dandie, scratching his head,—"it's lying high and exposed—it may feed a hog, or aiblins twa in a good year."

"And for this grazing, which may be worth about five shillings a year, you are willing to throw away a hundred pound or two?"

"Na, sir, it's no for the value of the grass," replied Dinmont; "it's for justice."

"My good friend," said Pleydell, "justice, like charity, should begin at home. Do you justice to your wife and family, and think no more about the matter."

Dinmont still lingered, twisting his hat in his hand—"It's no for that, sir—but I would like ill to be bragged wi' him—he threeps he'll bring a score o' witnesses and mair—and I'm sure there's as mony will swear for me as for him, folk that lived a' their days upon the Charlies-hope, and wadna like to see the land lose its right."

"Zounds, man, if it be a point of honour," said the lawyer, "why don't your landlords take it up?"

"I dinna ken, sir (scratching his head again), there's been nae election-dusts lately, and the lairds are unco neighbourly, and Jock and me canna get them to yoke thegither about it a' that we can say—but if ye thought we might keep up the rent—"

"No! no! that will never do," said Pleydell,—"confound you, why don't you take good cudgels and settle it?"

"Odd, sir," answered the farmer, "we tried that three times already—that's twice on the land and ance at Lockerby Fair.—But I dinna ken—we're baith gey good at single-stick, and it couldna weel be judged."

"Then take broadswords, and be d—d to you, as your fathers did before you," said the counsel learned in the law.

"Aweel, sir, if ye think it wadna be again the law, it's a' ane to Dandie."

"Hold! hold!" exclaimed Pleydell, "we shall have another Lord Soulis' mistake—Pr'ythee, man, comprehend me; I wish you to consider how very trifling and foolish a lawsuit you wish to engage in."

"Ay, sir?" said Dandie, in a disappointed tone. "So ye winna take on wi' me, I'm doubting?"

"Me! not I—go home, go home, take pint and agree." Dandie looked but half contented, and still remained stationary. "Anything more, my friend?"

"Only, sir, about the succession of this leddy that's dead, auld Miss Margaret Bertram o' Singleside."

"Aye, what about her?" said the counsellor, rather surprised.

"Ou, we have nae connection at a' wi' the Bertrams," said Dandie,—"they were grand folk by the like o' us—But Jean Liltup, that was auld Singleside's housekeeper, and the mother of these twa young ladies that are gane—the last o' them's dead at a ripe age, I trow—Jean Liltup came out o' Liddel water, and she was as near our connection as second cousin to my mother's half-sister—She drew up wi' Singleside, nae doubt, when she was his housekeeper, and it was a sair vex and grief to a' her kith and kin. But he acknowledged a marriage, and satisfied the kirk—and now I wad ken frae you if we hae not some claim by law?"

"Not the shadow of a claim."

"Aweel, we're nae puirer," said Dandie,—"but she may hae thought on us if she was minded to make a testament.—Weel, sir, I've said my say—I'se e'en wish you good night, and—" putting his hand in his pocket.

"No, no, my friend; I never take fees on Saturday nights, or without a memorial—away with you, Dandie." And Dandie made his reverence, and departed accordingly.

"Your majesty," said Mannering, laughing, "has solemnised your abdication by an act of mercy and charity—That fellow will scarce think of going to law."

"Oh, you are quite wrong," said the experienced lawyer. "The only difference is, I have lost my client and my fee. He'll never rest till he finds somebody to encourage him to commit the folly he has predetermined—No! no! I have only shown you another weakness of my character—I always speak truth of a Saturday night."

"And sometimes through the week, I should think," said Mannering, continuing the same tone.

"Why, yes; as far as my vocation will permit. I am, as Hamlet says, indifferent honest, when my clients and their solicitors do not make me the medium of conveying their double-distilled lies to the bench. But *oportet vivere!* it is a sad thing...

Aeneas Morrison
The Doom of William Brodie
1788

The civic worth and respectability of Deacon William Brodie, Burgess, Guild Brother of Edinburgh, Deacon of the Incorporation of Wrights, six times elected to the Town Council, ensured that his flight, pursuit, arrest in Amsterdam, trial and conviction as an accomplished longtime burglar and conspirator would prove a grave shock to Edinburgh in 1788. Calvinism and its secular legacy of manners had identified appearance with character. Brodie fled on 9 March and was denounced by his confederate George Smith the next day: after being brought back, Brodie was placed on trial with Smith on 27 and 28 August and they were executed on 1 October, despite Brodie's attempts to ensure he would be revived following removal from the gallows. Brodie is identified somewhat dubiously as the inspiration for Stevenson's Jekyll and Hyde, and his presiding judge, Robert Macqueen, Lord Braxfield (1722–1799), correctly as that for Weir of Hermiston. The Court appointed Aeneas Morrison to be Smith's solicitor and his account at the trial, much the best, was published on 6 September.

Lord Justice-Clerk. My Lords, you will now deliver your opinions as to the fentence to be pronounced againft the pannels at the bar.
Lord Hailes. My Lords, after the verdict of the jury, nothing remains for us but the melancholy talk of pronouncing the fentence of the law. It is not left in our option what punifhment to inflict; for the law has declared the crime of which thefe unhappy men have been convicted, capital. It is my opinion, my Lord, that the prifoners at the bar be carried back to the Tolbooth of Edinburgh, and that they be there detained, and that they be executed on Wednefday the firft day of October next.
Lord Efkgrove. My Lord, nothing is left for me but to agree with the opinion delivered by my honourable brother. I fincerely commiferate the fate of thefe unhappy men; one of them efpecially I pity much. Now that I fee him at the bar, I remember that I knew his father, who was a moft worthy man. Their fituation is a miferable one; and I hope that it will have the effect to deter others from being betrayed into the fame vices which have led thefe poor men to this ignominious condition.
Lords Stonefield and *Swinton* delivered fentiments to the fame purpofe.

ADDRESS TO THE PRISONERS.

Lord Justice Clerk. William Brodie and George Smith, It belongs to my office to pronounce the ſentence of the law againſt you. You have had a long and fair trial, conducted on the part of the public proſecutor with the utmoſt candour and humanity; and you have been aſſiſted with able counſel, who have exerted the greateſt ability and fidelity in your defence. I wiſh I could be of any uſe to you in your melancholy ſituation. To one of you it is altogether needleſs for me to offer any advice: You, William Brodie, from your education and habits of life, cannot but know every thing ſuited to your preſent ſituation which I could ſuggeſt to you. It is much to be lamented, that thoſe vices which are called gentlemanly vices are ſo favourably looked upon in the preſent age. They have been the ſource of your ruin; and, whatever may be thought of them, they are ſuch as aſſuredly lead to ruin. I hope you will improve the ſhort time which you have now to live, by reflecting upon your paſt conduct, and endeavouring to procure, by a ſincere repentance, forgiveneſs for your many crimes. God always liſtens to thoſe who ſeek him with ſincerity. The ſentence of the Law, and of this High Court, is, That you be carried back to the priſon from whence you came, there to be detained until Wednesday the 1ſt day of October next; and on that day to be taken forth of the tolbooth to the common place of execution, and there to be hanged on a gibbet by the neck until you are dead; and your moveable goods and gear to be eſcheat and inbrought to his Majeſty's uſe: And this is pronounced for doom.

The ſentence was afterwards read aloud; at the concluſion of which Mr Brodie reſpectfully bowed to the Court, and the pannels were then carried off to priſon.

Thus ended a trial which had excited the public curioſity to an extraordinary degree, and in which their expectations were not diſappointed. During the ſpace of 21 hours, the time it laſted, circumſtances continually followed each other to render it highly intereſting, and more particularly to the gentlemen of the law, on account of the great variety and importance of the legal topics which were diſcuſſed and decided. The pannels behaved in a manner different from each other; Smith appearing to be much dejected, eſpecially at receiving his dreadful ſentence, although in many inſtances he ſhowed very great acuteneſs in his remarks upon the depoſitions of the witneſſes, and in the queſtions to them which he ſuggeſted: Mr. Brodie, on the other hand, affected coolneſs and determination in his behaviour. When the ſentence of death was pronounced, he put one had in his breaſt and the other in his ſide, and looked full around him. It is ſaid that he accuſed his companion of puſillanimity, and even kicked him as they were leaving the Court; but we will not venture to vouch for this laſt circumſtance of his behaviour. He was genteely dreſſed, in a blue coat, a fancy veſt, black ſilk breeches, and white ſilk ſtockings, and he was otherwiſe remarkably clean and neat. Smith was but poorly clothed, having had no money ſince his confinement, which had already laſted ſix months.

Robert Burns
Ae Fond Kiss
1791

Burns, after the success of his poems with the literary circles of Edinburgh, went there in 1786 and on 4 December 1787 met Mrs Agnes Maclehose, whose husband was abroad. He revisited her there in 1788 and finally said farewell to her when he returned for the last time in November 1791. She became the 'Clarinda' of his verse, which under her spell grew coy, mannered, polite and derivative, but his two farewell poems, Gloomy December and this one, return to his true language and accents and Mrs Maclehose achieves a far more genuine identity as 'Nancy'. A very agreeable play on their relationship was written by Robert Kemp in The Other Dear Charmer but the evidence is entirely against its assumption of the propriety of their conduct.

Ae fond kiss, and then we sever;
Ae fareweel, and then for ever!
Deep in heart-wrung tears I'll pledge thee,
Warring sighs and groans I'll wage thee.—

Who shall say that Fortune grieves him,
While the star of hope she leaves him:
Me, nae chearful twinkle lights me;
Dark despair around benights me.—

I'll ne'er blame my partial fancy,
Naething could resist my Nancy:
But to see her, was to love her;
Love but her, and love for ever.—

Had we never lov'd sae kindly,
Had we never lov'd sae blindly!
Never met—or never parted,
We had ne'er been broken-hearted.—

Fare-thee-weel, thou first and fairest!
Fare-thee-weel, thou best and dearest!
Thine be ilka joy and treasure,
Peace, Enjoyment, Love and Pleasure!—

Ae fond kiss, and then we sever!
Ae fareweel, Alas, for ever!
Deep in heart-wrung tears I'll pledge thee,
Warring sighs and groans I'll wage thee.—

Henry, Lord Cockburn
The Birth of the Review
1802

Henry Cockburn (1779–1854) published his biography of his friend and Mentor Francis Jeffrey (1773–1850) in 1852, and left after his death his Memorials of his Time *(1856), one of the richest and wittiest memoirs in Scottish history, as well as his* Circuit Journeys *(1874). Both were zealous Whigs, all the more because of that party's near half-century in the political wilderness (1784–1806, 1807–30), when Jeffrey as editor of the* Edinburgh Review *(1802–1829) won distinction as literary critic and Cockburn as contributor wrote on legal and political subjects. Both became judges in 1834. The* Review *indeed won the highest of fame in its early years with such writers as the Whig wit and clergyman Sydney Smith (1771–1845) and the brilliant Maverick lawyer and future Lord Chancellor Henry Brougham (1778–1868); in his last years as editor Jeffrey brought in Carlyle and Macaulay as contributors. Jeffrey's successor Macvey Napier (1776–1847), the first professor of conveyancing at Edinburgh University, was largely successful in maintaining its quality, but it subsequently atrophied and entered on a long decline. This account is from the* Life of Jeffrey.*

AT LAST, ON THE 10th of October 1802, the first number of the Edinburgh Review appeared. Besides several other articles, it contained seven by Smith, four by Horner, four commonly ascribed to Lord Brougham, and five by Jeffrey, one of which, upon Mourier on the influence of the French Revolution, began the work.

The effect was electrical. And instead of expiring, as many wished, in their first effort, the force of the shock was increased on each subsequent discharge. It is impossible for those who did not live at the time, and in the heart of the scene, to feel, or almost to understand, the impression made by the new luminary, or the anxieties with which its motions were observed. It was an entire and instant change of every thing that the public had been accustomed to in that sort of composition. The old periodical opiates were extinguished at once. The learning of the new Journal, its talent, its spirit, its writing, its independence, were all new; and the surprise was increased by a work so full of public life springing up, suddenly, in a remote part of the kingdom. Different classes soon settled into their different views of it. Its literature, its political economy, and its pure science, were generally admired. Many thoughtful men, indifferent to party, but anxious for the progress of the human mind, and alarmed lest war and political confusion should restore a new course of dark ages, were cheered by the unexpected appearance of what seemed likely to prove a great depository for the contributions of able men to the cause of philosophy. Its political opinions made it be received by one party with demonstrations of its iniquity, with confident prophecies of the impossibility of so scandalous a publication lasting, much pretended derision, and boundless abuse of its audacious authors. On the opposite side, it was hailed as the dawn of a brighter day. It was not merely the intelligent championship of their principles that those on that side saw apparently secured, but the far higher end, that reason would be heard. The splendid career of the Journal, as it was actually run, was not anticipated, either by its authors or by its most ardent admirers; none of whom could forsee its long endurance, or the extent to which the mighty improvements that have reformed our opinions and institutions, and enabled us to engraft the wisdom of experience on the maintainable antiquities of our system, were to depend on this single publication. They only saw the present establishment of an organ of the highest order, for the able and fearless discussion of every matter worthy of being inquired into; but they could not then discern its consequences.

Nowhere was its pillar of fire watched with greater intensity than in Scotland, where the constitutional wilderness was the darkest. Many years had to pass before it could effect actual reform; but it became clearer every day that a generation was forming by which the seed sowing by this work must at last be reaped. To Edinburgh in particular it was of especial benefit. It extended the literary reputation of the place, and connected it with public affairs, and made its opinions important. All were the better of a journal to which every one with an object of due importance had access, which it was in vain either to bully or to despise, and of the fame of which even its reasonable haters were inwardly proud.

It was distinguished in its outset from similar publications, by its being kept quite independent of booksellers, and by the high prices soon paid for articles. The first kept its managers free; the second gave them the command of nearly all the talent in the market. Yet for the first two or three numbers they had an idea that such a work could be carried on without remunerating the writers at all. It was to be all gentlemen, and no pay. And it was during this state of matters that Jeffrey doubted its success, and meant to have a very short connection with it. But this blunder was soon corrected by a magnificent recurrence to the rule of common sense. Mr. Constable, who was their

155

publisher, though unfortunate in the end, was the most spirited book-seller that had ever appeared in Scotland. yet even he seems at one time to have been doubtful of the permanent success of the work, for Mr. Smith gave him the following advice, in a letter which is not dated, but must have been written within the first year of the Review's existence:—"Sir, You ask me for my opinion about the continuation of the E. Review. I have the greatest confidence in giving it to you, as I find every body here (who is capable of forming an opinion upon the subject) unanimous in the idea of its success, and in the hope of its continuation. It is notorious that all the reviews are the organs either of party or of booksellers. I have no manner of doubt that an *able, intrepid,* and *independent* review would be as useful to the public as it would be profitable to those who are engaged in it. If you will give £200 per annum to your editor, and ten guineas a sheet, you will soon have the best review in Europe. This town, I am convinced, is preferable to all others for such an undertaking, from the abundance of literary men it contains, and from the freedom which at this distance they can exercise towards the wits of the south. The gentlemen who first engaged in this review will find it too laborious for pleasure; as labour, I am sure they will not meddle with it for a less valuable offer.—I remain, Sir, you obedt. humble sert." &c.

"P.S.—I do not, by the expressions I have used above, mean to throw any censure on the trade for undertaking reviews. Every one for himself; God for all. It is fair enough that a bookseller should guide the public to his own shop. And fair enough that a critic should tell the public they are going astray."

Thomas Carlyle
The Outer Court
1809

The book known as Carlyle's Reminiscences *was written between 1866 and 1868, this passage forming part of a sketch of Jeffrey dated 3 January 1867. The book was published by Carlyle's future biographer James Anthony Froude a few weeks after Carlyle's death in 1881, arousing harsh controversy, as it had been composed in a time of bitter dejection after his wife, Jane Welsh Carlyle, had died while he was on holiday in his native Dumfries having come to Edinburgh to deliver his inaugural address as Rector in 1866. A superior text to Froude's was established by Charles Eliot Norton in 1887 and is used here, with the minor corrections added by Dr Ian Campbell. Carlyle lived intermittently in Edinburgh, 1809–14 and 1819–24, and settled there for two years in 1826 after marriage, but his memory of their extreme poverty embittered his recollection of it after her death.*

FEW SIGHTS HAVE BEEN more impressive to me than the sudden one I had of the "Outer House," in Parliament Square, Edinburgh, on the evening of 9th November 1809, some hours after my arrival in that City, for the first time. We had walked some twenty miles that day, the third day of our journey from Ecclefechan; my companion one "Tom Smail," who had already been to College last year, and was thought to be a safe guide and guardian to me: he was some years older than myself; had been at School along with me, though never in my class;—a very innocent conceited, insignificant, but strict-minded orthodox creature, for whom, knowing him to be of no scholarship or strength of judgment, I privately had very small respect, though civilly following him about in things he knew better than I. As in the streets of Edinburgh, for example, on my first evening there! On our journey thither he had been wearisome, far from entertaining; mostly silent, having indeed nothing to say, he stalked on generally some steps ahead; languidly whistling through his teeth some similitude of a wretched Irish tune, which I knew too well as that of a still more wretched doggrel song called "The Belfast Shoemaker,"—most melancholy to poor me, given up to my bits of reflections in the silence of the moors and hills.

How strangely vivid, how remote and wonderful, tinged with the hues of far-off love and sadness, is that Journey to me now, after fifty-seven years of time! My Mother and Father walking with me, in the dark frosty November morning, through the village, to set us on our way; my dear, ever-loving Mother and her tremulous affection; my etc. etc.—But we must get to Edinburgh, over Moffat, over Eric-stane (Burnswark visible there for the last time, and my poor little Sister Margaret "bursting into tears" when she heard of this in my first letter home): I hid my sorrow and my weariness, but had abundance of it, chequering the mysterious hopes and forecastings of what Edinburgh and the Student element would be. Tom and I had entered Edinburgh, after twenty miles of walking, between two and three P.M.; got a clean-looking, most cheap lodging ("Simon Square" the poor locality); had got ourselves brushed, some morsel of dinner doubtless; and Palinurus Tom sallied out into the streets with me, to show the novice mind a little of Edinburgh before sundown. The novice mind was not excessively astonished all at once; but kept its eyes well open, and said nothing. What streets we went through, I don't the least recollect; but have some faint image of St. Giles's High-Kirk, and of the Luckenbooths there, with their strange little ins and outs, and eager old women in miniature shops of combs, shoelaces and trifles; still fainter image, if any whatever, of the sublime Horse-Statue in Parliament Square hard by;—directly after which Smail, audaciously (so I thought) pushed open a door (free to all the world), and dragged me in with him to a scene which I have never forgotten.

An immense Hall, dimly lighted from the top of the walls, and perhaps with candles burning in it here and there; all in ·strange *chiaroscuro*, and filled with what I thought (exaggeratively) a thousand or two of human creatures; all astir in a boundless buzz of talk, and simmering about in every direction, some solitary, some in groups. By degrees I noticed that some were in wig and black gown, some not, but in common clothes, all well-dressed; that here and there on the sides of the Hall, were little thrones with enclosures, and steps leading up; red-velvet figures sitting in said thrones, and the black-gowned eagerly speaking to them,—Advocates pleading to Judges, as I easily understood. How they could be heard in such a grinding din was somewhat a mystery. Higher up on the walls, stuck there like swallows in their nests, sat other humbler figures these I found were the sources of certain wildly plangent lamentable kinds of sounds or echoes which from time to time pierced the universal noise of feet and voices, and rose unintelligibly above it, as if in the bitterness of incurable woe;—Cries of the Court, I gradually came to understand.

And this was Themis in her Outer House; such a scene of chaotic din and hurlyburly as I had never figured before. It seems to me there were four times or ten times as many people in that Outer House as there now usually are; and doubtless there is something of fact in this, such have been the curtailments and abatements of Law Practice in the Head Courts since then, and transference of it to the County jurisdictions. Last time I was in that Outer House (some six or seven years ago, in broad daylight), it seemed like a place fallen alseep, fallen almost dead.

David Haggart
His Last Poem
1821

*This poem by David Haggart (1801–1821) has its authenticity affirmed by his largely unsym-
pathetic counsel Henry Cockburn and is printed in his* Life *(1821), which is ostensibly an
autobiography but partly or wholly ghosted. Haggart was an attractive criminal, native to
Edinburgh, who after many adventures in Scotland, England and Ireland, was brought back to his
birthplace to be tried and convicted for murder and, after his disposition of his literary remains, duly
hanged. George Borrow has a memoir of a conversation with him in* Lavengro *and the novelist
Allan Massie includes a sensitive account of his career in* Ill-Met by Gaslight *(1980).*

Able and willing, you will me find,
Though bound in chains, still free in mind;
For with these things I'll ne'er be grieved,
Although of freedom I'm bereaved.

In this vain world there is no rest,
And life is but a span at best;
The rich, the poor, the old, the young,
Shall all lie low before it's long.

I am a rogue, I don't deny,
But never lived by treachery;
And to rob a poor man, I disown,
But them that are of high renown.

Now, for the crime that I'm condemn'd,
The same I never did intend;
Only my liberty to take,
As I thought my life did lie at stake.

My life, by perjury, was sworn away,
I'll say that to my dying day.
Oh, treacherous S——, you did me betray,
For all I wanted was liberty.

No malice in my heart is found,
To any man above the ground.
Now, all good people, that speak of me,
You may say I died for my liberty.

Although in chains you see me fast,
No frown upon my friends you'll cast,
For my relations were not to blame,
And I brought my parents to grief and shame.

Now, all you ramblers, in mourning go,
For the Prince of Ramblers is lying low;
And all you maidens, who love the game,
Put on your mourning veils again.

And all you powers of music chaunt,
To the memory of my dying rant—
A song of melancholy sing,
Till you make the very rafters ring.

Farewell relations, and friends also,
The time is nigh that I must go;
As for foes, I have but one,
But to the same I've done no wrong.

Robert Christison
Medicine and Law
1822

Robert Christison (1797–1882), son of an Edinburgh University professor of Humanity, became himself professor of Medical Jurisprudence and Police, and thence professor of Materia Medica there, holding his chairs from 1822 to 1877. He had previously studied in Edinburgh, London and Paris where he specialised in toxicology, a science in which he afterwards became the leading authority of his time. His range of expertise was extraordinary, including music, botany and most branches of medicine. He bitterly opposed the entry of women students to Edinburgh University during the campaign led by Sophia Jex-Blake in 1868–72. He personally investigated and testified in a variety of famous murder-cases including those of Burke and Hare, Madeleine Smith and William Palmer. He was made a baronet in 1871. This extract is from his unfinished autobiography which was printed in his Life by his sons (1885).

MY PROGRESS IN MEDICO-LEGAL KNOWLEDGE was greatly promoted, and the practical bearing lectures much enhanced, by constant practice as a reporter in precognitions and as a witness in courts of law, first in criminal trials, and soon in civil actions also. My earliest appearances were on the side of the prisoner in the Justiciary Court, the young counsel coming to me for the discovery of loopholes in the case for the Crown,—flaws which it was easy enough to find in the defective medico-legal inquiries of the day. But Solicitor-General Hope, afterwards Lord Justice-Clerk, saw the inconvenience arising from obstructions thus thrown in his way, and by his advice I became unacknowledged standing medical counsel "for his Majesty's interest." My previous training as witness on the prisoner's side, and the wise advice of my elder brother, with whom I continued to keep house, led me always to look at both sides of a question. So far as the medical relations of a case were concerned, I thus became umpire between the prosecutor and the prisoner in the precognition. In point of fact, I thus on several occasions put a stop to further procedure, either by eliciting proof of innocence, or by showing the inconclusiveness of evidence, and the futility of proceeding to trial. I followed the same rule in my inquiries and evidence in civil actions, in which it is even more necessary to be on guard against the one-sidedness of the preliminary investigations. Once during an inquiry of this kind, I was roundly charged by the agent with precognoscing for the opposite party rather than on the side for which I was employed. It would have served no good end to have informed this gentleman that, whatever might be his duty in the case, mine was to find out the truth. But I silenced his scruples by letting him see that, if my services as his witness were to be turned to good account, I must know as much as possible of the other side in order to stand cross-examination; that I could rely on him putting me well up to the facts on his own side, but that for those on the opposite side I had found I must always depend very much upon myself.

The consequence of this mode of procedure was, that I cannot recall a single instance of my evidence-in-chief having been shaken in cross-examination. In general, indeed, it was rather strengthened by points being brought out which had been over-looked in my primary evidence, and which the cross-examining counsel had better have let alone. Hence the leading members of the Bar ceased to cross-examine me; or when they did, it was to bring out some point in favour of their client, which they knew beforehand that I possessed, and was quite ready to produce if desired.

If there is any part of my professional duties on the discharge of which I look back with more satisfaction than another, it is that of reporter and witness in medico-legal questions. I know that I thus gained the approbation of both Bar and Bench. I make this remark, not out of self-satisfaction, but from earnest desire that all my brethren would profit by my experience, and put an end to the disgrace under which scientific equally with all sorts of professional evidence has for some time lain, of being rather the pleading of a counsel than the testimony of a witness. It cannot be denied that in all professions and sciences men may now be got to defend, on their oath as witnesses, any case in which there is a little show of reasonable doubt. In no profession has this practice become so common, and in degree so deplorable, as in that of civil-engineering—a fact which I can trace to nothing else but the shameful laxity of parliamentary committees in multitudinous costly railway cases, and heavy bribes in the shape of fees. But in medicine the fault is scarcely less flagrant; and naturally it is worst in similar circumstances—in cases connected with railway accidents. Every railway board of directors has its own surgeons, partly to look after the health of the men, but greatly also to help themselves through their legal troubles arising out of accidents. I am sorry for these brethren of mine, who seem to consider it a matter of duty and necessity that they must always be on the railway side of a question. I am sorry for them, but doubly so for the necessity they create for medical testimony as uncompromising as theirs on the side of the opposite party. I was early engaged in one case of the kind for the party injured. Fortunately my report carried impartiality so much on the face of it, that the directors were induced to compromise the action by a large solatium. But I saw enough then to determine me never to have anything to do with the trade of medical witness in a railway-accident trial.

Much mischief, however, had been done previously to the character of medical testimony in the Scottish law courts by a small section of men, belonging to the Extra-Academical School of Medicine, who could scarcely ever meet a University man on a public occasion without setting up their backs and spitting at him. It was quite enough that a professor was a professional witness in a court of law for one of this brotherhood to appear on the other side; nor did they ever seem taken aback by the sorry figure they were made to cut on divers occasions. One of them was rather vain of the frequency with which Henry Cockburn, then at the Bar, had him engaged whenever he was counsel. The witness would not have been so proud of his post had he known why he so often filled it. On one occasion the agent in a case in which Cockburn was counsel, remarking that a medical witness would be wanted, asked whether he should see Dr —— on the subject. "No, no!" said Cockburn, "go to Dr ——. He will say anything you like."

The following is a specimen I heard of a cross-examination of this friend of Cockburn. In a trial for poisoning with arsenic—the last occasion on which an attempt was made to dispute the validity of the chemical evidence in arsenical poisoning — Dr —— was employed to make a muddle of the professional testimony; and this was how he set about it. The proof, from symptoms during life and morbid appearances after death—apart from irrefragable chemical proof of the presence of arsenic in the stomach—was unusually strong, perhaps singly conclusive. But Dr —— had no difficulties. "He had great experience of disease. Vast experience in pathological dissections. There was nothing in the symptoms of the deceased during her life which he had not seen again and again arising from natural disease: nothing in the appearances in the dead body which he had not seen twenty times as arising from natural causes." "But, Dr ——," said the Lord Advocate, "the symptoms you have heard detailed, and which you say may have arisen from natural disease, are also such as arsenic may produce, are they not?" "They may be all produced by natural disease." "So you have already told us. But may they not also be produced by arsenic?" "They may; but natural disease may

164

equally cause them." "You need not repeat that information, Doctor. Give me a simple answer to my simple question: May these symptoms be produced by arsenic? Yea or Nay?" "Yes." "Now, Dr ——, you have also told us that the appearances found after death were such as natural disease may produce. Are they not also such as may be produced by arsenic?" "Natural causes may account for them all," &c. &c., through the same round of fencing, until he was compelled to admit that arsenic might produce them. "Now, Doctor," continued the Lord Advocate, "you have heard the evidence of arsenic having been found in the stomach of the woman. Are you satisfied that arsenic was discovered there?" "My Lord, I am no judge of chemical evidence." "Then, Dr ——, in that case I must tell you that it will be my duty to represent to the jury and judges that arsenic was unequivocally detected; and I ask you this—Suppose arsenic was detected, what in that case do you think was the cause of these symptoms, and of these signs in the dead body?" "Natural disease might cause them all." "Yes! yes! we all know that. But suppose that arsenic was found in the stomach, what then would be your opinion as to their cause?" A pause on the part of the Doctor, now run to earth. "Do you not think, sir, that in that case arsenic was the cause?" Softly and reluctantly came the inevitable answer, "Yes." "One more question, then, and I have done: In your opinion, did this person die of poisoning with arsenic?" "Yes." "Have you any doubt of it?" "No." "Then" (*sotto voce*, yet audibly enough), "what the devil brought you here?"

William Hazlitt

The Loveless City
1822

In January 1822, Hazlitt (1778–1830) set out from London for Edinburgh, the sole purpose of his visit being to divorce his wife under the more liberal Scots law. The necessary forty days of residence presumably accounted for the frustration evident in this comment on the city, published in his Liber Amoris, or the New Pygmalion *(1823): it separated him from Miss Walker, the current object of his devotion, who in any case later rejected him. His second marriage (1824–25) to Mrs Bridgewater ended with her leaving him; his first, to Sarah Stoddart, had taken place in 1808. Hazlitt's literary connection with Edinburgh was more fortunate at a distance, his essays for the* Edinburgh Review *beginning in 1814. He was the great pioneer of left-wing criticism of English literature, restoring the reputation of Swift and showing himself one of the finest commentators on Shakespeare of all time.*

——'STONY-HEARTED' Edinburgh! What art thou to me? The dust of thy streets mingles with my tears and blinds me. City of palaces, or of tombs—a quarry, rather than the habitation of men! Art thou like London, that populous hive, with its sunburnt, well-baked, brick-built houses—its public edifices, its theatres, its bridges, its squares, its ladies, and its pomp, its throng of wealth, its outstretched magnitude, and its mighty heart that never lies still? Thy cold grey walls reflect back the leaden melancholy of the soul. The square, hard-edged, unyielding faces of thy inhabitants have no sympathy to impart. What is it to me that I look along the level line of thy tenantless streets, and meet perhaps a lawyer like a grasshopper chirping and skipping, or the daughter of a Highland laird, haughty, fair, and freckled? Or why should I look down your boasted Prince's Street, with the beetle-browed Castle on one side, and the Calton Hill with its proud monument at the further end, and the ridgy steep of Salisbury Crag, cut off abruptly by Nature's boldest hand, and Arthur's Seat overlooking all, like a lioness watching her cubs? Or shall I turn to the far-off Pentland Hills, with Craig-Crook nestling beneath them, where lives the prince of critics and the king of men? Or cast my eye unsated over the Frith of Forth, that from my window of an evening (as I read of AMY and her love) glitters like a broad golden mirror in the sun, and kisses the winding shores of kingly Fife?

166

Oh no! But to thee, to thee I turn, North Berwick-Law, with thy blue cone rising out of summer seas; for thou art the beacon of my banished thoughts, and dost point my way to her, who is my heart's true home. The air is too thin for me, that has not the breath of Love in it; that is not embalmed by her sighs!

Sir Walter Scott
Burke and Hare
1828–29

William Burke (1792–1829) and William Hare (floruit 1818–1829) were Ulster Catholic immigrants to Scotland for work on the Union Canal which when completed in 1822 linked Falkirk to Edinburgh. Hare's wife owned a lodging-house where Burke and his mistress Helen MacDougal lodged. To offset Hare for the loss of money owed by a lodger who died, Burke advocated selling his cadaver to the anatomists, and its warm and unquestioning reception by the famous extra-mural lecturer and anthropologist Robert Knox (1791–1862) induced them to turn to murder. Their sixteenth victim, an Irishwoman, led to their arrest. Christison's tests could not prove murder had been committed; Burke and Hare had made suffocation a means impossible of detection. Hare and his wife accepted a promise of immunity, and so Burke and his (probably innocent) mistress were tried. Cockburn and James Moncreiff, Whigs, defended them, largely as a means of pillorying Scott's friend the Tory Lord Advocate Sir William Rae (1769–1842) for Hare's immunity. MacDougal was found not proven, Burke guilty (he was delighted at her escape). Margaret Hare ultimately fled to Ulster and the Crown ensured Hare's escape to England and oblivion. Maria Edgeworth (1767–1849), Scott's great exemplar in fiction, wrote to him about the case on 10 January 1829, satirically alluding to 'our enlightened and civilised times' which probably prompted his onslaught on the Scottish Enlightenment in his reply to her.

19 December 1828

. . . As for us we are killing each other not for the love of art but for the benefit of science. Our Irish importation have made a great discovery in OEconomics namely that a wretch who is not worth a farthing while alive becomes a valuable article when knockd on the head & carried to an anatomist and acting on this principle have cleard the streets of some of those miserable offcasts of society whom nobody missd because nobody wishd to [see] them again. . . .

[To his daughter Charlotte, Mrs John Gibson Lockhart]

... All Edinburgh is alarmd by a very odd and horrid discovery. Some Irish people have been for some time in the habit of decoying into secret places and murdering such wretches as they thought would be least missd for the sole purpose of selling their bodies for dissection and it would seem that the Anatomists have been in the habit of giving them from £7 to £10 for any corpse whatever no questions askd and what seems shocking that they saw marks of violence on the bodies without being startled or making enquiry how the party came to his end. It is supposed that upwards of twenty persons have perishd in this most miserable manner. But it is certain that three cases can be distinctly proved against Burke and his wife who kept a subterranean cellar in the Grassmarket where this horrid trade was driven. Their usual mode was to intoxicate the poor creatures & so strangle or smother them. But the fate of a poor idiot well known by the name of daft Jamie was particularly shocking. Having in that respect more wit than wiser folks he refused the liquor which they tried to forc[e] upon him and after a desperate defence was subdued and strangled by main forc[e]. The trial comes on on Monday. I am sorry I cannot be there. The murtherers are all Irish of the lowest ranks. There is a generall terror among the servant maids who think their pretty persons are especially aimd at. And two of Glengarrys savage Highlandmen are so completely cow'd that they dared not stir out after sunset for fear of being caught up and dissected.

They keep the thing as quiet as they can for fear of riot but if I were a Doctor I would be afraid of my windows on Monday and well if they get off with a pebbling.

I was shockd in the midst of all this by receipt of a very polite card from the Medical Society inviting me to dine with them. It sounded like a card from Mr [John] Thurtell [who was hanged with Hunt for the murder of Weir in 1824] inviting *one* to a share of his gig on a Roslin party.

After all it is horrid example how men may stumble and fall in the full march of Intellect. The thing is no doubt exaggerated in extent but I learn from the Crown Counsel that *many* cases have occurd besides the *three* which they expect to prove. One of the creaturs who perishd was a prostitute of uncommon personal beauty.

[To his son Charles]

23 January 1829

... In the mean time we have the horrors of the West-port to amuse us, and that we may appear wiser than our neighbours, we drive in our carriages filled with well dress'd females to see the wretched cellars in which those atrocities were perpetrated, and any one that can get a pair of shoes cobbled by Burke would preserve them with as much devotion as a Catholic would do the sandals of a saint which had pressd the holy soil of Palestine. I suspect Justice has done her worst or best to avenge these enormities, and our natural feelings revolt to think that so many of the perpatrators must escape punishment. But you must recollect that it is a thousand times better that the greatest villain should escape than that publick faith should be broken or the law wrested from its even tenour for the purpose of punishing them. The Lord Advocate [his friend Sir William Rae] could not have convicted Burke without the evidence of Hare & his wife, and even succeeded with difficulty, having their support. To break faith with the wretch would be to destroy, in a great measure, a great barrier which the publick has hitherto enjoy'd against crime from the want of reliance of the wicked on each other. Hare therefore I fear must be left to the vengeance of heaven, unless the rabble were to make another Porteous job of it. I did not go to the scene of action, although the newspapers reported me one of the visitors. ...

[To Mary Anne, Mrs Thomas Hughes of Uffington]

29 January 1829

... Your wishes have been nearly acomplished the She-hare has been well nigh hunted to death. She was recognized on the bridge with a blind sickly child in her arms and instantly assailed by the mob with snowballs & stones and even personal violence. I am told that she was at one moment suspended over the banisters of the highest arch & only held by the clothes. It was well for [her] that her supporters had no chilblains [from which he was then in great pain]. At length the police rescued her but I think it a chance that she loses her life if she ventures into the country, & in Edinburgh she cannot remain. Her Husband remains in jail till a deliverance is obtained from the court of Justiciary. The trial of the question comes on on Monday. This Hare is a most hideous wretch so much so that I was induced to remark him from having observed his extremely odious countenance once or twice in the Street where in general I am no observer of faces but his is one which there is no passing without starting & I recognized him easily by the prints. One was apt to say indeed I did say to myself that if he was not some depraved villain Nature did not write with a legible hand.

Burke was executed yesterday morning. He died with firmness though overwhelmed with the hooting cursing and execrations of an immense mob which they hardly suspended during the prayer & psalm which in all other instances in my memory have passed undisturbed, Governor [Joseph] Wall's [in 1802] being a solitary exception. The wretch was diseased with a cancer which the change of diet and the cold of his cell made cruelly painful. . . .

[To Mrs Hughes]

5 February 1829

. . . Our murders have gone on to a point that when all must have supd full with horrors. Yet our gentlemen of the press want not indeed to start a new hare but to have a new course at the old *Hare* a wretch who was to be sure a most abandoned villain but to whom the publick faith was pledged and to whose evidence specially given under promise of life it was owing that they convicted the murderer who has hanged. However the Court of Justiciary has refused to continue his confinement. You will have heard how we brutalized ourselves by shouts and insult even when the wretch that suffered was in his devotions [Scott having seen Burke's execution from a window]. Moreover Sanders was ass enough to purchase the rope he was hanged with at half a crown an inch. Item the hangman became a sort of favourite was invited into a house and treated with liquor for having done his miserable duty on such a villian. And all this in the full march of intellect. Burke was far from being an ignorant man. He wrote a good hand reckond readily and read a good deal chiefly religious books and works of controversy of which he could give some account. And with all these advantages he became a human carcase butcher by wholesale . . .

[To John Bacon Sawney Morritt]

7 February 1829

I return the paper [material relating to the report of the trial of Burke and McDougal being prepared anonymously by his friend Charles Kirkpatrick Sharpe]. There is a slip in which Burke's confession [to be published by Sharpe] differs from that of Hare [shown to Scott by Rae or the judges and later lost, probably intentionally]. They gave the same account of the number & the same descriptions of the victims but they differed in the order of time in which they were committed. Hare stated with great probability that the body of Joseph the Miller was the second sold (that of the old pensioner being the first) and of course he was the first man murdered. Burke with less likelihood asserts the first murder to have been that of a female lodger. I am apt to think that Hare was right for there was an additional motive to reconcile them to the deed in the Miller's case the fear that the apprehensions entertained through the fever would discredit [the Hares' lodging-house] and the consideration that there was as they might [think] less harm in killing a man who was to die at any rate. It may be worth your reporter's while to know this for it is a slip in the history of the crime. It is not odd that Burke should have [been mistaken] acted upon as he seems always to [have been] by ardent spirits and involved in a constant succession of murthers, should have misdated the two actions. On the whole Hare & he making separate confessions agree wonderfully.

[To John Stevenson, publisher to C.K. Sharpe]

4 February 1829

... Certainly I thought, like you, that the public alarm was but an exaggeration of vulgar rumour; but the tragedy is too true, and I look in vain for a remedy of the evils, though it [is] easy to see [where] this black and unnatural business has found its accursed origin. The principal source certainly lies in the feelings of attachment which the Scotch have for their deceased friends. They are curious in the choice of their place of sepulchre, — and a common shephered is often, at whatever ruinous expense to his family, transported many miles to some favourite place of burial which has been occupied by his fathers. It follows, of course, that any inteference with their remains is considered with most utter horror and indignation. To such of their superiors as they love from clanship or habits of dependence, they attach the same feeling of attachment. I experienced it when I had a great domestic loss [Charlotte, his wife, died on 14 May 1826]; for I learned afterwards that the cemetery was guarded, out of good will, by the servants and dependants who had been attached to her during life; and were I to be laid beside my lost companion just now, I have no doubt it would be long before my humble friends would discontinue the same watch over my remains, and that it would incur mortal risk to approach them with the purpose of violation. This is a kind and virtuous principle, which every one so far partakes, that, although an unprejudiced person would have no objection to the idea of his own remains undergoing dissection, if their being exposed to scientific research could be of the least service to humanity, yet we all shudder at the notion of any who had been dear to us, especially a wife or sister, being subjected to a scalpel among a gazing and unfeeling crowd of students. One would fight and die to prevent it. This current of feeling is encouraged by the law which, as distinguishing murderers and other atrocious criminals, orders that their bodies shall be given for public dissection. This makes it almost impossible to assign publickly the bodies of those who die in the public hospitals to the same fate; for it would be inflicting on poverty the penalty which, wisely or unwisely, the law of the country has denounced against guilt of the highest degree; and it would assuredly deprive all who have a remaining part of feeling or shame, of the benefit of those institutions of charity of which they are the best objects. This natural prejudice seems too deeply rooted to be eradicated. If not very liberal, it is surely natural, and so deeply-seated that many of the best feelings must be destroyed ere it can be eradicated. What then remains? The only chance I see is to permit importation from other countries. If a subject can be had in Paris for ten or twenty francs, it will surely pay the importer who brings it to Scotland, and if the medical men find it convenient to use more oeconomy they will teach anatomy for all practical purposes equally well, though they may not make such advances in physiology. Something much be done, for there is an end of the *Cantabit vacuus* [*coram latrone viator* ("The destitute traveller will sing when confronted by the thief")—Juvenal, tenth Satire], the last prerogative of beggary, which entitled him to laugh at the risk of robbery. The veriest wretch in the highway may be better booty than a person of consideration, since the last may have but a few shillings in his pocket, and the beggar, being once dead, is worth ten pounds to his murderer.

The great number of the lower Irish which have come over here since the peace, is, like all important occurrences, attended with its own share of good and evil. It must relieve Ireland in part of the excess of population, which is one of its greatest evils, and it accommodates Scotland with a race of hardy and idefatigable labourers, without which it would be impossible to carry on the very expensive improvements which have been executed. Our canals, our railroads, our various public works, are all wrought by Irish. I have often employed them myself at burning clay, and similar operations, and have found them labourers quiet and tractable, light-spirited, too, and happy to a degree beyond belief, and in no degree quarrelsome, keep whisky from them and them from whisky. But most unhappily for all parties they work at far too low a rate — at a rate, in short, which can but procure salt and potatoes; they become reckless, of course, of all the comforts and decencies of life, which they have no means of procuring. Extreme poverty brings ignorance and vice, and these are the mothers of crime. If Ireland were to submit to some kind of poor-rate — I do not mean that of England, but something that should secure to the indigent their natural share of the fruits of the earth, and enable them at least to feed while others are feasting — it would, apparently, raise the character of the lower orders, and deprive them of that recklessness of futurity which leads them to think only of the present. Indeed, when intoxication of the lower ranks is mentioned as a vice, we must allow the temptation is well-nigh irresistible; mean, clothes, fire, all that men can and do want, are supplied by a drop of whisky; and no one should be surprised that the relief (too often the only one within the wretches' power) is eagerly grasped at.

We pay back, I suspect, the inconveniences we receive from the character of our Irish importation, by sending you a set of half-educated, cold-hearted Scotchmen, to be agents and middle-men. Among them, too, there are good and excellent characters, — yet I can conceive they often mislead their English employers. I am no great believer in the extreme degree of improvement to be derived from the advancement of science; for every pursuit of that nature tends, when pushed to a certain extent, to harden the heart, and render the philosopher reckless of everything save the objects of his own pursuit; all equilibrium in the character is destroyed, and the visual nerve of the understanding is perverted by being fixed on one object exclusively. — Thus we see theological sects (although inculcating the moral doctrines) are eternally placing man's zeal in opposition to them; and even in the callous [Courts], it is astonishing how we become callous to right and wrong, when the question is to gain or lose a cause. I have myself often wondered how I became so indifferent to the horrors of a criminal trial, if it involved a point of law. — In like manner, the pursuers of physical studies inflict tortures on the lower animals of creation, and at length come to rub shoulders with the West Port. The state of high civilization to which we have arrived, is perhaps scarcely a national blessing, since, while the *few* are improved to the highest point, the *many* are in proportion brutalized and degraded, and the same nation displays at the same time the very highest and the very lowest state in which the human race can exist in point of intellect. *Here* is a doctor who is able to take down the whole clock-work of the human frame, and may in time find some way of repairing and putting it together again; and *there* is Burke with the body [of his] murdered countrywoman on his back, and her blood on his hands, asking his price from the learned carcass-butcher. After all, the golden age was the period for general happiness, when the earth gave its stores without labour, and the people existed only in the numbers which it could easily subsist; — but this was too good to last. As our numbers increased, our wants multiplied; and here we are, contending with increasing difficulties by the force of repeated inventions. Whether we shall at last eat each other, as of yore, or whether the earth will get a flap with a comet's tale first, who ... will venture to pronounce? ...

[To Maria Edgeworth]

Robert Louis Stevenson
The Body-Snatcher
1828

Certain circumstances touching the writing of this story have emerged in the course of its preparation for inclusion in this anthology, and as these include matter apparently previously unknown to Stevenson authorities and to the public at large it has been decided, exceptionally, to prepare a more detailed note than usual which in this case follows the story.

EVERY NIGHT IN THE YEAR, four of us sat in the small parlour of the George at Debenham—the undertaker, and the landlord, and Fettes, and myself. Sometimes there would be more; but blow high, blow low, come rain or snow or frost, we four would be each planted in his own particular armchair. Fettes was an old drunken Scotchman, a man of education obviously, and a man of some property, since he lived in idleness. He had come to Debenham years ago, while still young, and by a mere continuance of living had grown to be an adopted townsman. His blue camlet cloak was a local antiquity, like the church-spire. His place in the parlour at the George, his absence from church, his old, crapulous, disreputable vices, were all things of course in Debenham. He had some vague Radical opinions and some fleeting infidelities, which he would now and again set forth and emphasise with tottering slaps upon the table. He drank rum—five glasses regularly every evening; and for the greater portion of his nightly visit to the George sat, with his glass in his right hand, in a state of melancholy alcoholic saturation. We called him the Doctor, for he was supposed to have some special knowledge of medicine, and had been known, upon a pinch, to set a fracture or reduce a dislocation; but beyond these slight particulars, we had no knowledge of his character and antecedents.

One dark winter night—it had struck nine some time before the landlord joined us—there was a sick man in the George, a great neighbouring proprietor suddenly struck down with apoplexy on his way to Parliament; and the great man's still greater London doctor had been telegraphed to his bedside. It was the first time that such a thing had happened in Debenham, for the railway was but newly open, and we were all proportionately moved by the occurrence.

"He's come," said the landlord, after he had filled and lighted his pipe.

"He?" said I. "Who?—not the doctor?"

"Himself," replied our host.

"What is his name?"

"Doctor Macfarlane," said the landlord.

Fettes was far through his third tumbler, stupidly fuddled, now nodding over, now staring mazily around him; but at the last word he seemed to awaken, and repeated the name "Macfarlane" twice, quietly enough the first time, but with sudden emotion at the second.

"Yes," said the landlord, "that's his name, Doctor Wolfe Macfarlane."

Fettes became instantly sober; his eyes awoke, his voice became clear, loud, and steady, his language forcible and earnest. We were all startled by the transformation, as if a man had risen from the dead.

"I beg your pardon," he said, "I am afraid I have not been paying much attention to your talk. Who is this Wolfe Macfarlane?" And then, when he had heard the landlord out, "It cannot be, it cannot be," he added; "and yet I would like well to see him face to face."

"Do you know him, Doctor?" asked the undertaker with a gasp.

"God forbid!" was the reply. "And yet the name is a strange one; it were too much to fancy two. Tell me landlord, is he old?"

"Well," said the host, "he's not a young man, to be sure, and his hair is white; but he looks younger than you."

"He is older, though; years older. But," with a slap upon the table, "it's the rum you see in my face—rum and sin. This man, perhaps, may have an easy conscience and a good digestion. Conscience! Hear me speak. You would think I was some good, old, decent Christian, would you not? But no, not I; I never canted. Voltaire might have canted if he'd stood in my shoes; but the brains"—with a rattling fillip on his bald head—"the brains were clear and active, and I saw and made no deductions."

"If you know this doctor," I ventured to remark, after a somewhat awful pause, "I should gather that you do not share the landlord's good opinion."

Fettes paid no regard to me.

"Yes," he said, with sudden decision, "I must see him face to face."

There was another pause, and then a door was closed rather sharply on the first floor, and a step was heard upon the stair.

"That's the doctor," cried the landlord. "Look sharp, and you can catch him."

It was but two steps from the small parlour to the door of the old George Inn; the wide oak staircase landed almost in the street; there was room for a Turkey rug and nothing more between the threshold and the last round of the descent; but this little space was every evening brilliantly lit up, not only by the light upon the stair and the great signal lamp below the sign, but by the warm radiance of the bar-room window. The George thus brightly advertised itself to passers-by in the cold street. Fettes walked steadily to the spot, and we, who were hanging behind, beheld the two men meet, as one of them had phrased it, face to face. Dr. Macfarlane was alert and vigorous. His white hair set off his pale and placid, although energetic, countenance. He was richly dressed in the finest of broadcloth and the whitest of linen, with a great gold watch-chain, and studs and spectacles of the same precious material. He wore a broad-folded tie, white and speckled with lilac, and he carried on his arm a comfortable driving-coat of fur. There was no doubt but he became his years, breathing, as he did, of wealth and consideration; and it was a surprising contrast to see our parlour sot—bald, dirty, pimpled, and robed in his old camlet cloak—confront him at the bottom of the stairs.

"Macfarlane!" he said somewhat loudly, more like a herald than a friend.

The great doctor pulled up short on the fourth step, as though the familiarity of the address surprised and somewhat shocked his dignity.

"Toddy Macfarlane!" repeated Fettes.

The London man almost staggered. He stared for the swiftest of seconds at the man before him, glanced behind him with a sort of scare, and then in a startled whisper, "Fettes!" he said, "you!"

"Ay," said the other, "me! Did you think I was dead too? We are not so easy shut of our acquaintance."

"Hush, hush!" exclaimed the doctor. "Hush, hush! this meeting is so unexpected—I can see you are unmanned. I hardly knew you, I confess, at first; but I am overjoyed—overjoyed to have this opportunity. For the present it must be how-d'ye-do and good-bye in one, for my fly is waiting, and I must not fail the train; but you shall—let me see—yes—you shall give me your address, and you can count on early news of me. We must do something for you, Fettes. I fear you are out at elbows; but we must see to that for auld lang syne, as once we sang at suppers."

"Money!" cried Fettes; "money from you! The money that I had from you is lying where I cast it in the rain."

Dr. Macfarlane had talked himself into some measure of superiority and confidence, but the uncommon energy of this refusal cast him back into his first confusion.

A horrible, ugly look came and went across his almost venerable countenance. "My dear fellow," he said, "be it as you please; my last thought is to offend you. I would intrude on none. I will leave you my address, however——"

"I do not wish it—I do not wish to know the roof that shelters you," interrupted the other. "I heard your name; I feared it might be you; I wished to know if, after all, there were a God; I know now that there is none. Begone!"

He still stood in the middle of the rug, between the stair and doorway; and the great London physician, in order to escape, would be forced to step to one side. It was plain that he hesitated before the thought of this humiliation. White as he was, there was a dangerous glitter in his spectacles; but while he still paused uncertain, he became aware that the driver of his fly was peering in from the street at this unusual scene and caught a glimpse at the same time of our little body from the parlour, huddled by the corner of the bar. The presence of so many witnesses decided him at once to flee. He crouched together, brushing on the wainscot, and made a dart like a serpent, striking for the door. But his tribulation was not entirely at an end, for even as he was passing Fettes clutched him by the arm and these words came in a whisper, and yet painfully distinct, "Have you seen it again?"

The great rich London doctor cried out aloud with a sharp, throttling cry; he dashed his questioner across the open space, and, with his hands over his head, fled out of the door like a detected thief. Before it had occurred to one of us to make a movement the fly was already rattling toward the station. The scene was over like a dream, but the dream had left proofs and traces of its passage. Next day the servant found the fine gold spectacles broken on the threshold, and that very night we were all standing breathless by the bar-room window, and Fettes at our side, sober, pale, and resolute in look.

"God protect us, Mr. Fettes!" said the landlord, coming first into possession of his customary senses. "What in the universe is all this? These are strange things you have been saying."

Fettes turned toward us; he looked us each in succession in the face. "See if you can hold your tongues," said he. "That man Macfarlane is not safe to cross; those that have done so already have repented it too late."

And then, without so much as finishing his third glass, far less waiting for the other two, he bade us good-bye and went forth, under the lamp of the hotel, into the black night.

We three turned to our places in the parlour, with the big red fire and four clear candles; and as we recapitulated what had passed, the first chill of our surprise soon changed into a glow of curiosity. We sat late; it was the latest session I have known in the old George. Each man, before we parted, had his theory that he was bound to prove; and none of us had any nearer business in the world than to track out the past of our condemned companion, and surprise the secret that he shared with the great London doctor. It is no great boast, but I believe I was a better hand at worming out a story than either of my fellows at the George; and perhaps there is now no other man alive who could narrate to you the following foul and unnatural events.

In his young days Fettes studied medicine in the schools of Edinburgh. He had talent of a kind, the talent that picks up swiftly what it hears and readily retails it for its own. He worked little at home; but he was civil, attentive, and intelligent in the presence of his masters. They soon picked him out as a lad who listened closely and remembered well; nay, strange as it seemed to me when I first heard it, he was in those days well favoured, and pleased by his exterior. There was, at that period, a certain extramural teacher of anatomy, whom I shall here designate by the letter K. His name was subsequently too well known. The man who bore it skulked through the streets of Edinburgh in disguise, while the mob that applauded at the execution of Burke called loudly for the blood of his employer. But Mr. K—— was then at the top of his vogue; he enjoyed a popularity due partly to own talent and address, partly to the incapacity of his rival, the university professor. The students, at least, swore by his name, and Fettes believed himself, and was believed by others, to have laid the foundations of success when he acquired the favour of this meteorically famous man. Mr. K—— was a *bon vivant* as well as an accomplished teacher; he liked a sly illusion no less than a careful preparation. In both capacities Fettes enjoyed and deserved his notice, and by the second year of his attendance he held the half-regular position of second demonstrator, or sub-assistant in his class.

In this capacity the charge of the theatre and lecture-room devolved in particular upon his shoulders. He had to answer for the cleanliness of the premises and the conduct of the other students, and it was a part of his duty to supply, receive, and divide the various subjects. It was with a view to this last—at that time very delicate—affair that he was lodged by Mr.K—— in the same wynd, and at last in the same building, with the dissecting-rooms. Here, after a night of turbulent pleasures, his hand still tottering, his sight still misty and confused, he would be called out of bed in the black hours before the winter dawn by the unclean and desperate interlopers who supplied the table. He would open the door to these men, since infamous throughout the land. He would help them with their tragic burden, pay them their sordid price, and remain alone, when they were gone, with the unfriendly relics of humanity. From such a scene he would return to snatch another hour or two of slumber, to repair the abuses of the night, and refresh himself for the labours of the day.

Few lads could have been more insensible to the impressions of a life thus passed among the ensigns of mortality. His mind was closed against all general considerations. He was incapable of interest in the fate and fortunes of another, the slave of his own desires and low ambitions. Cold, light, and selfish in the last resort, he had that modicum of prudence, miscalled morality, which keeps a man from inconvenient drunkenness or punishable theft. He coveted, besides, a measure of consideration from his masters and his fellow-pupils, and he had no desire to fail conspicuously in the external parts of life. Thus he made it his pleasure to gain some distinction in his studies, and day after day rendered unimpeachable eye-service to his employer, Mr. K——. For his day of work he indemnified himself by nights of roaring, blackguardly enjoyment; and when that balance had been struck, the organ that he called his conscience declared itself content.

The supply of subjects was a continual trouble to him as well as to his master. In that large and busy class, the raw material of the anatomist kept perpetually running out; and the business thus rendered necessary was not only unpleasant in itself, but threatened dangerous consequences to all who were concerned. It was the policy of Mr. K—— to ask no questions in his dealings with the trade. "They bring the body, and we pay the price," he used to say, dwelling on the alliteration—"*quid pro quo.*" And, again, and somewhat profanely, "Ask no questions," he would tell his assistants, "for conscience' sake." There was no understanding that the subjects were provided by the crime of murder. Had that idea been broached to him in words, he would have recoiled in horror; but the lightness of his speech upon so grave a matter was, in itself, an offence against good manners, and a temptation to the men with whom he dealt. Fettes, for instance, had often remarked to himself upon the singular freshness of the bodies. He had been struck again and again by the hangdog, abominable looks of the ruffians who came to him before the dawn; and putting things together clearly in his private thoughts, he perhaps attributed a meaning too immoral and too categorical to the unguarded counsels of his master. He understood his duty, in short, to have three branches: to take what was brought, to pay the price, and to avert the eye from any evidence of crime.

One November morning this policy of silence was put sharply to the test. He had been awake all night with a racking toothache—pacing his room like a caged beast or throwing himself in fury on his bed—and had fallen at last into that profound, uneasy slumber that so often follows on a night of pain, when he was awakened by the third or fourth angry repetition of the concerted signal. There was a thin, bright moonshine; it was bitter cold, windy, and frosty; the town had not yet awakened, but an indefinable stir already preluded the noise and business of the day. The ghouls had come later than usual, and they seemed more than usually eager to be gone. Fettes, sick with sleep, lighted them upstairs. He heard their grumbling Irish voices through a dream; and as they stripped the sack from their sad merchandise he leaned dozing, with his shoulder propped against the wall; he had to shake himself to find the men their money. As he did so his eyes lighted on the dead face. He started; he took two steps nearer, with the candle raised.

"God Almighty!" he cried. "That is Jane Galbraith!"

The men answered nothing, but they shuffled nearer the door.

"I know her, I tell you," he continued. "She was alive and hearty yesterday. It's impossible she can be dead; it's impossible you should have got this body fairly."

"Sure, sir, you're mistaken entirely," said one of the men.

But the other looked Fettes darkly in the eyes, and demanded the money on the spot.

It was impossible to misconceive the threat or to exaggerate the danger. The lad's heart failed him. He stammered some excuses, counted out the sum, and saw his hateful visitors depart. No sooner were they gone than he hastened to confirm his doubts. By a dozen unquestionable marks he identified the girl he had jested with the day before. He saw, with horror, marks upon her body that might well betoken violence. A panic seized him, and he took refuge in his room. There he reflected at length over the discovery that he had made; considered soberly the bearing of Mr. K——'s instructions and the danger to himself of interference in so serious a business, and at last, in sore perplexity, determined to wait for the advice of his immediate superior, the class assistant.

This was a young doctor, Wolfe Macfarlane, a high favourite among all the reckless students, clever, dissipated, and unscrupulous to the last degree. He had travelled and studied abroad. His manners were agreeable and a little forward. He was an authority on the stage, skilful on the ice or the links with skate or golf-club; he dressed with nice audacity, and, to put the finishing touch upon his glory, he kept a gig and a strong trotting-horse. With Fettes he was on terms of intimacy; indeed, their relative positions called for some community of life; and when subjects were scarce the pair would drive far into the country in Macfarlane's gig, visit and desecrate some lonely graveyard, and return before dawn with their booty to the door of the dissecting-room.

On that particular morning Macfarlane arrived somewhat earlier than his wont. Fettes heard him, and met him on the stairs, told him his story, and showed him the cause of his alarm. Macfarlane examined the marks on her body.

"Yes," he said, with a nod, "it looks fishy."

"Well, what should I do?" asked Fettes.

"Do?" repeated the other. "Do you want to do anything? Least said soonest mended, I should say."

"Some one else might recognise her," objected Fettes.

"She was as well known as the Castle Rock."

"We'll hope not," said Macfarlane, "and if anybody does—well, you didn't, don't you see, and there's an end. The fact is, this has been going on too long. Stir up the mud, and you'll get K—— into the most unholy trouble; you'll be in a shocking box yourself. So will I, if you come to that. I should like to know how any one of us would look, or what the devil we should have to say for ourselves, in any Christian witness-box. For me, you know there's one thing certain—that, practically speaking, all our subjects have been murdered."

"Macfarlane!" cried Fettes.

"Come now!" sneered the other. "As if you hadn't suspected it yourself!"

"Suspecting is one thing——"

"And proof is another. Yes, I know; and I'm as sorry as you are this should have come here," tapping the body with his cane. "The next best thing for me is not to recognise it; and," he added coolly, "I don't. You may, if you please. I don't dictate, but I think a man of the world would do as I do; and I may add, I fancy that is what K—— would look for at our hands. The question is, Why did he choose us two for his assistants? and I answer, Because he didn't want old wives."

This was the tone of all others to affect the mind of a lad like Fettes. He agreed to imitate Macfarlane. The body of the unfortunate girl

183

was duly dissected, and no one remarked or appeared to recognise her.

One afternoon, when his day's work was over, Fettes dropped into a popular tavern and found Macfarlane sitting with a stranger. This was a small man, very pale and dark, with coal-black eyes. The cut of his features gave a promise of intellect and refinement which was but feebly realised in his manners, for he proved, upon nearer acquaintance, coarse, vulgar, and stupid. He exercised, however, a very remarkable control over Macfarlane; issued orders like the Great Bradshaw; became inflamed at the least discussion or delay, and commented rudely on the servility with which he was obeyed. This most offensive person took a fancy to Fettes on the spot, plied him with drinks, and honoured him with unusual confidences on his past career. If a tenth part of what he confessed were true, he was a very loathsome rogue; and the lad's vanity was tickled by the attention of so experienced a man.

"I'm a pretty bad fellow myself," the stranger remarked, "but Macfarlane is the boy—Toddy Macfarlane I call him. Toddy, order your friend another glass." Or, it might be, "Toddy, you jump up and shut the door." "Toddy hates me," he said again. "Oh, yes, Toddy, you do!"

"Don't you call me that confounded name," growled Macfarlane.

"Hear him! Did you ever see the lads play knife? He would like to do that all over my body," remarked the stranger.

"We medicals have a better way than that," said Fettes. "When we dislike a dead friend of ours, we dissect him."

Macfarlane looked up sharply, as though this jest were scarcely to his mind.

The afternoon passed. Gray, for that was the stranger's name, invited Fettes to join them at dinner, ordered a feast so sumptuous that the tavern was thrown into commotion, and when all was done commanded Macfarlane to settle the bill. It was late before they separated; the man Gray was incapably drunk. Macfarlane, sobered by his fury, chewed the cud of the money he had been forced to squander and the slights he had been obliged to swallow. Fettes, with various liquors singing in his head, returned home with devios footsteps and a mind entirely in abeyance. Next day Macfarlane was absent from class, and Fettes smiled to himself as he imagined him still squiring the intolerable Gray from tavern to tavern. As soon as the hour of liberty had struck he posted from place to place in quest of his last night's companions. He could find them, however, nowhere; so returned early to his rooms, went early to bed, and slept the sleep of the just.

At four in the morning he was awakened by the well-known signal. Descending to the door, he was filled with astonishment to find Macfarlane with his gig, and in the gig one of those long and ghastly packages with which he was so well acquainted.

"What?" he cried. "Have you been out alone? How did you manage?"

But Macfarlane silenced him roughly, bidding him turn to business. When they had got the body upstairs and laid it on the table, Macfarlane made at first as if he were going away. Then he paused and seemed to hesitate; and then, "You had better look at the face," said he, in tones of some constraint. "You had better," he repeated, as Fettes only stared at him in wonder.

"But where, and how, and when did you come by it?" cried the other.

"Look at the face," was the only answer.

Fettes was staggered; strange doubts assailed him. He looked from the young doctor to the body, and then back again. At last, with a start, he did as he was bidden. He had almost expected the sight that met his eyes, and yet the shock was cruel. To see, fixed in the rigidity of death and naked on that coarse layer of sackcloth, the man whom he had left well clad and full of meat and sin upon the threshold of a tavern, awoke, even in the thoughtless Fettes, some of the terrors of the conscience. It was a *cras tibi* which re-echoed in his soul, that two whom he had known should have come to lie upon these icy tables. Yet these were only secondary thoughts. His first concern regarded Wolfe. Unprepared for a challenge so momentous, he knew not how to look his comrade in the face. He durst not meet his eye, and he had neither words nor voice at his command.

It was Macfarlane himself who made the first advance. He came up quietly behind and laid his hand gently but firmly on the other's shoulder.

"Richardson," said he, "may have the head."

Now Richardson was a student who had long been anxious for that portion of the human subject to dissect. There was no answer, and the murderer resumed: "Talking of business, you must pay me; your accounts, you see, must tally."

Fettes found a voice, the ghost of his own: "Pay you!" he cried. "Pay you for that?"

"Why, yes, of course you must. By all means and on every possible account, you must," returned the other. "I dare not give it for nothing, you dare not take it for nothing; it would compromise us both. This is another case like Jane Galbraith's. The more things are

wrong the more we must act as if all were right. Where does old
K—— keep his money?"

" There," answered Fettes hoarsely, pointing to a cupboard in the
corner.

"Give me the key, then," said the other calmly, holding out his
hand.

There was an instant's hesitation, and the die was cast. Macfarlane
could not suppress a nervous twitch, the infinitesimal mark of an
immense relief, as he felt the key between his fingers. He opened the
cupboard, brought out pen and ink and a paper-book that stood in one
compartment, and separated from the funds in a drawer a sum
suitable to the occasion.

"Now, look here," he said, "there is the payment made—first
proof of your good faith: first step to your security. You have now to
clinch it by a second. Enter the payment in your book, and then you
for your part may defy the devil."

The next few seconds were for Fettes an agony of thought; but in
balancing his terrors it was the most immediate that triumphed. Any
future difficulty seemed almost welcome if he could avoid a present
quarrel with Macfarlane. He set down the candle which he had been
carrying all this time, and with a steady hand entered the date, the
nature, and the amount of the transaction.

"And now," said Macfarlane, "it's only fair that you should pocket
the lucre. I've had my share already. By-the-bye, when a man of the
world falls into a bit of luck, has a few shillings extra in his
pocket—I'm ashamed to speak of it, but there's a rule of conduct in
the case. No treating, no purchase of expensive class-books, no
squaring of old debts; borrow, don't lend."

"Macfarlane," began Fettes, still somewhat hoarsely, "I have put
my neck in a halter to oblige you."

"To oblige me?" cried Wolfe. "Oh, come! You did, as near as I can
see the matter, what you downright had to do in self-defence.
Suppose I got into trouble, where would you be? This second little
matter flows clearly from the first. Mr. Gray is the continuation of
Miss Galbraith. You can't begin and then stop. If you begin, you must
keep on beginning; that's the truth. No rest for the wicked."

A horrible sense of blackness and the treachery of fate seized hold
upon the soul of the unhappy student.

"My God!" he cried, "but what have I done? and when did I begin?
To be made a class assistant—in the name of reason, where's the harm
in that? Service wanted the position; Service might have got it.
Would *he* have been where *I* am now!"

186

"My dear fellow," said Macfarlane, "what a boy you are! What harm *has* come to you? What harm *can* come to you if you hold your tongue? Why, man, do you know what this life is? There are two squads of us—the lions and the lambs. If you're a lamb, you'll come to lie upon these tables like Gray or Jane Galbraith; if you're a lion, you'll live and drive a horse like me, like K——, like all the world with any wit or courage. You're staggered at the first. But look at K——! My dear fellow, you're clever, you have pluck. I like you, and K—— likes you. You were born to lead the hunt; and I tell you, on my honour and my experience of life, three days from now you'll laugh at all these scarecrows like a High School boy at a farce."

And with that Macfarlane took his departure and drove off up the wynd in his gig to get under cover before daylight. Fettes was thus left alone with his regrets. He saw the miserable peril in which he stood involved. He saw, with inexpressible dismay, that there was no limit to his weakness, and that, from concession to concession, he had fallen from the arbiter of Macfarlane's destiny to his paid and helpless accomplice. He would have given the world to have been a little braver at the time, but it did not occur to him that he might still be brave. The secret of Jane Galbraith and the cursed entry in the day-book closed his mouth.

Hours passed; the class began to arrive; the members of the unhappy Gray were dealt out to one and to another, and received without remark. Richardson was made happy with the head; and before the hour of freedom rang Fettes trembled with exultation to perceive how far they had already gone toward safety.

For two days he continued to watch, with increasing joy, the dreadful process of disguise.

On the third day Macfarlane made his appearance. He had been ill, he said; but he made up for lost time by the energy with which he directed the students. To Richardson in particular he extended the most valuable assistance and advice, and that student, encouraged by the praise of the demonstrator, burned high with ambitious hopes, and saw the medal already in his grasp.

Before the week was out Macfarlane's prophecy had been fulfilled. Fettes had outlived his terrors and had forgotten his baseness. He began to plume himself upon his courage, and had so arranged the story in his mind that he could look back on these events with an unhealthy pride. Of his accomplice he saw but little. They met, of course, in the business of the class; they received their orders together from Mr. K——. At times they had a word or two in private, and Macfarlane was from first to last particularly kind and jovial. But it was plain that he avoided any reference to their common secret; and even when Fettes whispered to him that he had cast in his lot with the lions and forsworn the lambs, he only signed to him smilingly to hold his peace.

At length an occasion arose which threw the pair once more into a closer union. Mr. K—— was again short of subjects; pupils were eager, and it was a part of this teacher's pretensions to be always well supplied. At the same time there came the news of a burial in the rustic graveyard of Glencorse. Time has little changed the place in question. It stood then, as now, upon a cross road, out of call of human habitations, and buried fathom deep in the foliage of six cedar trees. The cries of the sheep upon the neighbouring hills, the streamlets upon either hand, one loudly singing among pebbles, the other dripping furtively from pond to pond, the stir of the wind in mountainous old flowering chestnuts, and once in seven days the voice of the bell and the old tunes of the precentor, were the only sounds that disturbed the silence around the rural church. The Resurrection Man—to use a byname of the period—was not to be deterred by any of the sanctities of customary piety. It was part of his trade to despise and desecrate the scrolls and trumpets of old tombs, the paths worn by the feet of worshippers and mourners, and the offerings and the inscriptions of bereaved affection. To rustic neighbourhoods, where love is more than commonly tenacious, and where some bonds of blood or fellowship unite the entire society of a parish, the body-snatcher, far from being repelled by natural respect, was attracted by the ease and safety of the task. To bodies that had been laid in earth, in joyful expectation of a far different awakening, there came that hasty, lamp-lit, terror-haunted resurrection of the spade and mattock. The coffin was forced, the cerements torn, and the melancholy relics, clad in sackcloth, after being rattled for hours on moonless byways, were at length exposed to uttermost indignities before a class of gaping boys.

Somewhat as two vultures may swoop upon a dying lamb, Fettes and Macfarlane were to be let loose upon a grave in that green and quiet resting-place. The wife of a farmer, a woman who had lived for sixty years, and been known for nothing but good butter and a godly conversation, was to be rooted from her grave at midnight and carried, dead and naked, to that far-away city that she had always honoured with her Sunday's best; the place beside her family was to be empty till the crack of doom; her innocent and almost venerable members to be exposed to that last curiosity of the anatomist.

Late one afternoon the pair set forth, well wrapped in cloaks and furnished with a formidable bottle. It rained without remission—a cold, dense, lashing rain. Now and again there blew a puff of wind, but these sheets of falling water kept it down. Bottle and all, it was a sad and silent drive as far as Penicuik, where they were to spend the evening. They stopped once, to hide their implements in a thick bush not far from the churchyard, and once again at the Fisher's Tryst, to have a toast before the kitchen fire and vary their nips of whisky with a glass of ale. When they reached their journey's end the gig was housed, the horse was fed and comforted, and the two young doctors in a private room sat down to the best dinner and the best wine the house afforded. The lights, the fire, the beating rain upon the window, the cold, incongruous work that lay before them, added zest to their enjoyment of the meal. With every glass their cordiality increased. Soon Macfarlane handed a little pile of gold to his companion.

"A compliment," he said. "Between friends these little d——d accommodations ought to fly like pipelights."

Fettes pocketed the money, and applauded the sentiment to the echo. "You are a philosopher," he cried. "I was an ass till I knew you. You and K—— between you, by the Lord Harry! but you'll make a man of me."

"Of course we shall," applauded Macfarlane. "A man? I tell you, it required a man to back me up the other morning. There are some big, brawling, forty-year-old cowards who would have turned sick at the look of the d——d thing; but not you—you kept your head. I watched you."

"Well, and why not?" Fettes thus vaunted himself. "It was no affair of mine. There was nothing to gain on the one side but disturbance, and on the other I could count on your gratitude, don't you see?" And he slapped his pocket till the gold pieces rang.

Macfarlane somehow felt a certain touch of alarm at these unpleasant words. He may have regretted that he had taught his young companion so successfully, but he had no time to interfere, for the other noisily continued in this boastful strain:—

"The great thing is not to be afraid. Now, between you and me, I don't want to hang—that's practical; but for all cant, Macfarlane, I was born with a contempt. Hell, God, Devil, right, wrong, sin, crime, and all the old gallery of curiosities—they may frighten boys, but men of the world, like you and me, despise them. Here's to the memory of Gray!"

It was by this time growing somewhat late. The gig, according to order, was brought round to the door with both lamps brightly shining, and the young men had to pay their bill and take the road. They announced that they were bound for Peebles, and drove in that direction till they were clear of the last houses of the town; then, extinguishing the lamps, returned upon their course, and followed a by-road toward Glencorse. There was no sound but that of their own passage, and the incessant, strident pouring of the rain. It was pitch dark; here and there a white gate or a white stone in the wall guided them for a short space across the night; but for the most part it was at a foot pace, and almost groping, that they picked their way through that resonant blackness to their solemn and isolated destination. In the sunken woods that traverse the neighbourhood of the burying-ground the last glimmer failed them, and it became necessary to kindle a match and re-illumine one of the lanterns of the gig. Thus, under the dripping trees, and environed by huge and moving shadows, they reached the scene of their unhallowed labours.

They were both experienced in such affairs, and powerful with the spade; and they had scarce been twenty minutes at their task before they were rewarded by a dull rattle on the coffin lid. At the same moment, Macfarlane, having hurt his hand upon a stone, flung it carelessly above his head. The grave, in which they now stood almost to the shoulders, was close to the edge of the plateau of the graveyard; and the gig lamp had been propped, the better to illuminate their labours, against a tree, and on the immediate verge of the steep bank descending to the stream. Chance had taken a sure aim with the stone. Then came a clang of broken glass; night fell upon them; sounds alternately dull and ringing announced the bounding of the lantern down the bank, and its occasional collision with the trees. A stone or two, which it had dislodged in its descent, rattled behind it into the profundities of the glen; and then silence, like night, resumed its sway; and they might bend their hearing to its utmost pitch, but naught was to be heard except the rain, now marching to the wind, now steadily falling over miles of open country.

They were so nearly at an end of their abhorred task that they judged it wisest to complete it in the dark. The coffin was exhumed and broken open; the body inserted in the dripping sack and carried between them to the gig; one mounted to keep it in its place, and the other, taking the horse by the mouth, groped along by wall and bush until they reached the wider road by the Fisher's Tryst. Here was a faint, diffused radiancy, which they hailed like daylight; by that they pushed the horse to a good pace and began to rattle along merrily in the direction of the town.

They had both been wetted to the skin during their operations, and now, as the gig jumped among the deep ruts, the thing that stood propped between them fell now upon one and now upon the other. At every repetition of the horrid contact each instinctively repelled it with the greater haste; and the process, natural although it was, began to tell upon the nerves of the companions. Macfarlane made some ill-favoured jest about the farmer's wife, but it came hollowly from his lips, and was allowed to drop in silence. Still their unnatural burden bumped from side to side; and now the head would be laid, as if in confidence, upon their shoulders, and now the drenching sackcloth would flap icily about their faces. A creeping chill began to possess the soul of Fettes. He peered at the bundle, and it seemed somehow larger than at first. All over the country-side, and from every degree of distance, the farm dogs accompanied their passage with tragic ululations; and it grew and grew upon his mind that some unnatural miracle had been accomplished, that some nameless change had befallen the dead body, and that it was in fear of their unholy burden that the dogs were howling.

"For God's sake," said he, making a great effort to arrive at speech, "for God's sake, let's have a light!"

Seemingly Macfarlane was affected in the same direction; for, though he made no reply, he stopped the horse, passed the reins to his companion, got down, and proceeded to kindle the remaining lamp. They had by that time got no farther than the cross-road down to Auchendinny. The rain still poured as though the deluge were returning, and it was no easy matter to make a light in such a world of wet and darkness. When at last the flickering blue flame had been transferred to the wick and began to expand and clarify, and shed a wide circle of misty brightness round the gig, it became possible for the two young men to see each other and the thing they had along with them. The rain had moulded the rough sacking to the outlines of the body underneath; the head was distinct from the trunk, the shoulders plainly modelled; something at once spectral and human riveted their eyes upon the ghastly comrade of their drive.

For some time Macfarlane stood motionless, holding up the lamp. A nameless dread was swathed, like a wet sheet, about the body, and tightened the white skin upon the face of Fettes; a fear that was meaningless, a horror of what could not be, kept mounting to his brain. Another beat of the watch, and he had spoken. But his comrade forestalled him.

"That is not a woman," said Macfarlane, in a hushed voice.

"It was a woman when we put her in," whispered Fettes.

"Hold that lamp," said the other. "I must see her face."

And as Fettes took the lamp his companion untied the fastenings of the sack and drew down the cover from the head. The light fell very clear upon the dark, well-moulded features and smooth-shaven cheeks of a too familiar countenance, often beheld in dreams of both of these young men. A wild yell rang up into the night; each leaped from his own side into the roadway: the lamp fell, broke, and was extinguished; and the horse, terrified by this unusual commotion, bounded and went off toward Edinburgh at a gallop, bearing along with it, sole occupant of the gig, the body of the dead and long-dissected Gray.

A Note On *The Body-Snatcher*

Stevenson was living with his wife in Kinnaird Cottage, Pitlochry, in June 1881 when he began work on 'The Body Snatchers', as it was then termed: he had intended it as an item in a volume of 'crawlers' which would also have included 'Thrawn Janet', written immediately before it. The proposed book, to be entitled *The Black Man and Other Tales* was abandoned, and as early as July 1881 he was writing to his friend Sidney Colvin that 'The Body Snatchers' had been 'laid aside in a justifiable disgust, the tale being horrid'. But when Edmund Gosse approached him on behalf of the *Pall Mall Gazette* for something for its Christmas Extra in 1884, and his first offering 'Markheim' had proved too short, he resurrected and presumably made some surgical changes in his discarded horror. The *Pall Mall Gazette* was so excited by it as to launch a massive advertising campaign, with six plaster skulls made up by a theatrical properties expert, six pairs of coffin-lids, 'painted dead black, while white skulls and cross-bones in the centre for relief' constructed by a carpenter, six long white surplices bought from a 'funeral establishment'. (Thus New York *Current Literature*.) Gosse recalled many years later in his introduction to the work that two or three old women and an invalid gentlemen 'fainted dead away' on meeting the advertisement in the streets of London, and the Police had the commercial suppressed as a public nuisance. The *Extra* was reprinted several times in 1884–1885, but Stevenson insisted he had been overpaid and sent back part of his £40 despite complaints of W. E. Henley that such a gesture was unprofessional.

The affair caused some unpleasantness in the medical world of Edinburgh. Although Knox had had many enemies there, some of his former pupils were still living, and the medical world in general was still vulnerable to similar if less grave charges. It had been hoped that the Burke and Hare story had been disposed of when Henry Lonsdale's *Knox the Anatomist* had appeared in 1870, under the guidance of the most illustrious of all Knox's former pupils, Professor Sir William Fergusson (1808–1877). But in the same year as the *Pall Mall Extra*, George MacGregor's *History of Burke and Hare* was published, and Stevenson, both in the sensationalism of his content and the rising celebrity of his name, had clearly given a new lease of life to the old scandal in a manner likely to feed the worst of speculations. Professor John Goodsir wrote bitterly: 'It will be said, of course, that the *Body Snatcher* is only a piece of fiction. A pleasant piece of fiction, certainly, to attach the stigma of cold-blooded deliberate murder to the name and memory of a man who has relatives and friends and admirers amongst the few still living of his many thousands of pupils. Was it out of delicate consideration for their feelings that Mr Stevenson made use of the K——, when he well knew that he might just as well have written KNOX.' (He seems to have been dissuaded from publishing the protest which survives in the National Library of Scotland, MS 170, ff 48–67.)

But an entirely different suspicion was also raising questions as to the story's being primarily factual or fictional. On 3 February 1885 the *Pall Mall Gazette* carried 'A Key to Mr Stevenson's Body-Snatcher' by an anonymous correspondent who recorded:

Perhaps Mr Louis Stevenson will not take it as a compliment. The other day I put the *Pall Mall* Christmas Extra into the hands of a Scotch octogenarian who, in the time of 'Fettes' and 'Macfarlane', had spent many nights in a lonely northern churchyard, blunderbuss in hand, in wait for 'body-snatchers', or, as he called them, 'resurrectionists'. I had gloated over the 'creepy' tale myself, but till I saw those old eyes flashing and those wizened hands trembling with excitement I hardly realized what the 'Burking' time was. 'Is it a true picture?' he repeated, in answer to my interrogations. 'Faith, the man that wrote it knew juist ower mickle aboot his subject. . . .'

And this is the problem of the story. How did the young Stevenson, born long after these times, capture the atmosphere and circumstances of the whole business of resurrectionism with such authority? He certainly heard stories of those days from his old nurse, but the rumour and hearsay on which they would have been based are a long way away from the authentic tone of the story. He had Lonsdale's and other accounts, but these are at their briefest on the very point where the story is strongest: the macabre atmosphere among the students. Another personal source, his friend Professor Fleeming Jenkin (1833–1885), could have supplied academic gossip, but very much at several removes. The inference is that Stevenson was able to write the story at top speed at Pitlochry because it was based on some encounter, almost certainly in an Edinburgh public-house late at night, from some former medical student who claimed to have been in Knox's entourage during the episode of Burke and Hare. Goodsir clearly suspected something of this kind, and demanded who the actors were based on, being quite sure they were from life. His candidates included a few juniors who were around during the dissections at Knox's rooms, but he named the most obvious originals, Fergusson, Alexander Miller and Thomas Wharton Jones.

It was these three who received the first, and sole naturally deceased, corpse from Burke and Hare, and it was Wharton Jones who had told them, said Burke's confession, 'that they would be glad to see them again when they had any other body to dispose of'. It was Fergusson who had made the discovery ascribed to Fettes in the story that the body of the prostitute brought by Burke and Hare whom he was examining in his professional capacity had been known to him in hers. 'When in the guise of fiction', complained Goodsir, 'an author maligns in the most unmistakeable terms the memories of men who have not long departed, he should recollect that some one still may live who can answer and refute his calumnies.' But with Stevenson's mixing around of the identities and roles of the protagonists Fergusson was in part cleared, although it was Fergusson also who had quickly removed the twisted foot which might have drawn attention to Burke and Hare having provided the corpse of the well-known idiot 'Daft Jamie' Wilson. Wharton Jones seems closer to Wolfe Macfarlane, in his grim and cynical manner—Fergusson's was merely remote—and in the harsh pragmatism of his rapacity for cadavers. Ironically, Goodsir was wrong on one point: Wharton Jones (1808–1891) was not dead, but after a distinguished career as an opthalmic specialist and professor in London, with rooms at Hanover Square, he had retired to Ventnor in the Isle of Wight. He certainly had an excellent basis for libel against Stevenson had he wished, since the story absolutely charges Wolfe Macfarlane with murder. But unlike Fergusson, who rose to even greater heights in London, and who went to such lengths to see that Lonsdale gave the Burke and Hare story to the world in a form best liable to protect the reputations of Knox and his students, Wharton Jones refused to speak of the episode to anyone. The *Lancet* noted the point at his death.

For although the downfall of Knox in the end affected Wharton Jones not too badly and Fergusson hardly at all, Wharton Jones did not remain in Edinburgh and assist Knox in brazening it out. Fergusson did. Fergusson was too brilliant, it may be, to be kept down, and he was given a post as surgeon at the Edinburgh Royal Dispensary in 1831, winning fame by the tying of the subclavian artery the same year. Neither he nor Miller nor Wharton Jones risked themselves to the mercy of the Edinburgh University professor of Anatomy by presenting themselves for degree examinations, and none of them ever seem to have taken a formal degree. Knox raised Fergusson in rank and gave him part of the teaching, but as a new generation, nursed on the horror-stories of Burke, Hare and Knox, reached student age, they shunned the famous doctor whose students at the time had stood by him. Knox made an ill-advised new start in Glasgow, and finally left for London and declined thereafter. Fergusson moved steadily upward and wisely sought academic status in London rather than Edinburgh. Wharton Jones, who had lived in Edinburgh with his mother, had left very soon after the Burke and Hare case, had taken up opthalmic studies in Glasgow, had buried himself in Cork for several years, and thence also came to London where he, too, rose to eminence. Thomas Henry Huxley was numbered among his devoted pupils.

Of Alexander Miller, who alone of the three students merely resided with a landlady as opposed to his family, nothing is known thereafter. No entry for him ever appeared in a medical directory or medical register, granted that such records only commence in mid-century. Goodsir mentions him but knows nothing of his fate after the case. If he left not only Knox but medicine and became an Edinburgh drifter, he could presumably have survived long enough to meet Stevenson and provide some basis for Fettes. At least we can be sure that what was written at Pitlochry was memory as well as imagination.

Felix Mendelssohn
The Sound of Music
1829

Jacob Ludwig Felix Mendelssohn-Bartholdy (1809–1847), the Jewish composer whose 'Wedding March' has probably concluded more Christian weddings than any other work, is the single most significant musical symbol in the transmission of images of Scotland to the development of Romanticism in Europe in 1830–60. His 'Hebrides Overture' ('Fingal's Cave'), in B Minor (Opus 26), inaugurated the concert overture when it was first performed in 1832, and, like his third ('Scottish') Symphony, in A minor-major (Opus 56), first performed in 1842, was originally inspired by his journey to Scotland in 1829. The former work in particular reflected his own and the contemporary interest in the Ossian of James Macpherson (1736–1796), the pseudo-epic manufactured from Gaelic sources and traditions. Before his two weeks in the Highlands, Mendelssohn with his friend Carl Klingemann stayed in Edinburgh from 26 July to 1 August, during which time they visited Scott. David Jenkins and Mark Visocchi produced a comprehensive and profusely illustrated view of the journey in their Mendelssohn in Scotland *(1978), whence come these letters to his family.*

Edinburgh: July 28, 1829

It is Sunday when we arrive in Edinburgh; then we cross the meadows, going towards two desperately steep rocks, which are called Arthur's Seat, and climb up. Below on the green are walking the most variegated people, women, children, and cows; the city stretches far and wide; in the midst is the castle, like a bird's nest on a cliff; beyond the castle come meadows, then hills, then a broad river; beyond the river again hills; then a mountain rather more stern, on which towers Stirling Castle; then blue distance begins; further on you perceive a faint shadow, which they call Ben Lomond.

All this is but one half of Arthur's Seat; the other is simple enough, it is the great blue sea, immeasurably wide, studded with white sails, black funnels, little insects of skiffs, boats, rocky islands, and such like. Why need I describe it? When God Himself takes to panorama-painting, it turns out strangely beautiful. Few of my Switzerland reminiscences can compare to this; everything here looks so stern and robust, half enveloped in haze or smoke or fog.

It is beautiful here! In the evening a cool breeze is wafted from the sea, and then all objects appear clearly and sharply defined against the gray sky; the lights from the windows glitter brilliantly; so it was yesterday when I walked up and down the streets with Mr. Fergusson (an Edinburgh 'friend of mine', to whom Mr. Droop, a London 'friend of mine', has introduced me), and called at the post-office for your letter of the 13th inst. I read it with particular zest in Princes Street, Edinburgh. In Edinburgh, a letter from under the yew-tree in the Leipziger Strasse!

My swim in the sea was pleasant too today, and afloat on the waves I thought of you all, how very closely we are linked together, and yet I was in the deep Scotch ocean, that tastes very briny. Dobberan is lemonade compared to it.

William Cobbett
The Rural Rider
1832

The Rural Rides of William Cobbett (1762–1835), written in the 1820s to report on the agricultural condition of England and its real needs for improvement as opposed to those assumed by Government, were collected and published in 1830, but they related largely to the South. He therefore chose to follow them with his Tour in Scotland and in the Far Northern Counties of England, in the Autumn of the Year 1832, published in 1833, after his election as M.P. for Oldham following the Reform Bill of 1832. His perspective remained largely south English, and his Scottish material was employed greatly by him for comparative purposes, but his trenchant ideas, thrust of observation, independence of mind and scepticism about fashionable notions of improvement gave it some of the quality of its dynamic predecessor. Cobbett had started political life as a vehement conservative polemicist in America and, from 1801, in his native England, but he swung to the radical side from 1804 although he preserved a powerful sense of tradition and hostility to its violators.

I NOW COME BACK to this delightful and beautiful city. I thought that BRISTOL, taking in its heights and CLIFTON and its rocks and its river, was the finest city in the world; but EDINBURGH with its castle, its hills, its pretty little sea-port, conveniently detached from it, its vale of rich land lying all around, its lofty hills in the back ground, its views across the FIRTH: I think little of its streets and its rows of fine houses, though all built of stone, and though everything in LONDON and BATH is beggary to these; I think nothing of *Holyrood House*; but I think a great deal of the fine and well-ordered streets of shops; of the regularity which you perceive everywhere in the management of business; and I will think still more of the absence of all that foppishness, and that affectation of carelessness, and that insolent assumption of superiority, that you see in almost all the young men that you meet with in the fashionable parts of the great towns in England. I was not disappointed; for I expected to find Edinburgh the finest city in the kingdom. Conversations at NEWCASTLE, and with many Scotch gentlemen for years past, had prepared me for this; but still the reality has greatly surpassed every idea that I had formed about it. The *people*, however, still exceed the place: here all is civility; you do not meet with rudeness, or even with the want of a disposition to oblige, even in persons in the lowest state of life. A friend took me round the environs of the city: he had a turnpike ticket, received at the first gate which cleared five or six gates. It was sufficient for him to *tell* the future gate-keepers that he had it. When I saw that, I said to myself, 'Nota bene: Gate-keepers take people's word in Scotland; a thing that I have not seen before since I left *Long Island.*'

In this tour round the city we went by a very beautiful little country-house, at which Mr. JEFFREY, the Lord Advocate, lives. He did not do me the honour to attend my lectures, on account of ill-health, which cause I am very sorry for; for it will require health and spirits, too, for him to buffet the storm that is about to spring up, unless his party be prepared to do a great many things of which they appear not as yet to have dreamed. In the course of this little tour I went to, and to the top of, the ancient CRAIGMILLAR Castle, which stands on a rock at about three miles from EDINBURGH and from which you see the castle and all the city of EDINBURGH; and you look across the Firth of FORTH, and, beyond it, and over the county of FIFE, and the Firth of TAY, see the Highlands rise up. It appears that part of this castle was demolished by the English, when that merciless monster Henry the Eighth invaded Scotland, in order to *compel the young Queen of Scots to marry his son,* Prince Edward! So this ruffian, who was marrying and beheading wives himself all his lifetime, actually undertook a war for a purpose like this! This young queen lost her life at last, by the hands of the myrmidons of his savage daughter; but, at any rate she enjoyed some years of happiness in France; and one minute of it she never would have had, being in the hands of a TUDOR.

This castle has round it, with some exceptions as to form, a circle the diameter of which is about ten miles, of land, which lets on an average for seven pounds the English acre. It lets the higher certainly, for being in the neighbourhood of a city like Edinburgh; but not much higher. Here is an area of seventy-five square miles; and here ought to be, according to the scale of the county of Suffolk, about thirty-two churches and thirty-two villages around them; and with the exception of MUSSELBURGH, there is but one, or at least I could see but one; and is it possible that among so many *really* learned and *really* clever men as these are at Edinburgh, not one should be found to perceive the vast difference in this respect between this city and all the cities in England, and to perceive too, how much greater and more famous EDINBURGH would be, if it were surrounded, as it ought to be, with market-towns and numerous villages? You cannot open your eyes, look in what direction you will, without perceiving, that Scotland is robbed of its wealth and of its character by a stupid and unnational nobility. And, if the reformed Parliament do its duty, it will do by Scotland as HENRY *the Seventh* did by England; and we shall very soon see villages rise up in Scotland, and see a stop put to the caravan bringing back to the North vagrants from NEWCASTLE.

Queen Victoria
Landscape for Albert
1842

Victoria (1819–1904), Queen of the United Kingdom of Great Britain and Ireland, had succeeded her uncle, William IV, in 1837, and married her first cousin, Prince Albert (1819–1861) of Saxe-Coburg Gotha in 1840. In 1842 they made their first visit to Scotland, and she recorded her reactions to Edinburgh on 3 September 1842. Extracts from her journals relating to subsequent journeys to the Highlands were published at her instance in her lifetime, but the journal of this visit was printed in David Duff's Victoria in the Highlands *(1968). She had already borne two children by the time she came to Scotland: after twelve years, Balmoral Castle was completed and she would reside there every spring and autumn for the remainder of her life.*

Saturday, September 3

At ten o'clock we set off—we two in the barouche—all the others following, for Edinburgh. We drove in under Arthur's Seat, where the crowd began to be very great, and here the Guard of Royal Archers met us; Lord Elcho walking near me, and the Duke of Roxburgh and Sir J. Hope on Albert's side. We passed by Holyrood Chapel, which is very old and full of interest, and Holyrood Palace, a royal-looking old place. The procession moved through the Old Town up the High Street, which is a most extraordinary street from the immense height of the houses, most of them being eleven stories high, and different families living in each story. Every window was crammed full of people.

They showed us Knox's House, a curious old building, as is also the Regent Murray's House, which is in perfect preservation. In the Old Town the High Church, and St. Paul's in the New Town, are very fine buildings. At the barrier, the Provost presented us with the keys.

The girls of the Orphan Asylum, and the Trades in old costumes, were on a platform. Further on was the New Church, to which—strange to say, as the church is nearly finished—they were going to lay the foundation stone. We at length reached the Castle, to the top of which we walked.

The view from both batteries is splendid, like a panorama in extent. We saw from them Heriot's Hospital, a beautiful old building, founded, in the time of James, by a goldsmith and jeweller, whom Sir Walter Scott has made famous in his *Fortunes of Nigel*. After this, we got again into the carriages and proceeded in the same way as before, the pressure of the crowd being really quite alarming; and both I and Albert were quite terrified for the Archers Guard, who had very hard work of it; but were of the greatest use. They all carry a bow in one hand, and have their arrows stuck through their belts.

Unfortunately, as soon as we were out of Edinburgh, it began to rain, and continued raining the whole afternoon without interruption. We reached Dalmeny, Lord Roseberry's, at two o'clock. The park is beautiful, with the trees growing down to the sea. It commands a very fine view of the Forth, the Isle of May, the Bass Rock, and of Edinburgh; but the mist rendered it almost impossible to see anything. The grounds are very extensive, being hill and dale and wood. The house is quite modern: Lord Roseberry built it, and it is very pretty and comfortable. We lunched there. The Roseberrys were all civility and attention. We left them about half-past three, and proceeded home through Leith.

The view of Edinburgh from the road before you enter Leith is quite enchanting; it is, as Albert said, "fairy-like", and what you would only imagine as a thing to dream of, or to see in a picture. There was that beautiful large town, all of stone (no mingled colours of brick to mar it), with the bold Castle on one side, and the Calton Hill on the other, with those high sharp hills of Arthur's Seat and Salisbury Crags towering above all, and making the finest, boldest background imaginable. Albert said he felt sure the Acropolis could not be finer; and I hear they sometimes call Edinburgh "the modern Athens". The Archers Guard met us again at Leith, which is not a pretty town.

The people were most enthusiastic, and the crowd very great. The Porters all mounted, with curious Scotch caps, and their horses decorated with flowers, had a very singular effect; but the fishwomen are the most striking-looking people, and are generally young and pretty women—very clean and very Dutch-looking, with their white caps and bright-coloured petticoats. They never marry out of their class.

At six we returned well tired.

Hugh Miller
The Disruption
1843

The Disruption of the Church of Scotland was one of the greatest events of modern Scottish history. It turned on the question of appointment of ministers by local lairds, in practice an arrangement similar to what obtained in the Church of England, or the traditional Presbyterian, method of adoption by the congregation or its delegates. The Presbyterian church was not necessarily as representative of Scotland as it liked to imagine, but here it certainly symbolised the issue of whether Scotland was to accept English forms of elitist rule or retention of its older and more democratic usages. The decision of the most distinguished clergy, led by the Rev. Thomas Chalmers (1780–1847) a theologian and social critic of outstanding oratorical fire, to leave the established Church of Scotland as incurably deferential to Government, meant that they moved from fixed and sure sources of income to futures of the greatest uncertainty. Hugh Miller (1802–56) was their zealous lay supporter: a confirmed social radical and agitator against aristocratic injury to tenants and the environment, he was also hostile to the infant labour movement. He reported the Disruption in his evangelical newspaper the Edinburgh Witness on 20 May 1843. George Rosie's Hugh Miller (1981) which inspired the present extract includes a good brief sketch of his life and selection of his writings.

THE FATAL DIE had been cast. On Thursday last the Religion of Scotland was disestablished. The day that witnessed a transaction so momentous can be a day of no slight mark in modern history. It stands between two distinct states of things,—a signal to Christendom. It holds out its sign to these latter times, that God and the world have drawn off their forces to opposite sides, and that His sore and great battle is soon to begin.

The future can alone adequately develop the more important consequences of the event. At present we shall merely attempt presenting the reader with a few brief notes of the aspect which it exhibited. The early part of Thursday had its periods of fitful cloud and sunshine, and the tall picturesque tenements of the Old Town now lay dim and indistinct in shadow, now stood prominently out in the light. There was an unusual throng and bustle in the streets at a comparatively early hour, which increased greatly as the morning wore on towards noon. We marked, in especial, several knots of Moderate clergy hurrying along to the levee, laughing and chatting with a vivacity that reminded one rather of the French than of the Scotch character, and evidently in that state of nervous excitement which, in a certain order of minds, the near approach of some very great event, indeterminate and unappreciable in its bearings, is sure always to occasion.

As the morning wore on, the crowds thickened in the streets, and the military took their places. The principles involved in the anticipated Disruption gave to many a spectator a new association with the long double line of dragoons that stretched down the High Street, as far as the eye could reach, from the venerable Church of St Giles, famous in Scottish story, to the humbler Tron. The light flashed fitfully on their long swords and helmets, and the light scarlet of their uniforms contrasted strongly with the dingier vestments of the masses, in which they seemed as if more than half engulphed. When the sun glanced out, the eye caught something peculiarly picturesque in the aspect of the Calton Hill, with its imposing masses of precipices overtopped by towers and monuments, and its intermingling bushes and trees now green with the soft, delicate foliage of May.

Between its upper and under line of rock, a dense living belt of human beings girdled it round, sweeping gradually downwards from shoulder to base, like the sash of his order on the breast of a nobleman. The Commissioner's procession passed, with sound of trumpet and drum, and marked by rather more than the usual splendour. There was much bravery and glitter,—satin and embroidery, varnish and gold lace,—no lack, in short, of that cheap and vulgar magnificence which can be got up to order by the tailor and the upholsterer for carnivals and Lord Mayors' days. But it was felt by the assembled thousands, as the pageant swept past, that the real spectacle of the day was a spectacle of a different character.

The morning levee had been marked by an incident of a somewhat extraordinary nature, and which history, though in these days little disposed to mark prodigies and omens, will scarce fail to record. The crowd in the Chamber of Presence was very great, and there was, we believe, a considerable degree of confusion and pressure in consequence. Suddenly,—whether brushed by some passer by, jostled rudely aside, or merely affected by the tremor of the floor communicated to the partitioning,—a large portrait of William the Third, that had held its place in Holyrood for nearly a century and a half, dropped heavily from the walls. "There," exclaimed a voice from the crowd,—"there goes the Revolution Settlement."

For hours before the meeting of Assembly, the galleries of St Andrew's Church, with the space behind, railed off for the accommodation of office-bearers not members, were crowded to suffocation, and a vast assemblage still continued to besiege the doors. Immediately after noon, the Moderate members began to drop in one by one, and to take their places on the Moderator's right, while the opposite benches remained well-nigh empty. What seemed most fitted to catch the eye of the stranger was the rosy appearance of the men, and the rounded contour of face and feature. We were reminded, in glancing over the benches, of a bed of full-blown piony-roses glistening after a shower; and, could one have but substituted among them the monk's frock for the modern dress-coat, and given to each crown the shaven tonsure, they would have passed admirably for a conclave of monks met to determine some weighty point of abbey-income, or right of forestry.

The benches on the left began slowly to fill, and on the entrance of every more distinguished member a burst of recognition and welcome shook the gallery. Their antagonists had been all permitted to take their places in ominous silence. The music of the pageant was heard outside; the Moderator (the Rev. Dr Welsh, Professor of Church History Edinburgh University) entered, attired in his gown; and ere the appearance of the Lord High commissioner, preceded by his pages and mace-bearer, and attended by the Lord Provost, the Lord Advocate, and the Solicitor-General, the Evangelical benches had filled as densely as those of their opponents, and the cross benches, appropriated, in perilous times like the present, to a middle party careful always to pitch their principles below the suffering point, were also fully occupied.

Never before was there seen so crowded a General Assembly; the number of members had been increased beyond all precedent by the double returns; and almost every member was in his place. The Moderator opened the proceedings by deeply impressive prayer; but though silence within was complete, a Babel of tumultuary sounds outside, and at the closed doors, expressive of the intense anxiety of the excluded multitude, had the effect of rendering him scarcely audible in the more distant parts of the building. There stood beside the chair, though on opposite sides, the meet representatives of the belligerent parties. On the right we marked Principal McFarlan of Glasgow,—the man, in these altered times, who could recommend his students to organise themselves into political clubs, but dissuade them from forming missionary societies. On his left stood Thomas Chalmers, the man through whose indomitable energy and Christian zeal two hundred churches were added to the Establishment in a little more than ten years. Science, like religion, had its representatives on the Moderator's right and left. On the one side we saw *Moderate* science personified in Dr Anderson of Newburgh,—a dabbler in geology, who found a fish in the Old Red Sandstone, and described it as a beetle; we saw science *not Moderate*, on the other side, represented by Sir David Brewster.

The Moderator rose and addressed the House in a few impressive sentences. There had been an infringement, he said, on the Constitution of the Church,—an infringement so great, that they could not constitute its General Assembly without a violation of the union between Church and State, as now authoritatively defined and declared. He was therefore compelled, he added, to protest against proceeding further; and, unfolding a document which he held in his hand, he read, in a slow and emphatic manner, the protest of the Church.

For the first few seconds, the extreme anxiety to hear defeated its object,—the universal hush, hush, occasioned considerably more noise than it allayed; but the momentary confusion was succeeded by the most unbroken silence; and the reader went on till the impressive close of the document, when he flung it down on the table of the House, and solemnly departed. He was followed, at a pace's distance, by Dr Chalmers; Dr Gordon and Dr Patrick MacFarlan immediately succeeded; and then the numerous sitters on the thickly occupied benches behind filed after them, in a long unbroken line, which for several minutes together continued to thread the passage to the eastern door, till at length only a blank space remained. As the well-known faces and forms of some of the ablest and most eminent men that ever adorned the Church of Scotland glided along in the current, to disappear from the courts of the State institution for ever, there rose a cheer from the galleries, and an impatient cry of "Out, out", from the ministers and elders not members of Assembly, now engaged in sallying forth, to join with them, from the railed area behind. The cheers subsided, choaked in not a few instances by tears. The occasion was by far too solemn for the commoner manifestations of either censure or approval; it excited feelings that lay too deep for expression. There was a marked peculiarity in the appearance of their opponents,—a blank, restless, pivot-like turning of head from the fast emptying benches to one another's faces; but they uttered no word,—not even in whispers. At length, when the last of the withdrawing party had disappeared, there ran from bench to bench a hurried, broken whispering,—"How many?"—"How many?"—"A hundred and fifty?" "No;" "Yes;" "Four hundred?" "No;"—and then for a moment all was still again. The scene that followed we deemed one of the most striking of the day.

The empty vacated benches stretched away from the Moderator's seat in the centre of the building, to the distant wall. There suddenly glided into the front rows a small party of men whom no one knew,—obscure, mediocre, blighted-looking men, that, contrasted with the well-known forms of our Chalmerses and Gordons, Candlishes and Cunninghams, McFarlans, Brewsters and Dunlops, reminded one of the thin and blasted corn-ears of Pharoah's vision, and, like them too, seemed typical of a time of famine and destitution. Who are these? was the general query; but no one seemed to know. At length the significant whisper ran along the house, "The Forty". There was a grin of mingled contempt and compassion visible on many a broad Moderate face, and a too audible titter shook the gallery. There seemed a degree of incongruity in the sight that partook highly of the ludicrous. For our own part, we were so carried away by a vagrant association, and so missed Ali Baba, the oil kettle, and the forty jars, as to forget for a time that at the doors of these unfortunate men lies the ruin of the Scottish establishment. The aspect of the Assembly sank, when it had in some degree recovered itself, into that expression of tame and flat commonplace, which it must be henceforth content to bear, until roused, happily, into short-lived activity, by the sharp paroxysms of approaching destruction.

A spectacle equally impressive with that exhibited by the ministers and elders of the Free Church, as they winded in long procession to their place of meeting, there to constitute their independent Assembly, Edinburgh has certainly not witnessed since those times of the Covenant when Johnston of Warriston unrolled the solemn parchment in the churchyard of the Greyfriars, and the assembled thousands, from the peer to the peasant, adhibited their names. The procession, with Dr Chalmers, and the Moderator in his robes and cap of office, at its head, extended, three in depth, for a full quarter of a mile. The Lord Provost of the city rode on before.

Rather more than four hundred were ministers of the church; all the others were elders. Be it remembered, that the number of ministers ejected from their charges at the Restoration, and who maintained the struggle in behalf of Presbytery during the long persecution of twenty-eight years mounted in all to but three hundred and seventy-six; but then, as now, the religious principles which they maintained were those of the country. They were principles that had laid fast hold of the national mind, and the fires of persecution served only to render their impress ineradicable. Is it not strange how utterly the great lessons of history have failed to impress the mean and wretched rulers of our country in this the day of their visitation?

Eve Blantyre Simpson
Science in Society
1847

Evelyn Blantyre Simpson (1856–1920), who also wrote on Stevenson, and on Scottish folklore, published her biography of her father, Sir James Young Simpson (1811–1870), in 1896. Her literary accomplishments accounted for its being the commission by the publisher as one of a series of succinct lives of great Scots rather than a contribution to the Victorian tradition of massive memorials by devoted and verbose relatives. Her father, a vigorous exponent of the advancement of women in medical life and elsewhere, would presumably have been pleased. The son of a baker, he had won his Edinburgh University M.D. at the age of 21, and his professorship of midwifery at 28. In addition to his discovery of chloroform he is famous for having anticipated the discovery of Röntgen rays and having made valuable discoveries in obstetrics. His eccentric manner and advanced theological speculations disguised his brilliance of mind. He largely opposed Christison on university questions, and was called in by him to save his life, which he did.

. . . CONTEMPORARY ACCOUNTS as to its first trial differ slightly. Dr. George Keith and my aunt, Miss Grindlay, are the only two survivors. My aunt says the Professor came into the dining-room one afternoon, holding a little bottle in his hand, and saying, 'This will turn the world upside down.' He then poured some into a tumbler, breathed it, and fell unconscious. This may have been some other drug, for many were tried, but till recently, when dimmed by age, Miss Grindlay's memory was a veracious one. Miss Petrie, her niece, was much at Queen Street in these days, and in a journal she kept, mentions that my father 'tried everything on himself first,' and once, after swallowing some concoction, was insensible for two hours. Dr. Keith recalled another experiment, when, not content with chloroform, he tried a compound of carbon, which brought on such irritation in breathing that he had to be kept under chloroform to relieve him. In experimenting upon himself, he was ever 'bold even to rashness,' as Sir Lyon Playfair (now Lord Playfair) in 1883 asserted of him in the House of Commons. He was speaking of vivisection, and told how Sir James, still searching for something better, came to his laboratory, and Playfair put in his hand a new liquid. He wanted to inhale it there and then, but Playfair insisted on two rabbits being first dosed with it, and they speedily succumbed. 'Now, was not this,' he asked the House, 'a justifiable experiment on animals? Was not it worth the sacrifice of two rabbits to save the life of the most distinguished physician of his time, who by the introduction of chloroform has done so much to mitigate animal suffering?'

Seeing he was ever recklessly rash in regard to himself, it is not unlikely he may have had a private trial of chloroform, and laid it aside again, to start fair with his two assistants, who had worked so unflinchingly with him. Some other compounds were tried that night, and then chloroform, which was lying in its little phial among some papers, was unearthed, and the result of this, its first trial as an anæsthetic, 4th November 1847, is best described in Professor Simpson's own words in a letter to Mr. Waldie, who had previously drawn his attention to this heavy-smelling 'perchloride of formyle.'

'I am sure you will be delighted to see part of the good results of our hasty conversation. I had the chloroform for several days in the house before trying it, as, after seeing it such a heavy, unvolatile-like liquid, I despaired of it, and went on dreaming about others. The first night we took it, Dr. Duncan, Dr. Keith, and I all tried it simultaneously, and were all "under the table" in a minute or two.' Dr. George Keith, writing to me in 1891, says: 'Dr. Miller, in the appendix to his work on surgery, published soon after, gives a full account of the scene. It is pretty correct, only he says we all took the chloroform at once. This, with a new substance to try, would have been foolish, and the fact is, I began to inhale it a few minutes before the others. On seeing the effects on me, and hearing my approval before I went quite over, they both took a dose, and I believe we were all more or less under the table together, much to the alarm of your mother, who was present.' Professor Miller, his neighbour, who used to come in every morning to see if the experimenters had survived, says: 'These experiments were performed after the long day's toil was over, at late night or early morn, and when the greater part of mankind were soundly anæsthetised in the arms of common sleep.' He describes how, after a 'weary day's labour,' the trio sat down and inhaled various drugs out of tumblers, as was their custom, and chloroform was searched for and 'found beneath a heap of waste paper, and with each tumbler newly charged, the inhalers resumed their occupation. . . A moment more, then all was quiet, and then a crash. On awakening, Dr. Simpson's first perception was mental. "This is far stronger and better than ether," said he to himself. His second was to note that he was prostrate on the floor, and that among the friends about him there was both confusion and alarm. Of his assistants, Dr. Duncan he saw snoring heavily, and Dr. Keith kicking violently at the table above him. They made several more trials of it that eventful evening, and were so satisfied with the results that the festivities of the evening did not terminate till a late hour, 3 a.m.'

The onlookers to this scene were my mother, her sister Miss Grindlay, her niece Miss Petrie, and her brother-in-law Captain Petrie. Accustomed as they had grown to experiments, they were startled with the results of this first 'inhaling of chloroform.' My aunt often spoke of Dr. Keith's ghastly expression when, ceasing to kick, he raised his head to the level of the table and stared with unconscious eyes on them. She had such a horror of chloroform, she refused ever to try it. My father used to threaten to put her under its influence, and when she fled he gave chase; but, light of foot as he was in these days, she always escaped, for fits of laughter used to seize him and choke him off the pursuit. Great was my father's joy at his success, and in having, in so handy a form, so potent an agent to deaden the suffering he had daily to witness. . . .

Thomas Babington Macaulay
To the Electors of Edinburgh
1847

In some respects it is still unclear exactly why Thomas Babington Macaulay (1800–1859) was defeated in the election of 1847 at Edinburgh, which he had represented since 1839. William Gibson Craig (1797–1878), his colleague, had hardly differed from him on the issues and was re-elected. Macaulay was irritated by the pressures placed upon him by local issues such as the Disruption, and rather resented calls that reminded him too much of that Scottish ancestry from which he had very self-consciously evolved. He was also spending increasing time with his great History of England, *whose first volumes were to appear in 1848. But he was probably quite correct in his implicit assumption that it was caused by his support for an increased grant to the Catholic seminary in Ireland, St Patrick's College, Maynooth: unlike Craig, he had made a classical speech in its favour in 1845 in which he savagely denounced the bigotry of its Protestant extremist enemies. For all his English cast, he had been a local hero since his first essay had appeared in the* Edinburgh Review *in 1825, and he had reminded his admirers of the breadth and scope of his achievement by republishing the cream of his essays for it in 1843. He was re-elected in 1852, having refused to campaign, and was made Baron Macaulay of Rothley in 1857. He had been M.P. for Calne (1830–32), and Leeds (1832–34), until he entered the Indian civil service. This letter is consciously reminiscent of Edmund Burke's speech facing defeat at Bristol in 1780.*

London, August 2, 1847.

Gentlemen,

You have been pleased to dismiss me from your service, and I submit to your pleasure without repining. The generous kindness of those who to the last gave me their support I shall always remember with gratitude. If anything has occurred of which I might justly complain, I have forgiven and shall soon forget it.

The points on which we have differed I leave with confidence to the judgement of my country. I cannot expect that you will at present admit my views to be correct; but the time will come when you will calmly review the history of my connection with Edinburgh. You will then, I am convinced, acknowledge that if I incurred your displeasure, I incurred it by remaining faithful to the general interests of the Empire, and to the fundamental principles of the Constitution. I shall always be proud to think that I once enjoyed your favour. But permit me to say, I shall remember not less proudly how I risked and how I lost it.

With every wish for the peace and prosperity of your City, I have the honour to be, Gentleman,

Your faithful servant,

T. B. Macaulay.

Alfred Tennyson
The Daisy
1853

It is ironic that Tennyson (1809–1892) should be remembered so vividly in Edinburgh for his line 'the grey metropolis of the North' (which Hugh MacDiarmid, among others, coupled with Scott's 'Mine own romantic town') since The Daisy is a contrast of the city's bleakness with his journey to Italy in 1851 with his wife, Emily Sellwood, whom he married in 1850 after a long engagement. In that year he had published In Memoriam, his great lament for his friend Arthur Hallam (1811–1833), and was made Poet Laureate on the death of Wordsworth. The Daisy, written in 1853, was published in 1855.

O LOVE, what hours were thine and mine,
In lands of palm and southern pine;
   In lands of palm, of orange-blossom,
Of olive, aloe, and maize and vine.

What roman strength Turbia show'd
In ruin, by the mountain road;
   How like a gem, beneath, the city
Of little Monaco, basking, glow'd.

How richly down the rocky dell
The torrent vineyard streaming fell
   To meet the sun and sunny waters,
That only heaved with a summer swell.

What slender campanili grew
By bays, the peacock's neck in hue;
   Where, here and there, on sandy beaches
A milky-bell'd amaryllis blew.

How young Columbus seem'd to rove,
Yet present in his natal grove,
   Now watching high on mountain cornice,
And steering, now, from a purple cove

Now pacing mute by ocean's rim;
Till, in a narrow street and dim,
   I stay'd the wheels at Cogoletto,
And drank, and loyally drank to him.

Nor knew we well what pleased us most,
Not the clipt palm of which they boast;
   But distant colour, happy hamlet,
A moulder'd citadel on the coast,

Or tower, or high hill-convent, seen
A light amid its olives green;
   Or olive-hoary cape in ocean;
Or rosy blossom in hot ravine,

Where oleanders flush'd the bed
Of silent torrents, gravel-spread;
   And, crossing, oft we saw the glisten
Of ice, far up on a mountain head.

We loved that hall, tho' white and cold,
Those niched shapes of noble mould,
   A princely people's awful princes,
The grave, severe Genovese of old.

At Florence too what golden hours,
In those long galleries, were ours;
   What drives about the fresh Cascinè,
Or walks in Boboli's ducal bowers.

In bright vignettes, and each complete,
Of tower or duomo, sunny-sweet,
   Or palace, how the city glitter'd,
Thro' cypress avenues, at our feet.

But when we crost the Lombard plain
Remember what a plague of rain;
   Of rain at Reggio, rain at Parma;
At Lodi, rain, Piacenza, rain.

And stern and sad (so rare the smiles
Of sunlight) look'd the Lombard piles;
 Porch-pillars on the lion resting,
And sombre, old, colonnaded aisles.

O Milan, O the chanting quires,
The giant windows' blazon'd fires,
 The height, the space, the gloom, the glory!
A mount of marble, a hundred spires!

I climb'd the roofs at break of day;
Sun-smitten Alps before me lay.
 I stood among the silent statues,
And statued pinnacles, mute as they.

How faintly-flush'd, how phantom-fair,
Was Monte Rosa, hanging there
 A thousand shadowy-pencill'd valleys
And snowy dells in a golden air.

Remember how we came at last
To Como; shower and storm and blast
 Had blown the lake beyond his limit,
And all was flooded; and how we past

From Como, when the light was gray,
And in my head, for half the day,
 The rich Virgilian rustic measure
Of Lari Maxume, all the way.

Like ballad-burthen music, kept,
As on The Lariano crept
 To that fair port below the castle
Of Queen Theodolind, where we slept;

Or hardly slept, but watch'd awake
A cypress in the moonlight shake,
 The moonlight touching o'er a terrace
One tall Agavè above the lake.

What more? we took our last adieu,
And up he snowy Splugen drew,
  But ere we reach'd the highest summit
I pluck'd a daisy, I gave it you.

It told of England then to me,
And now it tells of Italy.
  O love, we two shall go no longer
To lands of summer across the sea;

So dear a life your arms enfold
Whose crying is a cry for gold;
  Yet here to-night in this dark city,
When ill and weary, alone and cold.

I found, tho' crush'd to hard and dry,
This nurseling of another sky
  Still in the little book you lent me,
And where you tenderly laid it by:

And I forgot the clouded Forth,
The gloom that saddens Heaven and Earth,
  The bitter east, the misty summer
And gray metropolis of the North.

Perchance, to lull the throbs of pain,
Perchance, to charm a vacant brain,
  Perchance, to dream you still beside me,
My fancy fled to the South again.

John Ruskin
The Aesthete on Edinburgh
1853

Ruskin (1819–1900), prophet of English aesthetics and social reform, was partly of Scottish antecedents, and delivered the lecture of which this is the opening on 1 November 1853 as the commencement of his 'Lectures on Architecture and Painting', which were written while he was living in a cottage in Glenfinlas. He had initially asserted the architectural principles on which his approach was founded in writings for Loudon's Magazine of Natural History (1834), reprinted in 1892 as The Poetry of Architecture. By 1853 he was already famous as the author of Modern Painters (volumes 1 and 2, 1843, 1846, new edition bearing his name, 1851), Seven Lamps of Architecture (1849) and Stones of Venice (1851–53). He had defended the Pre-Raphaelites in public letters in 1851. Unknown to him his marriage to Euphemia Chalmers Gray of Perth was disintegrating as he worked on these lectures, his wife leaving him for John Everett Millais (the marriage, which had taken place in 1848, was annulled in 1855). A vigorous advocate of the duties of the state to guard the social interests of its workers and destitute, he bitterly assailed the fashionable economics of acquisitiveness.

1. I THINK MYSELF peculiarly happy in being permitted to address the citizens of Edinburgh on the subject of architecture, for it is one which, they cannot but feel, interests them nearly. Of all the cities in the British Islands, Edinburgh is the one which presents most advantages for the display of a noble building; and which, on the other hand, sustains most injury in the erection of a commonplace or unworthy one. You are all proud of your city; surely you must feel it a duty in some sort to justify your pride; that is to say, to give yourselves a *right* to be proud of it. That you were born under the shadow of its two fantastic mountains,—that you live where from your room windows you can trace the shores of its glittering Firth, are no rightful subjects of pride. You did not raise the moutains, nor shape the shores; and the historical houses of your Canongate, and the broad battlements of your castle, reflect honour upon you only through your ancestors. Before you boast of your city, before even you venture to call it *yours*, ought you not scrupulously to weigh the exact share you have had in adding to it or adorning it, to calculate seriously the influence upon its aspect which the work of your own hands has exercised? I do not say that, even when you regard your

city in this scrupulous and testing spirit, you have not considerable ground for exultation. As far as I am acquainted with modern architecture, I am aware of no streets which, in simplicity and manliness of style, or general breadth and brightness of effect, equal those of the New Town of Edinburgh. But yet I am well persuaded that as you traverse those streets, your feelings of pleasure and pride in them are much complicated with those which are excited entirely by the surrounding scenery. As you walk up or down George Street, for instance, do you not look eagerly for every opening to the north and south, which lets in the lustre of the Firth of Forth, or the rugged outline of the Castle Rock? Take away the sea-waves, and the dark basalt, and I fear you would find little to interest you in George Street by itself. Now I remember a city, more nobly placed even than your Edinburgh, which, instead of the valley that you have now filled by lines of railroad, has a broad and rushing river of blue water sweeping through the heart of it; which, for the dark and solitary rock that bears your castle, has an amphitheatre of cliffs crested with cypresses and olive; which, for the two masses of Arthur's Seat and the ranges of the Pentlands, has a chain of blue mountains higher than the haughtiest peaks of your Highlands; and which, for your far-away Ben Ledi and Ben More, has the great central chain of the St. Gothard Alps: and yet, as you go out of the gates, and walk in the suburban streets of that city—I mean Verona—the eye never seeks to rest on that external scenery, however gorgeous; it does not look for the gaps between the houses, as you do here; it may for a few moments follow the broken line of the great Alpine battlements; but it is only where they form a background for other battlements, built by the hand of man. There is no necessity felt to dwell on the blue river or the burning hills. The heart and eye have enough to do in the streets of the city itself; they are contented there; nay, they sometimes turn from the natural scenery, as if too savage and solitary, to dwell with a deeper interest on the palace walls that cast their shade upon the streets, and the crowd of towers that rise out of that shadow into the depth of the sky.

2. *That* is a city to be proud of, indeed; and it is this kind of architectural dignity which you should aim at, in what you add to Edinburgh or rebuild in it. For remember, you must either help your scenery or destroy it; whatever you do has an effect of one kind or the other; it is never indifferent. But, above, all, remember that it is chiefly by private, not by public, effort that your city must be adorned. It does not matter how many beautiful public buildings you possess, if they are not supported by, and in harmony with, the

private houses of the town. Neither the mind nor the eye will accept a new college, or a new hospital, or a new institution, for a city. It is the Canongate, and the Princes Street, and the High Street that are Edinburgh. It is in your own private houses that the real majesty of Edinburgh must consist; and, what is more, it must be by your own personal interest that the style of the architecture which rises around you must be principally guided. Do not think that you can have good architecture merely by paying for it. It is not by subscribing liberally for a large building once in forty years that you can call up architects and inspiration. It is only by active and sympathetic attention to the domestic and every-day work which is done for each of you, that you can educate either yourselves to the feeling, or your builders to the doing, of what is truly great.

3. Well, but, you will answer, you cannot feel interested in architecture: you do not care about it, and *cannot* care about it. I know you cannot. About such architecture as is built nowadays, no mortal ever did or could care. You do not feel interested in *hearing* the same thing over and over again;—why do you suppose you can feel interested in *seeing* the same thing over and over again, were that thing even the best and most beautiful in the world? Now, you all know the kind of window which you usually build in Edinburgh: here is an example of the head of one, a massy lintel of a single stone, laid across from side to side, with bold square-cut jambs—in fact, the simplest form it is possible to build. It is by no means a bad form; on the contrary, it is very manly and vigorous, and has a certain dignity in its utter refusal of ornament. But I cannot say it is entertaining. How many windows precisely of this form do you suppose there are in the New Town of Edinburgh? I have not counted them all through the town, but I counted them this morning along this very Queen Street, in which your Hall is; and on the one side of that street, there are of these windows, absolutely similar to this example, and altogether devoid of any relief by decoration, six hundred and seventy-eight. And your decorations are just as monotonous as your simplicities. How many Corinthian and Doric columns do you think there are in your banks, and post-offices, institutions, and I know not what else, one exactly like another?—and yet you expect to be interested! Nay, but, you will answer me again, we see sunrises and sunsets, and violets and roses, over and over again, and we do not tire of *them*. What! did you ever see one sunrise like another? does not God vary His clouds for you every morning and every night? though, indeed, there is enough in the disappearing and appearing of the great orb above the rolling of the world, to interest all of us, one would

think, for as many times as we shall see it; and yet the aspect of it is changed for us daily. You see violets and roses often, and are not tired of them. True! but you did not often see two roses alike, or, if you did, you took care not to put them beside each other in the same nosegay, for fear your nosegay should be uninteresting; and yet you think you can put 150,000 square windows side by side in the same streets, and still be interested by them. Why, if I were to say the same thing over and over again, for the single hour you are going to let me talk to you, would you listen to me? and yet you let your architects *do* the same thing over and over again for three centuries, and expect to be interested by their architecture; with a farther disadvantage on the side of the builder, as compared with the speaker, that my wasted words would cost you but little, but his wasted stones have cost you no small part of your incomes.

4. "Well, but," you still think within yourselves, "it is not *right* that architecture should be interesting. It is a very grand thing, this architecture, but essentially unentertaining. It is its duty to be dull, it is monotonous by law: it cannot be correct and yet amusing".

Believe me, it is not so. All things that are worth doing in art, are interesting and attractive when they are done. There is no law of right which consecrates dulness. The proof of a thing's being right is, that it has power over the heart; that it excites us, wins us, or helps us. . . .

Anthony Trollope
Love and Literature
1870

The ensuing report first appeared in the Edinburgh Evening Courant, *29 January 1870.*
'Yes. I am going to lecture at Edinburgh but not till Friday the 28 January;—a long day, my lord, and I shall be very happy to be your guest; am indeed most thankful to you for asking me. Some learned pundit,—at least he was a doctor,—kindly offered to give me the "hospitality of the city", which, as it means a half-formed introduction to the pickled snakes and a visit to the public library & the like, I viewed with horror and did not accept' wrote Trollope (1815–1882) to John Blackwood (1818–1879) on 13 October 1869. Blackwood had recently undertaken for Trollope the risky experiment of running in his Magazine two stories without the best-selling author's signature: Nina Balatka *(July 1866–January 1867) and* Linda Tressel *(October 1867–May 1868) and they did surprisingly well as books. These and other considerations prompted Trollope to give Blackwood the unusual bread-and-butter letter of his royalties, in this case those for* The Commentaries of Caesar *which was published in June 1870 as a volume in Blackwood's series of Ancient Classics for English Readers. So clearly the visit was a success for both: Trollope, his Barsetshire series concluded and the Palliser novels as far advanced as* Phineas Finn the Irish Member, *was now at the height of his popularity. But the mid-Victorianism of his lecture must not conceal the courage of his work: he had just (1869) published* He Knew He Was Right, *dealing with a husband driving himself to insanity from jealousy.*

LAST NIGHT, Mr Anthony Trollope lectured on ["Prose Fiction as Rational Amusement"] in the Music hall, to the members of the Philosophical Institution. There was a crowded audience. Mr Smith occupied the chair, and briefly introduced the lecturer. Mr Trollope commenced by stating that he had come forward to defend his own profession, and the amusement of the novel-reading portion of the community. Having referred to the use and abuse of prose fiction as a branch of English literature, he touched upon the merits of early English prose romance, and said that the plays about the time of Charles II, were poor in incident, abominable in moral, destitute in language, and false to humanity, while the greatest fault of the novels was their terrible dulness. But coming down to a later period, they had the works of Richardson and Fielding, whom he classed together; and who, he said, were the first novelists to teach practically to their readers what virtues they should imitate, and what vices they should shun. He referred in eulogistic terms to the novels of Maria Edgeworth and Miss Austin, and proceeding to speak of the influence the public exercised on the writers of novels, he gave it as his opinion that novelists would always write what the people demanded. He held that if the reading of novels was good for the old, it was also good for the young. We all learn from the cradle to the grave of good or evil, and the lessons of mature years were at least as important as those of our youth. He thought honest manliness to be as necessary as feminine grace, and he was of opinion that vicious teaching marred the one as effectually as it defaced the other. We had become a novel-reading people, and that we received much that was good or evil from novels was beyond question. Now, generally speaking, love stories were the mainstay and very staff of a novel's existence. If, however, he were to enter a man's house to teach a family how to make love, he would be called an impudent fellow, and yet in taking his book they accepted of his teaching. And that it should be done was essentially necessary to our existence—(Laughter)—and that it should be done well was, perhaps, of all matters in our own private life the most important. It was the novelist who best represented those feelings that did his work as a teacher best. The reading community was utterly averse to the teaching of bad lessons in novels. Having dealt with the objections that the time devoted to the amusement of reading novels should be devoted to work, and that novelists were untrue because of their fiction, he stated his opinion that a novel must be both sensational and realistic, and said if it failed in this respect, it was so far a failure in art. He afterwards referred to the writings of Sir Walter Scott, the great master of modern fiction, Charlotte Bronte, and Thackeray, whose several merits as writers of fiction be brought prominently before his hearers. He concluded by condemning in severe language any attempts at pandering to a vitiated taste. On the motion of Lord Neaves, a cordial vote of thanks was awarded Mr Trollope.

Arthur Conan Doyle
A Rectorial Election
1877

Arthur Conan Doyle's first novel, The Firm of Girdlestone, *of which this concludes Chapter Six, was largely written in 1884 but not published until 1890: this part of the work, dealing with the career of the hero, Tom Dimsdale, at Edinburgh University, is obviously autobiographical with obvious alterations (such as Tom's English background and ultimate failure as a medical student). Conan Doyle studied at Edinburgh Medical School from 1876 to 1881 when he graduated M.B., followed by M.D. in 1885. It is clear from internal evidence and newspaper reports that the Rectorial election in which he took an interest in his time was that of 1877, when the nominal leader of the Liberal party during Gladstone's temporary retirement, Spencer Compton, Marquess of Hartington and later Duke of Devonshire, defeated the Tories' nominee Richard Assheton Cross, then Home Secretary in the Disraeli cabinet. Conan Doyle used memories of the turbulent meetings in his* The Lost World *(1911).*

A RECTORIAL ELECTION is a peculiarly Scotch institution, and, however it may strike the impartial observer, it is regarded by the students themselves as a rite of extreme solemnity and importance from which grave issues may depend. To hear the speeches and addresses of rival orators one would suppose that the integrity of the constitution and the very existence of the empire hung upon the return of their special nominee. Two candidates are chosen from the most eminent of either party and a day is fixed for the polling. Every undergraduate has a vote, but the professors have no voice in the matter. As the duties are nominal and the position honourable, there is never any lack of distinguished aspirants for a vacancy. Occasionally some well-known literary or scientific man is invited to become a candidate, but as a rule the election is fought upon strictly political lines, with all the old-fashioned accompaniments of a Parliamentary contest.

For months before the great day there is bustle and stir. Secret committees meet, rules are formulated, and insidious agents prowl about with an eye to the political training of those who have not yet nailed their colours to any particular mast. Then comes a grand meeting of the Liberal Students' Association, which is trumped by a dinner of the Undergraduates' Conservative Society. The campaign is then in full swing. Great boards appear at the University gates, on which pithy satires against one or other candidate, parodies on songs, quotations from their speeches, and gaudily painted cartoons are posted. Those who are supposed to be able to feel the pulse of the University move about with the weight of much knowledge upon their brows, throwing out hints as to the probable majority one way or the other. Some profess to know it to a nicety. Others shake their heads and remark vaguely that there is not much to choose either way. So week after week goes by, until the excitement reaches a climax when the date of the election comes round.

There was no need upon that day for Dr. Dimsdale or any other stranger in the town to ask his way to the University, for the whooping and yelling which proceeded from that usually decorous building might have been heard from Prince's Street to Newington. In front of the gates was a dense crowd of townspeople peering through into the quadrangle, and deriving much entertainment from the movements of the lively young gentlemen within. Large numbers of the more peaceable undergraduates stood about under the arches, and these quickly made a way for the new-comers, for both Garraway and Dimsdale as noted athletes commanded a respect among their fellow-students which medallists and honours men might look for in vain.

The broad open quadrangle, and all the numerous balconies and ter-races which surround it, were crowded with an excited mob of students. The whole three thousand odd electors who stand upon the college rolls appeared to be present, and the noise which they were mak-ing would have reflected credit on treble their number. The dense crowd surged and seethed without pause or rest. Now and again some orator would be hoisted up on the shoulders of his fellows, when an oscil-lation of the crowd would remove his supporters and down he would come, only to be succeeded by another at some other part of the as-sembly. The name of either candidate would produce roars of applause and equally vigorous howls of execration. Those who were lucky enough to be in the balconies above hurled down missiles on the crowd beneath—peas, eggs, potatoes, and bags of flour or of sulphur; while those below, wherever they found room to swing an arm, returned the fusillade with interest. The doctor's views of academical serenity and the high converse of pallid students vanished into thin air as he gazed upon the mad tumultuous scene. Yet, in spite of his fifty years, he laughed as heartily as any boy at the wild pranks of the young politicians, and the ruin which was wrought upon broad-cloth coat and shooting jacket by the hail of unsavoury projectiles.

223

The crowd was most dense and most noisy in front of the class-room in which the counting of the votes was going forward. At one the result was to be announced, and as the long hand of the great clock crept towards the hour, a hush of expectation fell upon the assembly. The brazen clang broke harshly out, and at the same moment the folding doors were flung open, and a knot of men rushed out into the crowd, who swirled and eddied round them. The centre of the throng was violently agitated, and the whole mass of people swayed outwards and inwards. For a minute or two the excited combatants seethed and struggled without a clue as to the cause of the commotion. Then the corner of a large placard was elevated above the heads of the rioters, on which was visible the word "Liberal" in great letters, but before it could be raised further it was torn down, and the struggle became fiercer than ever. Up came the placard again—the other corner this time—with the word "Majority" upon it, and then immediately vanished as before. Enough had been seen, however, to show which way the victory had gone, and shouts of triumph arose everywhere, with waving of hats and clatter of sticks. Meanwhile, in the centre the two parties fought round the placard, and the commotion began to cover a wider area, as either side was reinforced by fresh supporters. One gigantic Liberal seized the board, and held it aloft for a moment, so that it could be seen in its entirety by the whole multitude:

LIBERAL MAJORITY,
241

But his triumph was short-lived. A stick descended upon his head, his heels were tripped up, and he and his placard rolled upon the ground together. The victors succeeded, however, in forcing their way to the extreme end of the quadrangle, where, as every Edinburgh man knows, the full-length statue of Sir David Brewster looks down upon the classic ground which he loved so well. An audacious Radical swarmed up upon the pedestal and balanced the obnoxious notice on the marble arms of the professor. Thus converted into a political partisan, the revered inventor of the kaleidoscope became the centre of a furious struggle, the vanquished politicans making the most desperate efforts to destroy the symbol of their opponents' victory, while the others offered an equally vigorous resistance to their attacks. The struggle was still proceeding when Dimsdale removed his father, for it was impossible to say what form the riot might assume.

"What Goths! what barbarians!" cried the little doctor, as they walked down the Bridges. "And this is my dream of refined quiet and studious repose!"

"They are not always like that, sir," said his son apologetically. "They were certainly a little jolly today."

"A little jolly!" cried the doctor. "You rogue, Tom. I believe if I had not been there you would have been their ringleader."

He glanced from one to the other, and it was so evident from the expression of their faces that he had just hit the mark, that he burst into a great guffaw of laughter, in which, after a moment's hesitation, his two young companions heartily joined.

James Barrie
Kidnapped
1879

Conan Doyle never met Stevenson at Edinburgh, but they drank in the same public-house, Rutherford's, opposite Old College: whether James Matthew Barrie (1860–1937) ever entered its portals is doubtful, but he remained haunted by his failure to have met Stevenson in his own years at Edinburgh University from 1878 to 1882 and when Rosaline Masson published her anthology of memoirs I Can Remember Robert Louis Stevenson (1922) he contributed an epilogue while acknowledging he had no meeting to memorialise. But when the book appeared he was led to write to Miss Masson on 4 December 1922 regretting his denial of an encounter, and she used it in her edition of 1925. The body of the letter occasionally hoodwinks scholars: by the conclusion of his writing it, the meeting had clearly become very real to Barrie, most appropriately for a playwright who specialised so deeply in the realism of the might-have-been whether in The Admirable Crichton *(1902),* Peter Pan *(1904),* Dear Brutus *(1917) or* Mary Rose *(1920), not to speak of the mystery play which left its outcome to its audience,* Shall We Join the Ladies? *(1921).*

Adelphi Terrace House 4 December '22

Dear Miss Masson

I am depressed to read my own fell admission that I never saw or spoke to him. Such a galaxy you have found, who even in the 'Seventies (Scotch canniness) were qualifying for future admission to your pages, while I kept hitting my forehead in vain, to recall some occasion when I touched the velvet coat. Why did I not, for instance, hang about the Fleeming Jenkins's door? If only I had this much to go upon we should soon have got started.

Even without it? Why not?

It is a lasting regret to me that I met R.L.S. but once. This was in the winter of '79 when I was in Edinburgh, my first year at the University, Masson my great man. One snowy afternoon, cold to the marrow, I was hieing me to my Humanities, and was crossing Princes Street, nigh the Register House, my head sunk in my cravat, when suddenly I became aware, by striking against him, of another wayfarer. Glancing up I saw a velvet coat, a lean figure with long hair (going black) and stooping shoulders, the face young and rather pinched but extraordinarily mobile, the manner doggedly debonair. He apologised charmingly for what was probably my fault, but I regarded him with stern disapproval. My glowering look was meant less for the chevalier himself than for his coat and hair, which marked him dandiacally as one of a class I had read about as having dinner every day. When he had passed he turned round to survey me, and I was still standing there, indicating in silence my disapproval of his existence. He went on, stopped and looked again. I had not moved. He then returned and, addressing me with exquisite reasonableness, said, 'After all, God made me.' To which I replied, 'He is getting careless.' He raised his cane (an elegant affair) and then there crossed his face a smile more winning than I had ever before seen on mortal. I capitulated at that moment.

'Do I know you?' he enquired.

'No,' I replied with a sigh, 'but I wish you did.'

At that he laughed outright, and was for moving on, when perhaps struck by my dejection, he said, 'I say, let us pretend that I do.' We gripped hands, and then taking me by the arm (I had never walked thus before) he led me away from the Humanities to something that he assured me was more humane, a howff called Rutherford's where we sat and talked by the solid hour. I had never been in this auberge (as he called it) before, nor have I been since, but I am sure it was a house of call of d'Artagnan and company in the days when they visited Newcastle and found it on the Scottish border. I associate that night indeed (for the afternoon wandered into night) with the four musketeers for various reasons, one being that we drank burgundy, and Chambertin at that, he reminding me that it was the favourite drink of Athos, and therefore the only drink for us, and when he ordered it he always said 'a few more bottles' in the haughty Athos way. It was served in tankards and there was froth on the top, but we drank on the understanding that it was Chambertin. As for his talk, it was the most copious and exhilarating that I ever heard come from man's lips, and ranged over every variety of subject. You will be interested to learn that I was not one of those who let great talk pass on unheeded like a spate, to regret afterwards that I took no notes. I could write shorthand in those days, and I 'took him down' in my class note-book (holding it beneath the table) till I had filled that bulky book. Alas that this record of wonderful hours should be lost. I lost it that night before we rose from the table. I had a vague recollection next morning that he had sold it to the waiter for a few more bottles of Chambertin. The waiter had proved to be a university student of my year, who valued, not the pages of talk, but other pages about the Differential Calculus.

I say that the work was lost before we rose, but I have a notion that we rose more than once. The first time was the result of his discovery that someone in Edinburgh had said in public that he considered the works of Robert Burns to have an immoral tendency. Who this person was he had no idea; but my companion's proposal was that we should go out into the streets and ring every door-bell until we found him. The intention was then to argue with him. We did go out (I think) and ring many bells, but without success, and the snow was still falling heavily, so I agreed with alacrity when he proposed that we should return to Rutherford's.

We had no more money (I had had none from the start) but he sold them his *velvet coat for a few more bottles of Chambertin. As the hours sped we seem to have become quarrelsome, just as Athos and his friends sometimes did. I think the reason was that one of us maintained that he was a 'braw singer' (I am not sure which one) and insisted on putting it to the proof with inharmonious results. I am certain that I left Rutherford's pursued through the blinding snow by my erstwhile friend, who kept shouting 'stop thief!' and describing me (happily incorrectly) as a man with wooden leg and a face like a ham. Long after all the rest of Edinburgh was a-bed he was chasing me through the white empty streets of the New Town and the Old Town, and I was panting hard when I at last reached my lodging in Frederick Street.*

I had no idea of his name, nor would it have conveyed much to me, but I always longed to meet him again however risky it might have been, and I searched for him and for a velvet coat (for I suppose he had more than one). I remembered him as The man in the velvet coat until years afterwards, when I saw his portrait in a newspaper, and discovered that my friend of a night had been no other than Robert Louis Stevenson.

Alas.

Heigho.

It might have been.   Yours sincerely, J. M. Barrie

William Ewart Gladstone

The Midlothian Campaign 1879

William Ewart Gladstone (1809–1898), who was of Scottish ancestry, resolved on contesting the Midlothian seat at the next election after he had been brought back into politics by the Balkan crisis of 1876. (The seat was the county around Edinburgh, normally Tory.) He transformed British political life with his 'Midlothian Campaign' of 24 November–6 December 1879, which agitated political issues before the masses to a degree never employed previously by a potential future Prime Minister. He had retired after his first ministry (1868–74), but after his victory at Midlothian in the election of March–April 1880 which his campaign had partly induced, it proved impossible to exclude him and he held office for the second of his four governments from 1880 to 1885. This address, fifth speech of the Campaign, was delivered on Saturday, 29 November 1879, at the Waverley Market, Edinburgh, before an audience of more than 20,000 people, hitherto unrivalled 'at least within the walls of any building in Scotland'. He was sponsored here by a Committee of Working Men representing the various trades of Edinburgh, and the meeting was chaired by the young Scottish Liberal leader, Archibald Primrose, Earl of Rosebery (1847–1929) who succeeded him when he finally left office in 1894.

MY LORD ROSEBERY, my Lords, Ladies, and Gentlemen,—There is nothing that I can say, or that much better and wiser men could say, to this meeting, that is one-half as remarkable as the meeting itself. It is no light cause that has brought together—that has called off from their usual occupations to stand in such compressed mass before me—this great ocean of human life. I fear, gentlemen, you have suffered; you must have suffered inconvenience, notwithstanding the admirable order that prevails; but although, gentlemen, I can tell you nothing that, as I have said, can in the least degree add to the intense interest of such an assemblage, yet neither can I part from you without a brief interchange of sentiments for a few moments on some of the questions in which our hearts are alike engaged. I say, gentlemen, an interchange of sentiment, for you have already expressed to me what your feelings are on behalf of the working classes at large. I am glad to see that you do not fear to call yourselves the working men of 'Edinburgh, Leith, and the district.' In this character you have given me your sentiments, and I wish to echo them back with corresponding sentiments of my own. An assemblage of this nature does not afford the place appropriate for minute criticism. My strength would not suffice; your patience must be exhausted. I will therefore avoid such criticisms; I will avoid what is in the nature of censure or blame; I will fall back, gentlemen, upon a positive principle upon which I would hope there can be no difference of sentiment among us, even if there be within the limits of this hall some few whose opinions are not wholly those of the majority, but still whose opinions and feelings we should endeavour, upon so noble an occasion, scrupulously to respect.

Gentlemen, you have spoken, in one line of your Address, of the unhappy position in which England stands, in which Great Britain will stand—the United Kingdom will stand—if it should be found to be in opposition to the interests of the struggling provinces and principalities of the East. Now, gentlemen, I wish to lay before you my view upon that subject, because there are some who tell us that we are not contending for liberty, but contending for despotism, and that the result of our policy will be that when the power of the Turkish Government ceases to sway the Eastern provinces of Europe, it will be replaced by another despotic Empire—the Empire of Russia. That, gentlemen, is not your view nor your desire, neither is it mine, and I wish to avail myself of this occasion for the purpose of clearly putting and clearly answering one question of vast importance—'Who is it that ought to possess, who is it that ought to sway, those rich and fertile countries which are known as composing what is called the Balkan Peninsula?'

It seems, gentlemen, to be agreed that the time has come, that the hour is about to strike, if it has not struck already, when all real sway of Turkish power over those fair provinces must cease, if it were only by reason of impotence. Who, then, is to have the succession to Turkey? Gentlemen, from the bottom of my heart, and with the fullest conviction of my understanding, I will give you the reply—a reply which, I am perfectly certain, will awaken a free, a generous, an unanimous echo in your bosoms. That succession is not to pass to Russia. It is not to pass to Austria. It is not to pass to England, under whatever name of Anglo-Turkish Convention or anything else. It is to pass to the people of those countries; to those who have inhabited them for many long centuries; to those who had reared them to a state of civilisation when the great calamity of Ottoman conquest spread like a wild wave over that portion of the earth, and buried that civilisation under its overwhelming force. Those people, gentlemen, are already beginning to enjoy the commencement of liberty. Four or five million Roumanians, who were formerly subject to Turkey, are now independent. Two million Servians, once political slaves, are now absolutely free. Three hundred thousand heroes such as Christendom cannot match—the men of Montenegro—who for four hundred years have held the sword in the hand, and never have submitted to the insolence of despotic power—those men at last have achieved not only their freedom, but the acknowledgment of their freedom, and take their place among the States of Europe. Bulgaria has reached a virtual independence. And, gentlemen, let me say a word on another province, that which was the scene of the terrible massacres and horrors of 1876—the province of Eastern Roumelia. It is inhabited by perhaps a population of a million. Well, gentlemen, at the Congress at Berlin we were told by Prince Bismarck and others that the Congress had restored to the Sultan a fair and rich province—namely, the province of Eastern Roumelia. Some were then afraid that the meaning of those words must be held to imply that the ancient despotism was still to prevail in Eastern Roumelia. The words that were used were ominous and dangerous words. It was said that the province was restored to the direct authority—political and military—of the Sultan. Gentlemen, I can a little console you on that subject; I hold in my hand—and if we were a less extended assembly I might be tempted to read to you—but I hold in my hand an account of the opening of the First Representative Chamber assembled in Eastern Roumelia. It has been freely elected by the people. It is, as was to be expected, a Bulgarian Chamber, but along with Bulgarians there sit in it Greeks, and, I believe, also, in one or two cases, Turks, by the title of freemen, and about to learn, as I hope, to act in that character. On the day of the meeting you will not be sorry to hear that the Governor-General entertained the representatives of this country, which four years ago was an enslaved country—he entertained them at dinner to the number of eighty-four. After dinner, toasts were drunk in our manner, and among those who proposed the toasts one was a Turk, in perfect harmony with the rest, who asked the company to drink to the health of the Sultan for having given them such an excellent Governor-General. Gentlemen, this is what I call progress. When you uproot slavery, when you put an end to suffering and shame, when you give security to life, property, and honour, which have previously only existed at the will of every representative of the Turkish power, of every one professing the Mahomedan religion, you accomplish a great and blessed work—a work in which the uttermost ends of the civilised world ought to rejoice, do rejoice, and will rejoice. The end of it all, gentlemen, is thus far, that not less than eight or ten millions of people have in one form or another been brought out of different degrees of political servitude, and have been made virtually freemen.

Gentlemen, I appeal to you to join me in the expression of the hope that under the yoke of no Power whatever will those free provinces again be brought. It is not Russia alone whose movements ought to be watched with vigilance. There are schemes abroad of which others are the authors. There is too much reason to suspect that some portion of the statesmen of Austria will endeavour to extend her rule, and to fulfil the evil prophecies that have been uttered, and cause the great change in the Balkan Peninsula to be only the substitution of one kind of supremacy for another. Gentlemen, let us place the sympathies of this country on the side of the free. Rely upon it, those people who inhabit those provinces have no desire to trouble their neighbours, no desire to vex you or me. Their desire is peacefully to pass their human existence in the discharge of their duties to God and man; in the care of their families, in the enjoyment of tranquillity and freedom, in making happiness prevail upon the earth which has so long been deformed in that portion of it by misery and by shame. But we say, gentlemen, that this is a fair picture which is now presented to our eyes, and one which should not be spoiled by the hand of man. I demand of the authorites of this country, I demand it of our Government, and I believe that you will echo the demand, that to no Russian scheme, that to no Austrian scheme, to no English scheme, for here we bring the matter home, shall they lend a moment's countenance; but that they shall with a kindly care cherish and foster the blessed institutions of free government that are beginning to prevail—nay, that are already at work in those now emancipated provinces. So that if we have been late in coming to a right understanding, if we have lost many opportunities in the past, at least we shall see and lay hold on those that remain, so that when in future times those countries again shall arrive at the prosperity and civilisation which they once enjoyed, they shall have cause to remember the name of Great Britain among the names of those who have contributed to the happy and the blessed change.

I think, gentlemen, that I have had sufficient evidence in the demeanour of this meeting that this is your opinion. I hope I am right in saying that such a meeting is not a mere compliment to an individual, or a mere contribution to the success of a party. Your gathering here to-day in almost countless thousands I regard as a festival of freedom, of that rational freedom which is alone secure, of that freedom best known to us, which is essentially allied with order and with loyalty. And I hope, gentlemen, that you will carry with you a determination, on the one hand, to do all you can in your civil and your social capacities for maintaining that precious possession of yours, and for handing it down to your posterity; and, on the other hand, for endeavouring by every lawful and honourable means, through the exercise of the vast moral influence of this country, and through all instruments which may from time to time be conformable to the principle of justice, for the extension of that inestimable blessing to such races and nations of the world as hitherto have remained beyond the range of its happy and ennobling influence.

Gentlemen, I thank you for the extraordinary kindness which has enabled me to convey the remains of a somewhat exhausted voice I hope even almost to the farther limits of this enormous building. That kindness is only a portion of the affectionate reception, for I can call it no less, which has been granted to me at every turn since my arrival in this country; and through you I desire, I will not say to discharge, for a discharge there can never be, but at least warmly, truly, cordially to acknowledge the debt that I owe to the people of Scotland.

Oscar Wilde
To his Wife
1884

Sir Rupert Hart-Davis notes in his authoritative edition of The Letters of Oscar Wilde *(1962) that except for brief notes 'this is the only letter from Wilde to his wife which is known to have survived'. Wilde (1854–1900) 'lectured twice in the Queen Street Hall, Edinburgh, on Saturday, 20 December. At 3 p.m. his subject was "Dress", and at 8 p.m. (when the* Scotsman *reported "a meagre attendance") "The Value of Art in Modern Life".' Wilde and Constance Mary Lloyd (1857-1898), also an Irish Protestant, were married on 29 May 1884. His lectures were part of his crusade for the furtherance of aesthetics, which had taken him to America in 1882; in these he sought to popularise the ideas of Ruskin and others.*

Tuesday [*Postmark 16 December 1884*]   *The Balmoral, Edinburgh*

Dear and Beloved, Here and I, and you at the Antipodes. O execrable facts, that keep our lips from kissing, though our souls are one.

What can I tell you by letter? Alas! nothing that I would tell you. The messages of the gods to each other travel not by pen and ink and indeed your bodily presence here would not make you more real: for I feel your fingers in my hair, and your cheek brushing mine. The air is full of the music of your voice, my soul and body seem no longer mine, but mingled in some exquisite ecstasy with yours. I feel incomplete without you. Ever and ever yours

OSCAR

Here I stay till Sunday.

William McGonagall
Edinburgh
1887

William Topaz McGonagall is agreed to have died in 1902, but reported his birth variously as having taken place in 1825 and 1830. Of Ulster parents, he was born and died in Edinburgh, but is generally associated with Dundee where for a time he was a worker in the jute industry. In 1887, according to himself, some supernatural or praeternatural force impelled him to commence writing what he took to be verse. Presumably his birthplace was one of the earliest subjects to suggest itself to him. The work appeared in his Poetic Gems *(1890), which was followed by two further volumes. The content of all his work is wholly serious in intention, and ludicrously funny in realisation, but his case is in fact a tragic one. He was mercilessly lampooned and assaulted, sometimes during his public readings; he bore it in the name of the art he seemed convinced he was serving. There is a brilliant essay on him in Hugh MacDiarmid's* Scottish Eccentrics *(1936) which stresses how much the McGonagall cult encouraged Philistinism.*

BEAUTIFUL city of Edinburgh!
Where the tourist can drown his sorrow
By viewing your monuments and statues fine
During the lovely summer-time.
I'm sure it will his spirits cheer
As Sir Walter Scott's monument draws near,
That stands in East Princes Street
Amongst flowery gardens, fine and neat.
And Edinburgh castle is magnificent to be seen
With its beautiful walks and trees so green,
Which seems like a fairy dell;
And near by its rocky basement is St. Margaret's well,
Where the tourist can drink at when he feels dry,
And view the castle from beneath so very high,
Which seems almost towering to the sky.
Then as for Nelson's monument that stands on the Calton hill,
As the tourist gazes thereon, with wonder his heart does fill
As he thinks on Admiral Nelson who did the Frenchmen kill.
Then, as for Salisbury crags, they are most beautiful to be seen,
Especially in the month of June, when the grass is green,

There numerous mole-hills can be seen,
And the busy little creatures howking away,
Searching for worms amongst the clay;
And as the tourist's eye does wander to and fro
From the south side of Salisbury crags below,
His bosom with admiration feels all aglow
As he views the beautiful scenery in the valley below;
And if, with an observant eye, the little loch beneath he scans,
He can see the wild ducks swimming about and beautiful white
swans.
Then, as for Arthur's seat, I'm sure it is a treat
Most worthy to be seen, with its rugged rocks and pastures green
And the sheep browsing on its sides
To and fro, with slow-paced strides,
And the little lambkins at play
During the livelong summer-day.
Beautiful city of Edinburgh! the truth to express,
Your beauties are matchless I must confess,
And which no one dare gainsay,
But that you are the grandest city in Scotland at the present day!

James Connolly
The Socialist Challenge
1894

James Connolly (1868–1916), the most noteworthy Left–wing political thinker to emerge in these islands in the last hundred years, was born at 107 Cowgate, an Edinburgh slum running under the wealthy Bridges linking the Old and New Towns. His parents were Irish Roman Catholic immigrants to Scotland. He worked as printer's 'devil', baker's boy, British soldier, and carter, before emigrating to Dublin in 1896. He subsequently worked in the Industrial Workers of the World in the U.S.A. and played an important part in bringing syndicalist thought into prominence in Ireland and Scotland especially in his Socialism Made Easy *which was reprinted in Scotland shortly after his execution for being one of the leaders of the Easter Week Rising of 1916. He was an active member of the Marxist body, the Scottish Socialist Federation while in Scotland, and was its candidate in the Edinburgh local elections of 1894 and 1895. At this time he had a personal column entitled 'Plain Talk' and signed 'R. Ascal' in the* Edinburgh Labour Chronicle, *a spirited but short-lived monthly where this, his third article, appeared on 1 December 1894.*

THE CZAR IS DEAD and the elections are over. The new Czar has issued a manifesto, and Bailie McDonald is now Lord Provost. The peace of Europe is still maintained, the Nihilists are plotting in silence, and Councillor Waterston has been and gone and done it.

A Tory Lord Provost rules over Liberal Edinburgh, and Councillor Sir James Russell sits and sighs and wishes his name was Blaikie.

Edinburgh Town Council attended Divine Service in Hope Park U.P. Church on Sunday, 18th November, *in honour of the Lord Provost*, who is a member of that congregation. I wonder if they meant it.

The Liberals have threatened to oppose Mr Waterston because he voted for Provost McDonald. Councillor Robertson declared at the Council meeting he was in favour of the honours going round, and would have voted against Sir James Russell had a really capable man been brought forward, but he would not vote for McDonald.

And yet they all went to church in honour of Lord Provost McDonald. Otherwise, I presume, they would not have gone at all.

This is the final outcome of the municipal elections: all the old gang are returned to office, and the municipal life of Edinburgh in the ensuing year will be marked by the same scrupulous regard to economy (in wages) and efficiency (in jobbery) to which we have been so well accustomed in the past.

The Social Democrats were defeated. On the authority of the celebrated representative of culture, Mr Francis McAweeney, we are told they received 'a crushing blow,' yet a more jubilant lot of men and women it would have been impossible to find on the day after the election.

An opponent passing under the windows of their Committee Room an hour after the result of the poll was declared, on hearing the jubilant speeches and enthusiastic cheering of the Socialists, was constrained to remark to a companion, that the Social Democrats receive a defeat better than their enemies do a victory.

And he was right. Some defeats are better than victories. A defeat endured as the result of contest conducted in a fair and honourable manner is a thousand times more creditable to the defeated party than a victory gained by all the mean and unscrupulous arts of the wirepullers.

The Socialists did not send any carriages for their lady supporters; they did not have committee rooms outside the polling booth, and, waylaying unfortunate voters, rush them in, and then escort them between tall hats and frock coats, to record their votes in favour of the rights of property; they did not tell Irish Catholics that Mr Connolly was a Freethinker, who wanted to overthrow the Church, and then tell old Scotch women of both sexes that Mr Connolly was an Irish Papist who wanted to introduce the Scarlet Woman; they did not seek the support of the Unionists by telling of the letter of recommendation from a leading Edinburgh Unionist; and seek the support of the Home Rulers by calling to their aid every quondam Home Ruler, or leader, who could be induced to sell his name, and voice, and birthright for the ill-smelling pottage of Liberal promises.

The Social Democrats were defeated. But last year the vote polled in George Square Ward for the I.L.P. candidate was only one-thirteenth of the total poll, whereas in St Giles, the vote for the avowed Social Democrat reached one-seventh of the total poll. A great advance, truly.

The official Liberal, backed by all the strength, reputation, and admirable electioneering organisation of the combined Liberal and Nationalist parties, and aided by the avowed support of the most influential Unionists in the ward, with a known man and a lawyer as their candidate, was yet only able to obtain a majority of four to one over a party the most revolutionary and the most recent in public life,

238

with no electioneering organisation, and with a candidate known to earn his bread by following an occupation most necessary in our city life, but nevertheless universally despised by the public opinion of aristocratic Edinburgh.

It is to be hoped that next year the Ward will not be troubled with the presence of another bogus Unionist candidate.

Had there been no Unionist, and had the advanced working-class voters been left free to choose between the revolutionary Social-Democrat and the orthodox Liberal and defender of the rights of property, there is little doubt the result of the poll would not have brought much comfort to the enemies of Socialism.

But hundreds of men, who would otherwise have voted Socialist, cast their votes reluctantly for Mr Mitchell as the candidate most likely to ensure the defeat of the Tory.

They will now have twelve months in which to meditate on the difference between the Liberal Tweedledee and the Tory Tweedledum, and after having so meditated they are invited to record the result of their studies at the polling booth on the first Tuesday of November 1895, if not before.

There is great heartburning in certain Liberal circles in Edinburgh over a matter which does not affect the working-class voter. It is an invitation to an 'At Home,' to be held in the Waterloo Rooms, Glasgow, by Lady Helen Ferguson of Novar.

All the gentlemen whose purses are in the habit of opening for the relief of distressed M.P.s and huckstering politicians in general, together with a few who have remained obdurate in spite of the pathetic appeals of Messrs Donworth and Dillon, are invited to this great social function.

Class the first will be thanked for their splendid devotion to the cause of Liberalism, and class the second will, it is hoped, be so overwhelmed with the magnificent display, and so enchanted by the bright smiles of the delegates from the Ladies' Liberal Association that they will open their hearts and their purses also, and all will be well.

By such means are replenished the Liberal coffers, and the Liberal working-man throws his cap in the air, and when he meets his Socialist comrade asks—'Where is the Tory gold?'

And his Socialist comrade, who has been stinting himself of his glass of beer in order to pay the election expenses of *his* candidate usually scratches his head and wonders also—'Where is the Tory gold?'

Gold of any kind or colour is a very scarce commodity in a Socialist committee room. *N.B.*—Those who do not believe this should come and join us and get a share of the plunder. Entry-money, sixpence; weekly subscription, one penny.—ADVT.

Any orthodox Liberal or Tory politician will tell you that one cause of the great misery among the working-class is to be found in the alarming prevalence of early marriages.

Yet in face of this lamentable fact, we are informed that his Grace the Duke of Argyll, who is 71 years of age, is about to get married to his third wife. As this step may lead to a still further increase in our pauper population, it is to be hoped wiser counsels will prevail and prevent the young couple taking the final disastrous step.

Ambrose Malvern, aged 68, committed suicide by jumping from a hotel window. This young man had married a widow the previous day. So I read in a contemporary. If some one will undertake to send this to his Grace the Duke of Argyll he might yet pause in his headlong career, and the nation be saved from an impending calamity.

Mr William M'Ewan, M.P., gave £50,000 to assist in building a new wing to Edinburgh University. We gave thanks. Edinburgh Town Council, having a love for the beautiful, spent £70,000 in obtaining for the citizens a better view of M'Ewan's £50,000. Again we gave thanks. The first act of the newly-elected Town Council was to accept an estimate for the proposed widening of the North Bridge and refuse to insert in it a clause requiring the payment of the current rate of wages. The labouring people who voted for the return of the old gang to office are still giving thanks.

We are a great people.

I hear the Rev. Mr Jackson, at a meeting in the Albert Hall, on Sunday, 18th November, declared his Socialism was of the kind endorsed by the Trades Union Congress at their recent meeting in Norwich. If this is true the rev. gentleman is eligible for membership of the I.L.P. or S.S.F., and I would advise him to enter into communication with one or other of these bodies, and take his proper place in the communion of the faithful.

But before admission he might, as a public character, be required to give some practical proofs of his sincerity. Not that we would expect him, as a follower of Him of Nazareth, to 'sell all he has and give it to the poor,' as one would-be follower was required to do. Oh, no, our latter-day Christianity is far too 'practical' to adopt such hare-brained theories of restitution as that implied in the aforementioned utterance of their Master.

But a certain colleague of Mr Jackson on the School Board has recently made an effort to deprive the women cleaners employed by that body of their wages, that is of their means of life, during sickness. Will Mr Jackson preach a sermon on the subject, taking for his text the injunction, 'Rob not the poor because he is poor.'

Or will he allow the Edinburgh Socialists the free use of his hall, or church, for the purpose of conducting a fortnight's mission to clergymen. Subject of mission: Instruction in the use of the Divine command, 'Love thy neighbour as thyself.'

Until our reverend friend is prepared to give such practical proofs of his Socialism will he please remember that 'Faith without works is dead.'

The conduct of the Edinburgh School Board, coupled with the conduct of the Town Council in refusing to insert the fair wages clause in a most important contract, should help to clear the cobwebs from the eyes of the intelligent voters and enable them to appreciate the necessity for an infusion of new Socialistic blood into all our public bodies.

For some time to come the work of Socialists on all such bodies will not be so much to pass new laws as to infuse into their administrator the spirit of the new life, to use all power to inaugurate the reign of justice, to convert our industrial system from a machine for making profit into an instrument for sustaining life, to transform our politics from the government of men into the wise and well-ordered administration of things, to relegate to the limbo of exploded superstitions the old doctrine of freedom of contract between affluence and starvation, and thus, by constantly placing our doctrines and our efforts upon the same platform as the class interests of the workers, to create such a public feeling in our favour as shall enable us to bridge the gulf between the old order and the new, and lead the people from the dark Egypt of our industrial anarchy, into the Promised Land of industrial freedom.

The return of a Socialist candidate does not then mean the immediate realisation of even the programme of palliatives commonly set before the electors. Nay, such programmes are in themselves a mere secondary consideration, of little weight, indeed, apart from the spirit in which they will be interpreted.

The election of a Socialist to any public body at present, is only valuable in so far as it is the return of a disturber of the political peace.

Until Socialism attains such a foothold in this country as shall enable the Socialists to return a majority to the public bodies which rule the country, every fresh seat captured must simply be regarded as a fresh means of spoiling the little games of the Jabezian philanthropists, financial jobbers, and political thimbleriggers, who thrive on their reputations as Liberal and Tory politicians.

If only for the value of letting the light of public opinion in on the doings of officialdom, we should never relax our efforts until every representative body has its full quota of Socialist members.

While on this matter, it would be as well to keep in mind the fact, that under the Local Government (Scotland) Act, which comes into force in April of 1895, the Poor Law system of this country will be at last placed under democratic control.

The workers will then have an opportunity of humanising this iniquitous system, by placing upon every Parish Council a sufficient number of Social Democrats to counteract the despotic tendencies of our Liberal and Tory taskmasters.

The poor paupers, the war-worn veterans who have fallen in the battle of life, who are imprisoned in those bastiles of poorhouses, may now have the closing years of their lives lightened and brightened by the action of an intelligent Social Democracy.

To every upholder of the present system the poorhouse inmates are a mere burden on the rates, or an intolerable nuisance to honest folk, who are well done for if they are fed and sheltered at all. But to the Social Democrat they are unfortunate victims of an evil social system. They are our brothers and sisters, crushed beneath the wheels of a remorseless competition. They are the effect of which the landlord and capitalist are the cause.

We have so long been accustomed to receive without question the teachings of the master class, that it is no wonder the poorhouse dole and poor-relief should be regarded amongst us as degrading to the recipient instead of to society at large. But it is on society at large, and on its supporters and apologists, the real stigma should rest. Indeed, it would be well for the workers as a whole if they could come to look upon the poor-rates as their first means of relief instead of as their last resource.

Man, as a social animal, has a claim upon the society which gave him birth. This claim is his right to live as long as he is willing to perform his share of the labour necessary to his own maintenance and the maintenance of society at large. This claim involves, in the first place, the right of free access to the means of life; in the second place, the duty of contributing to the support of the weaker members of the community, *i.e.,* children, the sick, infirm, and the aged.

Our Poor Law system is a grudging admission of the truth of this thesis, granted by the classes as an alternative to a troubled social upheaval. It has been surrounded since its inception with every form

242

of insult and degradation their mean and petty minds could devise, until, today, the hideous uniform of the pauper is loathed more than the garb of the convict.

Thus, our masters have striven to debase this institution, whose existence in our midst they feel to be a standing reproach to the devil-take-the-hindmost theory, with which they wish to govern society.

To rescue our Poor Law from their hands, to relieve it from the false ideals with which its administration has been cursed, and to make its administrators in very truth guardians of the poor, this should be the aim of the workers. By so directing their efforts they may create, out of the framework of our Parish Councils, a public body, who, in solicitude for the public welfare and thoughtful provision for the weaker members of our human family, will find the same incentive to effort as the Liberal and Tory politicians find in the grosser pursuit of the glittering spoils of office.

But such a body can only arise out of that higher conception of human rights and duties which will flow from a wide and general acceptance of the principles of enlightened Social Democracy.

Wilfred Owen
Six o'Clock in Princes Street
1917

The meeting in August 1917 of the soldier poets Siegfried Sassoon (1886-1967) and Wilfred Owen (1893-1918) in Craiglockhart War Hospital for Nervous Disorders where the military authorities had sent them from the front, is commemorated in Sassoon's Siegfried's Journey 1916-1920 *(1945), Owen's* Letters, *and, most recently, Stephen MacDonald's award-winning play,* Not About Heroes, *one of the outstanding successes at the Edinburgh Festival Fringe in 1982. Both men were in horrified revulsion against the slaughter of the war and the jingoism which continued to feed it. Of these days Owen wrote to his mother on 8 August 1917; 'At present I am a sick man in hospital, by night; a poet, for quarter of an hour after breakfast; I am whatever and whoever I see while going down to Edinburgh on the tram: greengrocer, policeman, shopping lady, errand boy, paper-boy, blind man, crippled Tommy, bank-clerk, carter, all of these in half an hour; next a German student in earnest; then I either peer over bookstalls in back-streets, or do a bit of a dash down Princes Street,—according as I have taken weak tea or strong coffee for breakfast.' This poem was presumably written shortly after the letter, and roughly when he first met Sassoon. For all of his hatred of the war, Owen ultimately went back and was killed, on 4 November 1918, one week before the Armistice.*

In twos and threes, they have not far to roam,
    Crowds that thread eastward, gay of eyes;
Those seek no further than their quiet home,
    Wives, walking westward, slow and wise.

Neither should I go fooling over clouds,
    Following gleams unsafe, untrue,
And tiring after beauty through star-crowds,
    Dared I go side by side with you;

Or be you on the gutter where you stand,
    Pale rain-flawed phantom of the place,
With news of all the nations in your hand,
    And all their sorrows in your face.

David Daiches
Two Worlds
1927

David Daiches, one of the leading modern critics of English literature, was born in 1912, son of a distinguished Rabbi. He was educated at George Watson's College in Edinburgh. His Two Worlds *(1957), whence this derives, is an account of his Edinburgh Jewish youth. He is also the author of many works on English and Scottish literature, which include a multi-volume* Critical History of English Literature *and a study of Stevenson which inaugurated the modern affirmation of the latter's literary stature. He has taught in many English and American universities, culminating in his professorship of English and American Studies at the University of Sussex; since his retirement he has been director of the Institute of Advanced Studies at Edinburgh University.*

I HAVE TALKED about the development of my literary ambitions which I associate with the summer of 1927 and the solitary walking and brooding that I indulged in at that time. I remember one Monday evening about this time, after I had been playing for Miss Brown a piece, by Frank Bridge whose name I forget but whose opening cadences I can still remember: I liked the pieces and played it well, and the music was running through my head as I leaned out of my bedroom window and listened to the sounds of Edinburgh coming up from the streets below—housewives beating carpets in the back greens of Livingstone Place, boys playing cricket in the Meadows, and the distant sound of bagpipes from the East Meadows, where public concerts were provided by the Corporation. Gradually the strains of the distant pipe music ousted the piano music from my consciousness, and I listened, unspeakably moved. I found the sound of bagpipes deeply moving; it awakened my sense of Scottish history with its violence and its pageantry and its fatal predilection for the lost cause. As I grew up Scotland became for me more and more an emotion rather than a country, and I would surrender myself to the emotion with a pleasing melancholy.

But of course I was Jewish, and my ancestors had no part in this romantic history: theirs had been a darker and more glorious destiny. My pride in Jewish history and my feeling for its particular kind of sadness existed side by side with my attitude to Scotland. It was largely a matter of mood (how much, in my childhood, was largely a matter of mood!). The Scottish mood rose to the sound of the bagpipes or the sight of Edinburgh Castle fading in the purple darkness; the Jewish mood came with the elegiac synagogue chants and the plaintive melodies of Jewish liturgy and folksong. Each mood excluded the other: in the Scottish mood the Jewish world seemed distant and unimportant, and in the Jewish mood Scottish history and traditions seemed modern and shabby. It was now that I became acutely aware of living in two worlds, or rather of moving freely between one and the other. Bagpipe music and synagogue melody represented the two poles between which my sensibility moved. I accepted this dualism as part of the nature of things, and looking back now I wonder at the ease with which I did so.

Muriel Spark
The World of Miss Jean Brodie
Circa 1932

The Prime of Miss Jean Brodie, *whence this extract is taken, was first published in 1961, and has been outstandingly successful as novel, play and film. Muriel Spark was born in Edinburgh in 1918 and was educated at Gillespie's School where her experiences have been credited with some of the inspiration for that work. She is also the author of many other novels, short stories, and critical studies of nineteenth-century figures.*

THE DAYS PASSED and the wind blew from the Forth.

It is not to be supposed that Miss Brodie was unique at this point of her prime; or that (since such things are relative) she was in any way off her head, She was alone, merely, in that she taught in a school like Marcia Blaine's. There were legions of her kind during the nineteen-thirties, women from the age of thirty and upward, who crowded their war-bereaved spinsterhood with voyages of discovery into new ideas and energetic practices in art or social welfare, education or religion. The progressive spinsters of Edinburgh did not teach in schools, especially in schools of traditional character like Marcia Blaine's School for Girls. It was in this that Miss Brodie was, as the rest of the staff spinsterhood put it, a trifle out of place. But she was not out of place amongst her own kind, the vigorous daughters of dead or enfeebled merchants, of ministers of religion, University professors, doctors, big warehouse owners of the past, or the owners of fisheries who had endowed these daughters with shrewd wits, high-coloured cheeks, constitutions like horses, logical educations, hearty spirits and private means. They could be seen leaning over the democratic counters of Edinburgh grocers' shops arguing with the Manager at three in the afternoon on every subject from the authenticity of the Scriptures to the question what the word 'guaranteed' on a jam-jar really meant. They went to lectures, tried living on honey and nuts, took lessons in German and then went walking in Germany; they bought caravans and went off with them into the hills among the lochs; they played the guitar, they supported all the new little theatre companies; they took lodgings in the slums and, distributing pots of paint, taught their neighbours the arts of simple interior decoration; they preached the inventions of Marie Stopes; they attended the meetings of the Oxford Group and put Spiritualism to their hawk-eyed test. Some assisted in the Scottish Nationalist Movement; others, like Miss Brodie, called themselves Europeans and Edinburgh a European capital, the city of Hume and Boswell.

They were not, however, committee women. They were not school-teachers. The committee spinsters were less enterprising and not at all rebellious, they were sober churchgoers and quiet workers. The school-mistresses were of a still more orderly type, earning their keep, living with aged parents and taking walks on the hills and holidays at North Berwick.

But those of Miss Brodie's kind were great talkers and feminists and, like most feminists, talked to men as man-to-man.

'I tell you this, Mr Geddes, birth control is the only answer to the problem of the working class. A free issue to every household...'

And often in the thriving grocers' shops at three in the afternoon:

'Mr Logan, Elder though you are, I am a woman in my prime of life, so you can take it from me that you get a sight more religion out of Professor Tovey's Sunday concerts than you do out of your kirk services.'

Hugh MacDiarmid
Talking with Five Thousand People in Edinburgh
1939

Modern Scottish nationalism dates from the appearance of a poem, Hugh MacDiarmid's A Drunk Man Looks at the Thistle *(1926), which proclaimed the validity of old traditions, the vindications of the Lallans language and the worthlessness of a cosy, acquiescent and amusing precious Scottishness: as well as a great poem it was also a manifesto in response to which all subsequent Scottish literary self-assertion has had to express itself. MacDiarmid was born Christopher Murray Grieve (1892-1978) and remained to the end an explosive critic of complacency, in prose and poetry, at once demanding nationalism and internationalism. This poem first appeared in* Poetry Scotland No. 2 *(1945). But for all of his force as a polemicist, he was also a lyricist of exceptional delicacy.*

God forbid that I should justify you: till I die I will not remove mine integrity from me.
JOB XXVII.5.

TALKING with five thousand people in Edinburgh yesterday
I was appalled at their lack of love for each other,
At their lack of ecstasy at the astounding miracle
Of being alive in the flesh and together with one another,
And amazed that men and women each superficially so different
Should be so obviously the product of the same temperament,
Dyed in the same vat to a uniform hue.
In each the mood, the atmosphere, the peculiar nature
Of the tension produced, all the intangibles in fact,
Were almost identical—the same unresolved discords,
The same sultry hates, the same murderous impulses
Below the surface of decorous lives, the same
Hopeless struggle against an evil no one dares name
—The same growing understanding that the substitute names
They use for it are wide of the mark, that the name must be
   spoken,
That it will be impossible soon not to speak it out plump and
   plain,
The whole five thousand of them, as with a single voice.

But yesterday I listened to the mutual criticisms,
The sneers, the belittlings, the cynical acceptances,
Misunderstandings, indifferences, looking down their noses,
Pursing their mouths, giving meaning looks, till I saw all these
     people
As specialists in hates and frustrations, students of helpless
     rages,
Articulators of inarticulate loathings, and suddenly understood
That the trouble was no one knew where the centre lay
Of the system of discontent in which they were pent,
All emotionally suspended and dubious
(Saying all sorts of things with the single exception
Of what they ought to be saying—what they needed to say;
Their powers of speech all hopelessly misapplied)
Because their talk evaded, deserted, their real theme.
They expressed themselves in despairs, doubts, grumblings and
     fears.
None of them had yet made clear contact with the sources of his
     or her power.
They were all fascinated by their hatred of something—but of
     what?
The passion of that nameless hatred got itself partially expressed
By seizing on this or that—on anything—in lieu of its true object.
These were occasions for the rages but not the causes.
Edinburgh produces and sustains agonising tensions of life
—Edinburgh, a blinded giant who has yet to learn
What the motive spirit behind his abilities really is.

So that as I spoke with these five thousand people
Each of us was more or less lost
In the midst of the events so powerfully presented.
All who should help to open the way for true expression
—The teachers, the ministers, the writers—are living like
     maggots
On dead words in an advanced state of decomposition,
Big words that died over twenty years ago
—For most of the important words were killed in the First World
     War—
And Edinburgh has not given birth to new words yet
In which it can say anything worth saying, make anything but
     animal noises.

Edinburgh—But Edinburgh is no worse than anywhere else;
All the big centres of mankind are like thunder-clouds to-day
Forming part of the horrific structure of a storm
That fills the whole sky—but ere long
Will disappear like the fabric of a dream.

Perhaps Edinburgh's terrible inability to speak out,
Edinburgh's silence with regard to all it should be saying,
Is but the hush that precedes the thunder,
The liberating detonation so oppressively imminent now?
For what are its people standing in their own light,
Denying life infinitely more abundant,
Preferring darkness to light, and death to life?
Edinburgh is capable here and now of a human life
As illimitably greater than any it has yet known,
As any human being's is to the lowest order of animal existence.
All they need to do is to lift up their hearts
And conceive nobler conditions of life, acquire
The feelings which will give forms to such a life, and at once
The necessary organs of these will appear,
Just as life at first put out arms and legs.
All they need to do is to be true to themselves
And not like some foolish woman who cries
There's thunder in the air and stuffs her ears with cotton wool
And goes to bed and hides herself under the blankets
Afraid of the thunder and lightning—the bridegroom who enters
    in.

There is no one really alive in Edinburgh yet.
They are all living on the tiniest fraction
Of the life they could easily have,
Like people in great houses who prefer
To live in their cellars and keep all the rest sealed up.

There is nothing to prevent them except themselves
Having all that the mind of man can know
Or the heart of man conceive.

Total strangers to all the events
Taking place around and in and through them.

No one with either the scientific training
Or the courage and desire to learn
What is going on beneath the surface of life.

Few, if any, of life's collisions here
Are on the purely individual plane.
There is no general scheme behind it,
No real general purpose,
No genuine fighting spirit.
Is there no one to fight this decline of honour,
This hypocrisy, meanness, and boredom?

Let the demagogues denounce me, [1]and betray me too
As Burns was betrayed and Bakunin and Maclean;
Serve me as Utin served Marx, with vile slanders to expel
Bakunin and James Guillaume. *Veritas odium parit.*
Friends, you know. I am guilty of it. Let it rest.
At the worst, *in magnis et voluisse sat est.*
I stand to my position, do what I can,
And will never be turned into a 'strong, silenced man,'
For I am corn and not chaff, and will neither
Be blown away by the wind, nor burst with the flail,
      But will abide them both
      And in the end prevail.

For I am like Zamyatin. I must be a Bolshevik
Before the Revolution, but I'll cease to be one quick
When Communism comes to rule the roost,
For real literature can exist only where it's produced
By madmen, hermits, heretics,
Dreamers, rebels, sceptics,
—And such a door of utterance has been given to me
As none may close whosoever they be.

Let a look at Edinburgh be called
Just an educational film then
Such as we see any day on the screen.
'The Abortion,' say, or 'Why Does It Rain?'
Or 'How Silk Stockings Are Made,' or, finally,
'What Is the Difference Between A Man and A Beaver?'

[1] 'Au milieu de douces imbéciles, c'est l'homme d'esprit qui est une bête.' Maria Star.

It's far too late in the day
  For a fellow like this
Trying to organise a conspiracy of feelings
  In Edinburgh of all places.

Let us fall in with the wishes of Authority,
Hush to treasonable rubbish like 'The Red Flag';
Let us study—and in the end be content to be
Each of us no better than a carted stag.

Sorley Maclean
Poem to Eimhir
1939

Sorley Maclean, the greatest Gaelic poet now living, was born in 1911, on the island of Raasay, and educated at Portree, Skye, where he later taught. He first came to Edinburgh in 1928, but this poem was probably written there in 1939 when he was teaching at Boroughmuir High School. (He has corrected its text for this edition.) It appeared in his Dáin do Eimhir *(1943), later translated from the Gaelic by Iain Crichton Smith as* Poems to Eimhir *(1979), but the present translation is by O.D.E. Sorley Maclean lives on Skye: his most recent book of poems is* Spring-Tide and Neap-Tide *(Canongate).*

Tric 's mi gabhail air Dùn-éideann
baile glas gun ghathadh gréine,
's ann a lasadh e le d' bhòidhche
baile lòghmhor, geal-reultach.

*   *   *   *

Often I walk in Edinburgh alone
grey town uninterrupted by the sun,
and see, whenever your light beauty soars,
a radiant City, shining like the stars.

Sydney Goodsir Smith
King and Queen o the Fowr Airts
1944

Sydney Goodsir Smith (1915-1975) was born in New Zealand, the son of the professor of
Forensic Medicine at Edinburgh University, Sir Sydney Smith (who wrote, among more scientific
works, an engaging book of memoirs Mostly Murder). Sydney Goodsir Smith was a poet of
elegance, humanity and high comedy. This poem first appeared in his So Late into the Night
(1952) but was written between 1944 and 1948. His Collected Poems was published after his
death; a vivid account of him appears in Trevor Royle's literary history of Edinburgh,
Precipitous City.

A Ballant

O, King and Queen o the fowr airts
My luve and I yon day,
They sang o us in Tara Haas,
They carolled in Cathay.

For us the mirkie lift was gowd,
The causie gowd beneath,
Emerants drapt frae ilka tree
And siller ran the Water o Leith.

The Dean Brig lowpt a Hieland Fling
Our regal whim to gratifie,
Schir Wattie sclimmed his steeple's tap
The better to view sic majestie.

Och, we were the sun and the sickle mune,
The wee speugs triumphed round our wey,
Sanct Giles cast doun his muckle croun
And aa the damned made holiday.

Tamburlane was a shilpiskate,
Ozymandias a parvenu,
Our Empire o the Embro streets
Owrepassed the dwaums o Xanadu.

But fient the pleisure-dome we fand,
Waif peacocks mang the laicher breeds,
We ained the birlan mapamound
—But damn the neuk to lay our heids.

The birds hae nests, the tods dens,
The baillie skouks aneath his stane,
But we, the minions o the race,
We hadna howff and we hadna hame.

Ay, King and Queen o the fowr airts,
Our crounit heids abune the cloud,
Our bed yon nicht was the munelicht gress
—I wadna changed for Holyrood!

Moray McLaren
A Trifle Unnecessary
1945

Moray McLaren (1901–1971) published this story in his A Dinner with the Dead, and Other Stories *(1947). He wrote extensively on Scotland (he was born in Edinburgh), beginning with* Return to Scotland *(1930), and including* The Scots, *written for Pelican Books in 1951. He was first BBC Programme Director for Scotland and first Assistant Editor of* The Listener. *He styled himself 'an ardent European as well as an ardent Scot'.*

I HAD NOT BEEN in Edinburgh for some years; and it was with pleasure mingled with a not wholly disagreeable melancholy that I had been wandering through those familiar streets and squares. How little the place had altered! In the New Town my eye recalled many half-forgotten beauties of form and line. I even discovered in my heart an affection for some of the uglier nineteenth-century solid excesses. I was glad that they had, with all their ponderousness and lack of economy, not been removed. They had been the circumstances of my childhood.

Then I turned towards the Old Town, that straggles down the hillside on the other side of Princes Street Gardens. Someone had told me that a good deal of 'improvement' had been going on there. I was interested to see what had been done. The person who had told me had been Roy Crann, the president of the St Ninian's Society of Edinburgh. Roy, whom I had known for years, was an earnest, pushful young man, who would probably remain unchangingly earnest, pushful and young from the age of twenty-five to fifty-five. What would happen to him after that one could but guess. He was now, I suppose, about forty. I had run across him in my club in London and he had spoken most earnestly, and indeed eloquently, of the work the St Ninian's Society was doing in cleaning up Edinburgh architecturally.

'I hope you are not being too drastic,' I had said at length.

'No, no,' he assured me. 'Our aim is to strip Edinburgh of its Victorianism —'

'A formidable task,' I interrupted. But he went on as if I had not spoken.

'To strip it of its Victorianism and get down to the eighteenth-century form and the medieval quality which is still there, but so terribly overlaid.'

'It sounds good, Roy. I wish you luck.'

'You should come up and see what we are doing,' urged Roy.

'I will. I have to come north next month. And I hope to spend a few days in Edinburgh.'

'Come and call at our offices in George Street and I'll show you round. Or if I'm not there I'll get someone to take you.'

Roy's eyes, behind his powerfully lensed glasses, glistened eagerly.

'Really, Roy, I don't need anyone to lead me on a conducted tour of my native city. I'll have a look round by myself first. Then I'll come and call on you.'

It was, therefore, with the vague idea of seeing what Roy and his St Ninian's Society had been doing in the Old Town that I turned into the High Street. I decided to make first for MacGregor's Close. Roy had told me that this was one of their most notable improvements. Moreover it was a corner of Edinburgh which had made a deep impression on me in my youth. I cannot say that I had visited it often. But in the old days, just after the War of 1914, it was a place which, once seen, was not easy to forget. It had been one of the most noisome corners of Edinburgh's slums. It had also been the most picturesque remnant of Edinburgh's medieval domestic architecture. Its atmosphere combined a sense of the decay of the past with the rottenness of the present that was truly startling. In its macabre way it was one of the show-places of the town.

When I entered the Close from the High Street and saw the reformation that had been achieved I was compelled, perhaps a little reluctantly, to admit that Roy had done an effective job of work. The old scarred and peeling walls had been stripped and cleaned, and were now attractively white-harled. The outside stairs had been mended or tastefully rebuilt. The original line of the rooftops against the sky to the north had been carefully preserved. And a sixteenth-century sundial had been dug up from somewhere and placed in the centre of the court. Its appearance was certainly in harmony with its surroundings. But I could not help wondering what use it served. Very little sunlight could ever penetrate to the centre of MacGregor's Close, however much 'improved'. There was only one thing that remained unalterably the same—the smell, that peculiar rancid, sweet sour smell of an Edinburgh Close.

Still, as I have said, it was an effective job of work. And who was I, from the seclusion of my fairly comfortable existence, to allow even a shadow of regret for the old romantic squalor to cross my mind? If such a thought did touch me I instantly rejected it. In doing so I felt myself warming a little towards Roy Crann. People might say that he was pushful, earnest and professionally young, but at least he did the job. While other people had spent decades in talking about improving Scotland and Edinburgh, Roy in one lustrum had, in one practical direction, achieved more than all of them put together. I knew that this was only one specimen of his and his society's efforts.

'Ay, it's a bonny sicht, is it no?'

The words, uttered in a cracked old female voice, broke in upon my thoughts. I turned to see who had spoken them. They came from a figure strangely out of keeping with the improved MacGregor's Close. Huddled in a corner of the Close hard by its entrance was an old woman, with a shawl of faded and filthy tartan round her head and a tray of shoe-laces, which she was presumably offering for sale, upon her knee. Here was a living revocation of the past, a creature of the Edinburgh of my childhood.

'Yes,' I agreed, 'they've certainly cleaned the old place up.'

'Ay, they have that.'

'Do you like it better as it is now?'

'Weel, Ah...'

Seeing that I was inclined for conversation the old woman beckoned me closer to her, and said in a lowered voice:

'D'ye want tae see the sichts o' Edinburgh? I can show them tae you, sir.'

'No, no Mother,' I laughed. 'I know them as well as you do. I was born here—in Edinburgh, I mean.'

'Ay, ye micht hae been. But I wis born here long afore you, sir.'

'How old are you, Mother?'

'Ah'll no be seeing seventy-fower again. Ah can show you sichts ye hae never seen in all your born days. Ah can tak ye—'

'No, no. I don't think I'll bother you to stir your old bones.'

'Then gie me a shilling for my auld banes, and Ah'll tell ye things, sir, aboot Edinburgh that'll mak yer hair staun on end.'

'What can you tell me, Mother, that I don't know already?' I asked her, as I handed her a florin. She clutched it in her claw-like hand and raised it quickly to her mouth. For a moment I thought she was going to swallow it, but she was only readjusting her teeth, which had come loose in her excitement at seeing the coin. As soon as she had regained her composure she spoke.

'Weel, tae begin with ....

And here I may say she used a Scotticism much more vigorous and crude than the English words which I am compelled to write.'

'Tae begin with, I was the mistress of Lawrence MacMarr.'

It was enough. This was a statement to which I could not bear the thought of additions or decorations. It was complete in itself. I wished to do no more than to have heard it, believed it and leave it. I gave her five shillings and hurried out of the Close.

Lawrence MacMarr. What, I wondered, would have been the effect of the statement I had just heard on other Edinburgh folk of my acquaintance. Some of the older people, those of my parents' generation, would, I think, have been profoundly shocked; not so much at the old woman's voluntary defamation of her long-defunct chastity as at the thought that Lawrence MacMarr could have ever had a mistress, let alone one drawn from such a class. Some of my own generation, or those a little bit younger than I am, would have been, in an equally tiresome way, delighted. They would have cross-questioned the old woman, worried the last detail out of her, and have written the whole thing up in a psycho-analytical way in some up-to-date journal devoted to denigration of the idols of the past. And what about the very young? The sad thing is, I think, that they would just not have been interested at all. But they would have been wrong; and I am fairly sure that those who come after them, in a hundred years or so, will agree with me.

As I walked up the High Street I wondered whether the old woman could possibly be speaking the truth. I made a rapid calculation of dates. Yes, it might be true. MacMarr had left Edinburgh about the middle nineties, and had died just after the turn of the century in the South of France. And from what one knew of his life in Edinburgh it was not improbable that .... I hesitated, and almost turned round to go back and talk to my old friend in the Close. But no, it was better to leave things as they were. If ever a statement was self-sufficient hers was. I walked on in the direction of Roy Crann's offices in George Street.

Lawrence MacMarr. What a stir his memory had made in the Edinburgh of my youth! What a conflict of opinions had raged about him in the years that had passed since then! He died in the year before I was born, but I have the fancy that I am one of the not very large number of his fellow-citizens who understand him, appreciate him at his true worth, neither idolizing nor contemptuous of him. I rather think that my view of him is the one that posterity will take (if it takes one at all), for, by the accident of my birth, childhood and youth in

Edinburgh during the early part of this century, I became aware of Lawrence MacMarr just between the two waves of opinion about him—adulation and denigration.

Lawrence MacMarr was one of those strange freaks that are thrown up by the Scottish genius once every hundred years, freaks that now and again touch the hem of the garment of international greatness. He really was an astonishing and fascinating creature. Born of an Edinburgh middle-class family, and intended by his parents for the pursuit of some ordinary Edinburgh profession, he had early displayed a remarkable versatility and industry in the arts, and, so one is led to believe, to a lesser degree in the sciences. It was this versatility that, in the high noon of his post-mortem popularity, had earned him, amongst his most reckless Edinburgh admirers, the ridiculous soubriquet of 'The Scottish Leonardo da Vinci'.

It is true, however, that like Leonardo he is, and probably will be, most remembered by his paintings. Apart from those in private collections, there are two of his paintings in the National Gallery of Scotland, two in the Tate, and a number in galleries in the United States, where, twenty years ago, there was a great vogue for him. He was much under the influence of the French Post-Impressionists, but if his style derived from then there was something not only in his subjects but his manner that was highly individual and national. You feel, when you look at even one of his least significant works, that it is painted by a Scotsman and that that Scotsman is undoubtedly Lawrence MacMarr.

It is the same, but only more so, with his poetry and verse. Here, too, the influence of Baudelaire, Verlaine and the rest of them is felt. But there is something about the delicate vigour in his choice and use of English words and rhythms that shows that it is a Scotsman who is using them. Now and again, too, he bursts out into the use of the Scots tongue in his lyrics with an effect that is almost, but not quite, Burnsian in its quality.

His prose, by which he is less well known, has for me a little too rigid and Latin a flavour about it. It was in the lyric, expressed either in paint or verse, that he was at his most successful. I have heard that he was a skilful musician, but have no more evidence of this than the existence of two or three quite pleasant settings of his own verse. He studied science at Edinburgh University. And the scientists, in their own arid phraseology, tell me that some of his post-graduate work there was 'quite useful.'

Despite all this, Edinburgh did not think very much of him when he lived there; and it was only after he had left Scotland, had died in

France, and had through his paintings achieved a measure of international reputation, that the people of his native city woke up to the fact of Lawrence MacMarr. Once having woken up, they certainly made up for their neglect. Articles, criticisms, reminiscences and imitations filled the Press and Journals. Halls were crowded to hear lectures on him and his works. For a brief period it might have seemed that Raeburn, Scott, Stevenson and Burns were all cast into the shade. And Edinburgh took all the credit.

Then, after the War of 1914, the reaction set in. His very talents were selected for derision. In an age of specialization his versatility was dismissed a superficial. His industry, at a time when slipshod writing and slapdash painting were the fashion, was sneered at by clever writers from London as being more craft that art. And Edinburgh sat back, a little shocked and surprised.

As with his work, so with his private life. MacMarr, like many men condemned to die early, had a strong gusto for life. He took it where he found it. Mingled with his native puritanism was a powerful dash of what it was then fashionable to call *La nostalgie de la boue*. The public-houses, dance halls and places of less savoury reputation in Leith Walk had known him well at one time. All this was conveniently forgotten as soon as he was dead and famous. Humanity has a passion to model its heroes of the moment after itself. It makes its gods in its own image; and there is no use complaining about it. It is the inevitable fate of any artist to be made, if only temporarily, into a plaster saint as soon as he becomes popular. Be that as it may, there must have been some who smiled to hear Lawrence MacMarr's sayings quoted with approval from a dozen Edinburgh pulpits and his less felicitous 'verse prayers' collected together into a volume that practically amounted to a manual of devotion. I do not say that these utterances and writings of his were not genuine: they certainly represented one side of the man. All I do say is that there must have been some who perhaps excusably smiled when they heard or saw them.

The reaction to this too set in. For my part I found it much more irritating and tiresome than the process of whitewashing, which was, at least, an innocent if muddle-headed pursuit. With truffle-nosed industry the C.I.D. of the post-1918 literary world plunged into Leith Walk, London and Paris, returning with (to them) rich prizes in the shapes of salacious and vinous anecdotes. This time Edinburgh did not sit back, but sat up shocked and surprised.

However, the great healer set to work, and, by the time at which the history that I am recounting begins, those who cared for

Lawrence MacMarr as an artist and a man had begun to see him in something of a true perspective. The controversy was over and, after his own not quite first-class fashion, MacMarr had begun to join posterity.

Apart from anything else, it really had been an extraordinary coincidence that the old woman in the Close had mentioned MacMarr's name to me. For the last twenty-four hours he had been much in my mind, having been absent from it for a long period. Coming up in the train from London the day before I had been reading a book which had been sent to me for review. It was called *Lawrence MacMarr—A Garland of Remembrances*. It was a voluminous collection of MacMarriana by a certain Miss Prudence Muir, who, years before, I had known in Edinburgh. Miss Muir, so she informed us in her preface, had as a young girl in Edinburgh met MacMarr. After his death she had devoted her life to collecting unpublished anecdotes and reminiscences of her hero. These, with the assistance of many pens from all corners of the globe, she had collected together in her 'Garland'. She now published them 'in defence of the fair name of the great Scottish painter and poet'. It must have taken her about forty years to compile. It was an astonishing monument of industry and piety.

Despite the somewhat excessive odour of lavender and forget-me-not that seemed to hang about its pages the book was, to me, quite interesting. And so, despite some rather severe memories I had of Miss Muir when I had been a young man in Edinburgh, I determined to give the book a good review. After all, I could quite honestly praise its interest, its industry and its piety. I had just finished it when a peculiar little incident occurred.

We were leaving Berwick, and had just crossed the line which marks the Border between Scotland and England. I had noticed earlier on an elderly taciturn man of the Edinburgh lawyer type who was sitting opposite me. As we crossed the Border he suddenly spoke:

'We're in Scotland now.'

'I'm very glad to hear it,' I said.

Having broken the ice the elderly man went on:

'I see you're reading a book about Lawrence MacMarr. I once met him.'

'Really, sir? That's very interesting. Are you one of the contributors to this book?'

'I said I *once* met him. Once was quite enough. I never wished to see him again.'

'Indeed, sir?' I said. 'Why?'

'He came to my aunt's house in Drummond Place to dinner. But he was obviously in liquor when he arrived *before* dinner. He was unable to come down from the drawing-room to the dinner-table. He had to be sent home in a cab.'

'That must have been very awkward.'

'It was disgusting.'

No further remarks were made until we got to Edinburgh, where my companion bade me good night. For a moment I had toyed with including this anecdote in my review of the book. But I quickly dismissed it from my mind. I had no very pleasant memories of Miss Muir's treatment of me years ago, but that seemed no justification for a public and ill-mannered gibe such as including this incident in my review would be.

And now on the top of this there had come this adventure in MacGregor's Close. I stepped on my way to Roy's office rather more quickly. It was too good a story to waste. I looked forward to telling it to him.

When I got to the offices of the St Ninian's Society in George Street I was kept waiting in the hall outside Roy's office for ten minutes. This affectation of Roy's (for I felt sure it was an affectation to make himself appear more important in my eyes) never failed to irritate me. He had practised it every time I had called on him. Now, when I really did want to see him, it had the effect of considerably lowering the temporary warmth of feeling for him that I had succeeded in arousing. When at length I was ushered into his room he rose with an air of gaunt abstraction from a table on which maps and plans were scattered in a manner which I could not help feeling had been prepared. He adjusted his large horn-rimmed spectacles and, with the genial smile of the busy man who is good enough to spare a few moments of his time, greeted me.

'Ah, so you've come to see what we've been doing.'

'Yes, Roy. I've had a glance at some of the suppurating wounds on the body of our mother-city on which you have been spreading your antiseptic.'

Roy did not quite like this.

'Oh, ah, I see what you mean. What have you had a look at?'

'I've seen MacGregor's Close. You've done an extraordinarily good job there, Roy. Honestly you have.'

Roy sat back, and put the tips of his fingers together in a Gothic vane.

'Yes, we took a good deal of trouble over that. I think we succeeded. We cleaned it right up, but we managed to preserve everything essential from the old place.'

'Including the essential smell.'

'Oh, you noticed that, did you? It's a nuisance, but we can't do anything about it. The architect thinks it's something to do with the earth underneath.'

'I confess to a slight feeling of relief that even you can't change the quality of the earth.'

Roy smiled his wintry smile, but said nothing; so I went on: 'And there are other things that remain there too. I met an astonishing old woman who sells shoe-laces and matches at the corner of the Close.'

Roy shook his head disapprovingly.

'Yes, we didn't like to clear off all the old people at once. But they'll soon die off.'

'Well, I strongly advise you to get hold of this old woman before she dies off.'

'Why?'

'She claims with some vigour, and with a ring of truth in her voice, that she was the mistress of Lawrence MacMarr.'

I used the stronger, more vivid Scottish phrase. I saw Roy obviously wince.

'What has that to do with me?' he asked.

'You ought to get her to deliver a lecture to the St Ninian's Society.'

Roy pursed his lips in genuine disapproval.

'Oh, I wouldn't dream of doing such a thing.'

I had not, of course, made the suggestion completely seriously. But something in Roy's tone and attitude so irritated me that I gave wings to my fantasy and went on:

'Why ever not? If you could resuscitate Jean Armour you wouldn't hesitate to get her to give a lecture on Burns. A hundred years from now, if the St Ninian's Society is still in existence, members would pay a hundred guineas to hear what this old lady had to say—if they could bring her alive again.'

Roy thought for a moment. Then, with an air of conspiracy he said, in a lowered voice:

'We might arrange with the B.B.C. to get her voice recorded and locked away. But it would be rather awkward with the Director . . . .'

'I've got an even better idea, Roy. She's very old. Give her five pounds for the use of her body after she's dead. She'd probably drink herself dead at once on the money, so you wouldn't have long to wait for your money's worth. Then you could get her stuffed, and put in the hall here in a glass case with a notice under it "This was the mistress of Lawrence MacMarr." You might include some lines from *Ae Fond Kiss*, or a verse or two of MacMarr's own poem to Jeannie.'

Roy's face was now a sight to behold, but I went on:

'It would, apart from the local interest, be the most poignant reminder to members of your society that "Beauty vanishes, Beauty passes." That is to say, if any of them need reminding of it.'

Roy could stand no more.

'I think that's the most disgusting idea I have ever heard of,' he said.

'I'm sorry Roy,' I apologized. 'But when will you dear fellow-citizens of mine learn to distinguish between fact and fantasy?'

'I'm glad to hear you did not mean the suggestion seriously,' Roy replied, still looking at me acidly.

'No, I did not,' I said, as I took my leave.

As I wandered down from George Street into Princes Street I found myself, I am afraid, in an unwarrantable state of petulance. By now I ought long ago to have learned to accept certain facets in the Edinburgh mentality as inevitable and not to have bothered about them. But there was something in Roy Crann's extravagantly prosaic Edinburgh attitude that had ruffled me—perhaps it was because he was not an Edinburgh man.

When I was walking along Princes Street towards my hotel in Charlotte Square I passed a big bookshop. One entire window was completely full of copies of Prudence Muir's *Garland of Remembrances*. It was the sight of this window that evoked a long-dead memory in me and prompted me to a foolish and ill-mannered action.

In a flash I was back twenty-odd years in time. I, a shy, eager youth, reputed to be interested in literary matters, had been kindly asked to one of Miss Prudence Muir's literary at-homes in her house in Queen Street. Even at that date Miss Muir was something out of Edinburgh's literary past. She had grown enormously fat, but preserved a fashion of dressing which allowed women to be fat and still keep their dignity. She was also large in build and had a swarthy complexion and a hooked nose. Altogether an alarming person. She ruled her salons with the authority that Queen Victoria used to exercise over her Court. Her literary productions had up till then been slight; but it was always with a shock of surprise that one recollected that this commanding personality had been the authoress of such fragrant fragments.

On the evening which I recalled there were about a dozen people present. Some were nondescript; some were those subfuse eccentrics which Edinburgh manages to produce each decade. The

266

conversation, as it always did at these gatherings, eventually came round to Lawrence MacMarr. I was then thrilled to hear for the first time authentic stories about the great man which have since become familiar to me. I longed to contribute something to the discussion. Then there was a pause, and the moment came. I remembered seeing in some French paper some mildly interesting reminiscences of the short time when MacMarr was studying in Paris in the Quartier Latin. It was, therefore, with no *arrière-pensée* that I said:

'I believe some very interesting stuff could be collected about the Bohemian side of MacMarr's life.'

Yes, the innocent epithet Bohemian was the word I used, but there was no doubt of the construction placed upon it by the literary salon and its queen. There was an audible silence. Then she spoke:

'I always think that those who mention that side of poor Lawrence's life are a trifle unnecessary.'

As I write these words they do not appear particularly oppressive. At the time, in the manner, and in the circumstances in which they were uttered, they were devastating. I was at the age of eighteen damned, cast into literary outer darkness, for ever dismissed as a 'trifle unnecessary.'

It was only when I had made my escape from Queen Street that I fully realized what Miss Muir had been driving at. Even that did not diminish my discomfort and anger. Why should one side of MacMarr's life, which had gone to his making as a man and an artist, be the subject of an absolute taboo? I agreed that those who dwelt upon it did so from prurient or stupidly iconoclastic motives. Was it not a sign of an equally prurient mind to pretend that it had never existed? Why had I not had the courage to say so? How humiliated, how angry I was!

All this had happened more than twenty years ago. Yet the sight of that well-stocked window in the Princes Street bookshop brought it all before me again with painful distinctness. There was only one difference now. I had the courage of my opinions. Had I not been so exacerbated by the morning's proceedings, however, I do not think I would have behaved as badly as I did.

I turned in to my hotel in Charlotte Square where I was staying. I took a sheet of notepaper and wrote the following letter:

Dear Miss Muir, You may not remember it, but years ago you were kind enough to receive me at your monthly literary gatherings. For my part, I have the liveliest recollections of the discussions and arguments we had, particularly about Lawrence MacMarr. I have just been reviewing your book for—and have devoted what skill I have with my pen to praising its industry and its piety. I hope the review will please you.

By a strange coincidence I met, upon my return to Edinburgh today, someone who claims to have known Lawrence MacMarr well, whose memoirs, however, do not appear in the pages of your book. Should you be contemplating a second edition I feel that you might care to include what she has to say: and I would be only too pleased to arrange an introduction.

She is an old lady who sells matches and shoe-laces at the corner of MacGregor's Close. My talk with her was of the briefest. Nevertheless what she said seemed to me to have the ring of truth about it. Her Scots is broad, antique and vigorous. But I feel sure that you, who are so great an amateur of our native Doric, will have no difficulty in understanding her.

She says (and since I am writing in English I will put what she said into English, though she expressed it much more forcibly), she says that she was the mistress of Lawrence MacMarr. Believe me, yours very sincerely,

Moray McLaren

No sooner had I posted the letter in the large post office opposite the hotel than I was seized with remorse. I would have given a sovereign to have recalled it. Almost I contemplated going into the post office and trying to get it back. But I knew that would be no good. What an ill-mannered, foolish, wanton thing to have done. What a needless insult to an inoffensive old lady. If I had outgrown my youthful timidity I did not appear to have outgrown my gaucherie. A little later I did my best to excuse myself. After all was it so wanton? The Fates in making me meet in twenty-four hours the old lawyer in the train, the old lady of the Close and finally Roy Crann had clearly pointed the way. I had but obeyed. It was the best excuse I could offer myself.

Two mornings later as I was dressing I wondered if there would be a reply for me when I came down to breakfast. Once again I tried to palliate my offence. After all, I had not used the old woman's words, I had only said 'she says she was the mistress of Lawrence MacMarr.' In these days that would not pass for a very strong remark.

On my breakfast-table there was only one communication for me. It was a postcard in the thin Italianate hand which I now remembered over the years:

Moray McLaren, Esquire,
at The —— Hotel,
Edinburgh

I paused for half a minute before I turned it over. When I did so I received the most stunning rebuke I have ever had administered to me. Whether Miss Muir had been stung by jealousy or by my ill manners into what would have been for her a fantastic falsehood, or whether she calmly produced on a postcard a secret over half a century old I do not know. In either event it was a knock-out for me.

On the other side of the postcard above her signature there were written only three words:

So was I.

Sir Thomas Beecham
The Edinburgh Festival
1949

The Edinburgh International Festival, whose first director was Rudolf Bing (afterwards knighted), was born in 1947, and two years later Sir Thomas Beecham (1879–1961) arrived to conduct Berlioz's King Lear, *having announced in Glasgow in February 1948 that 'The people of Scotland are damned fools to throw away £60,000 on a musical festival'. Beecham was conducting the Royal Philharmonic Orchestra which he had formed in 1946. The son of the millionaire baronet who invented Beecham's pills, Sir Thomas could afford to indulge himself. Among other things, he conducted the Hallé Orchestra at the age of 20 and introduced the Russian ballet to London in 1911. This press conference was reported in the* Scotsman *on 22 August 1949. The music critics replied in kind, accusing Beecham of choosing a piece of the 'banality' of the Berlioz to throw his own virtuosity into sharper relief.*

RECLINING IN THE DEPTHS of an armchair in the artists' room at the Usher Hall yesterday, where he had been rehearsing the Royal Philharmonic Orchestra for three hours, Sir Thomas Beecham, in shirt-sleeves, braces, and flannel trousers, told about 20 representatives of the Press that he was not going to criticise anything or anybody.

"I am going to have a pleasant time," he said. "This is my holiday. On Tuesday, I go 100 miles into Scotland where nobody else goes."

"Do you feel it an honour or a privilege to be playing in the Edinburgh Festival now?" he was asked.

"Good God, no," retorted Sir Thomas. "It is an honour and a privilege to the Festival for me to come here. This is about the 390th festival in which I have taken part. It seems to be a very nice affair, and if so, it is entirely due to my friend, Mr Bing."

The Edinburgh Festival, he ventured, should not be dependent on a "dubious organisation" like the Arts Council. It should be a Scottish affair entirely. Asked if he thought the Festival should have a central theme, he declared: "Who wants a one-man festival any longer? No man living is worth a festival to himself. That is what ruins these things. These things are dead."

His reply to a question concerning the 1951 Festival of Britain was:

"You mean that exhibition? I consider it the most monumental piece of imbecility and iniquity. We are broke. We have been misgoverned worse than any nation in the world for the last 50 years. One set of lunatics dragged us into the first world war without being prepared. We were dragged into the last war by another set of incompetent lunatics. And we are going to celebrate 50 years of the most abominable misgovernment at the expense of the United States of America. That is an achievement for you."

Sir Thomas was resting after his exertions on the rostrum when the Press representatives were shown into his room. With a cigar between his fingers and a glass of ginger ale on the table at his side, he spoke forcefully and freely for about half-an-hour in reply to questions.

The first query concerned comments which Sir Thomas made on Edinburgh's Festival in the early days of the undertaking. He denied that he had ever criticised the Festival as such. At the beginning, he said, he had questioned the advisability of holding what he thought to be a stunt in preference to tackling seriously the problem of having a Scottish orchestra. When the Festival was eventually organised and proclaimed he saw it was something quite different to what he had anticipated.

"Kindly make this clear. If you don't I shall write to your editors," he told the newspapermen, emphasising the point with a wave of his cigar.

"It was a serious artistic endeavour, likely to stimulate the whole musical population of Scotland and to increase appreciation of the value of good orchestral playing. Therefore, I began to see that something good might come of it."

Sir Thomas mentioned his very great objection to taxpayers providing money for musical enterprises. In the first place, we had not got the money and therefore, as we could not afford our necessities, it followed that we could not afford our luxuries. The Americans were paying for about a quarter of our necessities and, therefore they were paying for all our luxuries.

"They are paying for our music and they are about to make one godammed row about it," he said.

"On the first Festival about £21,000 was lost. The last Festival cost about £11,000. I am told there is a fair chance of the present Festival even paying its way, and therefore I rejoice. I also hope and I damn well expect that all those hundreds of thousands of people who are coming to this Festival will realise and get it into their addled heads that you have got to have a first-rate Scottish orchestra equal to anything that comes into this town. If you don't get it, the greatest use and value of the Festival goes."

Sir Thomas fastened on an American lady member of the company: "Are you taking this in, Madam?" When she assured him that she was, he observed: "Well, you put in what I say about American money. We can't pay for raw materials. How do you think we are paying for music and national theatres? Bah! The country's gone to pot. Nobody has got any moral sense. I haven't got much myself. Maybe a little more than most people. Ask me another question."

Commenting that many foreign orchestras got money from their Governments, Sir Thomas asked the Press representatives if they realised that the Royal Philharmonic did not get a farthing from the Government or the Arts Council.

When a foreign journalist asked him about the association of the orchestra with the Arts Council, Sir Thomas said it was for tax redemption only. "Not one penny do we get from them" he said, "and to hell with the Arts Council."

Sir Thomas was obviously in good fettle. Someone asked him whether he felt that, if the loss on the Edinburgh Festival was somewhat less this year, it would be because the Festival had established a record of good music.

"How can anyone establish a record of good music," he retorted. "We have all been making good music for 100 years and more. What are you talking about? Don't you think there was good music here before the Edinburgh Festival? I presume you know what you do mean, so ask me the question again."

He was then asked if he thought the standard was higher.

"I don't know whether it has improved. There are orchestras here which play tolerably well. Some of the ballet companies disport themselves on the stage with fair propriety of movement. This is my first visit."

Regarding his stay in Edinburgh, he said he was going to the opera to-night and hoped to see a play or two later.

"The other orchestras I am familiar with. I never go to concerts other than my own. I find my own are unpleasant enough without listening to others which I am sure are worse."

Later he remarked: "The good thing about the Festival is that it almost invariably interests a large number of people by the publicity and general high standard of performances. These are people who would not otherwise be roused. It is also very popular among the shopkeepers."

It was then that he urged the Festival to be independent of the Arts Council. "The shopkeepers will pay for the thing," he suggested. "Why be allied to an English organisation? I'm all in favour of Scottish Home Rule."

Norman MacCaig
Edinburgh Spring
1954

Norman Alexander MacCaig was born in 1910 and educated at Edinburgh University, where he has since been writer in residence as at many other universities in Britain and North America. The author of many volumes of poetry, he included the present work, which he ascribes to 1954, in his Riding Lights (1955). As schoolmaster and as poet, he has been essentially a classicist.

I WALK my paint-box suburb. The clear air
Is flecked with green and ultramarine and rose.
The wind hangs nursery rhymes on branches;
The sun leans ladders against the apple trees.

And all my defence against the advancing summer
Is to trim hedges, gush the gutters sweet,
Tie the doomed rose against the wall
And watch myself being young and innocent.

Trams from my innocence thunder by like suns
Through my familiar city to where I know
Slatternly tenements wait till night
To make a Middle Ages in the sky.

A buzzing gas-lamp there must be my rose
Eating itself away in the ruined air
Where a damp bannister snakes up and
Time coughs his lungs out behind a battered door.

There craggy windows blink, mad buildings toss
Dishevelled roofs, and dangerous shadows lean,
Heavy with centuries, against the walls;
And Spring walks by ashamed, her eyes cast down.

She's not looked at. O merry midnight when
Squalid Persepolis shrugs its rotting stone
Round its old bones and hears the crowds
Weeping and cheering and crying, 'Tamburlaine'.

Tom Nairn
Festival of the Dead
1967

Tom Nairn was born in 1932 in Freuchie, and graduated M.A. in philosophy from Edinburgh University in 1956. He has been a member of the editorial board of the New Left Review *since 1962, and has held various academic posts in Britain and Europe. A tough Marxist critic of British anti-internationalism and Scottish parochialism, he published* The Left Against Europe? *in 1972 and* The End of Britain *in 1978. His positive criticism of Scottish nationalism, initially expressed in highly adverse essays, played a major part in the rethinking of Scottish Nationalism in the 1970s and he proved the most radical proponent of Scottish devolution during the debate up to 1979. The present essay appeared in the* New Statesman *on 1 September 1967.*

THIS IS THE 21st EDINBURGH FESTIVAL. A time for serious questions, as the *Scotsman* reminds us from its pulpit. More Drama, or less, within the overall glory of the thing? Will Lord Provost Brechin and his cronies cut the Festival Grant by one third next year, to celebrate the majority in the proper Presbyterian style? Time even to revive the hoariest nut of all: when, how will this songless city get its own Opera House?

Huddled in the dense gentility of the Festival Club on a Sabbath afternoon, to the rhythmic strains of that genuine voice of bourgeois Edinburgh, the Freda Winston String Trio, dreadful doubts assail one. The sour anglicised whine of these polite cultural exchanges in the Edinburgh tongue puts such questions into much better perspective than the *Scotsman* can. Behind the appalling artificial waterfall and a thousand carefully-poised teacups, a truly serious question is forced upon one: what *is* this Festival, after 21 years, what has it become? The answer is: it was Culture, it has become Scotland. It has not merely succeeded; it has turned fatally and permanently into another Scottish Thing, another structural element in the tiresome fantasy-life the Scots have been doping themselves with for the past three centuries to avoid their real problem. Festival time in Edinburgh seems to have joined tartanry, militarism, Burns and Scott—those 'mummied housegods in their musty niches', as Edwin Muir put it—as a constituent of the Great Scottish Dream.

The Scottish Dream is a function of the Scottish Neurosis. This collective neurosis was brought about in the 18th century by the partial suppression of Scottish nationhood in the Union Treaty of 1707. Nationality is of course the 'normality' in relation to which the basis of modern Scottish history must appear as pathology. Whatever its limitations—these are more evident every day now, and this fact is of importance to the Scots—the nation was the necessary framework of society throughout this time. Deprival of it inflicted an intolerable strain upon the Scots, and there has never been a real solution to the problem; consequently, there had to be a fantasy solution to make the situation tolerable, a dream-nationhood to take the place of the real one. A very great part of modern Scottish culture, and almost all of Scottish Nationalism has been poisoned at the root by this obsessive need. Essentially, it has been a magic incantation to raise the dead, a spell to recreate that whole social culture which—already deeply compromised and unsure of itself after the Reformation and the departure of the Stuart court—was finally decapitated in 1707.

A certain sense of identity, the convergence of thoughts and feelings around certain ideas, certain themes or attitudes, is a normal part of national society. The conditions of modern Scotland destroyed this self-image. The dilemma of the Scots has been to feel (again in Muir's words) that

> we are a people; race and speech support us, ancestral rite and custom, roof and tree .... And something that, defeated, still endures

but to have lost all idea of *what* people they really are. Some societies could perhaps survive the loss of statehood, the political means to construct their own destiny. The precarious and bloody earlier history of Scotland made it absolutely vital to preserve these means. Hence, the loss of them was an insufferable void, and Scottish cultural history is the dismal record of the attempts to escape from this void—either by literal escape to the south, or by fantasy-escape, a peopling of the emptiness with romantic shadows. This is why Scotland was so significant within European romanticism, as both subject and creator of myths: by its situation, it was made for the romantic posture. And to this day, a profoundly false, wish-fulfilling nostalgia remains the characteristic Scottish emotion.

The worst part of this insoluble problem lay in what *was* genuinely inherited and preserved, as the 'something that endures'. By and large, it was the odious hell-religion of Scottish Calvinism which endured, and still endures as the cultural substratum of the country.

The three-week Festival is exactly like an interminable church fête in atmosphere. People comment ceaselessly upon how little effect it has had upon the real, continuing life of the city—but what do they expect? The soil Scotland offers to this fragile festive culture is mildewed religiosity a mile deep, and what could thrive in this? Edinburgh's soul is bible-black, pickled in boredom by centuries of sermons, swaddled in the shabby gentility of the Kirk—what difference could 21 years of Festival make to this? In Edinburgh the iron age of Calvinism has long since turned into rust, and it is this rust which chokes and corrodes the eye and the ear.

The crisis of identity was rendered permanent—and even more insoluble—by the total impossibility of accepting the Kirk as a national self-image. Every human being provided with a minimum of intelligence and sensibility has recoiled from this idea, as from a sentence of death. But the Kirk *was* reality. Consequently, in Scotland the real must become unreal, and the unreal be seen at all costs as real—to state the matter frankly, the Scots Neurosis is absolutely incurable.

In Waverley Market there is an exhibition commemorating the 200th anniversary of Edinburgh's Georgian 'New Town'. Here one can study the plans for this Heavenly City of the 18th-century philosophers. Although the Nationalists naturally mention these giants in their trumpetings, they fail to see that this was in its day simply the most positive and brilliant escape from the tragedy of being Scottish. The great intellects of the New Town held elocution classes to expel dialect from their speech and Craig's 1767 plan refers to Edinburgh as 'the Ancient Capital of North-Britain'. The driving impulse of this great era was escape from the particularity of Scotland, on to the plane of the Universal—to an abstract truth and a cosmopolitan culture-owing nothing to their origins. In this moment of grandeur, Scotland discovered the right way of not being herself. When these conditions changed, and Romanticism took their place, she ws doomed. Doomed to being merely herself; that is, to the intolerable contradictions mentioned.

Of course this had already been prepared during the Edinburgh Enlightenment itself, by the revived interest in popular and folk culture. The search for the past had already begun, in the time of Robert Burns's success, and was swollen to chronic dimensions by Walter Scott. Scotland had found herself. This, not the bracing intellectual monuments of the Golden Age, was the definitive formula—the dream from which Scotland never recovered.

Now as ever, the only really popular part of the Festival is the Military Tattoo staged on the esplanade of Edinburgh Castle. Massed

277

on this dominating height, the folk who have assembled from every part of Scotland turn their solid backs on the Music and Drama, and enjoy themselves. Intellectuals who slink in in search of High Camp will be richly punished. But they had better be prepared to join in the vociferous choruses of *Abide with me* and stand bolt upright for *The Queen*. This corking spectacle begins with massed pipes and drums, and mounts up colourfully with swelling enthusiasm through every known level of corniness to the great climax of the lone, spot-lit piper puffing a tearful farewell on the battlements.

This culture and its profound popularity reflect the most important footnote added to the Tartan Ideology after Scott. Within the context of an expanding English imperialism, the Scots discovered another sub-identity, as the pioneers and military servants of the Empire. They were not merely exploited into this role—they avidly appropriated it, as another solution to the perennial problem of how to exist.

Nowadays of course, the Nationalist intellectuals have to dismiss this in the way they have always dismissed the Kirk. That is, too easily. They fail to observe that the really ugly truth of the spectacle lies less in its hideous content than in its semantic relationship to reality. The dream *works*. The utter feebleness of Scottish political Nationalism is the consequence of this: political Nationalism in Scotland is a contradiction in terms, everyone feels this, and hence the subject is a joke.

In Milne's Bar, the crowds of poets come and go among the portraits of MacDiarmid, Goodsir Smith, MacCaig and the other heroes. The prominent part of alcohol in the National spiritual life is well-known. The function of the mental whisky that also flows at Milne's is less appreciated: poetry. Next to tartan and soldiers, poetry is the greatest curse of contemporary Scotland. It is the intellectuals' special form of dope, which they can indulge in with a good conscience while the crowds go mad up on the Castle esplanade.

The meaning of the extraordinary prevalence of poetry in modern Scottish literature is evident. Prose is too risky. After Scott's fantasies, Scotland parted company with the great mainstream of the European novel: this was a developing tradition of realism, based on the dialectical exploration of appearance and reality in society. Scottish society could not face this kind of exposure. Here, precisely where speech is needed, there is a zone of silence, guarded by the ceaseless babble of versifying. Poetry, which ought to arise out of a prose culture, instead has to be a *substitute* for it, as in MacDiarmid. Poetry has to conjure up the national culture, as well as the nation itself, through an impossible, encyclopedic lyricism. Devoted to this false task, the poets actually fail to disturb the real, terrible silence of Scotland.

The crowds troop in nightly to see Pop Theatre Shakespeare and Molière, through the dank courtyard of the Church of Scotland's Assembly Hall, past the forbidding image of black Knox himself. As long as his tradition holds the tongue of Scotland in its grip, the sounds within the Hall will never have their proper resonance. This is the worst thing their twisted history has done to the Scots. Society is language; Scotland is silence.

The poet's wish is above all to burst through this heart of inarticulacy, to cry the Word which could restore all things whole. But the loss is far too deep for this. Presbyterianism appropriated the country's tongue and, merely by being what it is, killed it.

Scotland has no voice, and no present. This is the country of 'the dead, who lodge in us so strangely, unremembered, yet in their place', while the 'common heels' come and go 'And are content, with their poor frozen life and shallow banishment'. Yet even Muir, the poet who could feel these truths, could go on to state the problem in these words:

> For how can we reject
> The long last look on the every-dying face
> Turned backward from the other side of time?
> And how offend the dead and shame the living
> By these despairs?

This distinctive, hopelessly nostalgic feeling is itself a trap. For Scotland, reality and speech obviously lie somewhere on the other side of rejection. The offence of the dead and the shame of the living are conditions of sanity. Hope, as that well-known Scotsman R.D. Laing might well have put it, can only be beyond absolute despair.

'I find it hard to believe,' pomps Magnus Magnusson in the *Scotsman*'s centre page, 'that anyone could disagree that the Edinburgh International Festival has exalted Edinburgh into a real capital city after a lapse of centuries ....' Unerringly, he focuses upon the new element of delusion the Festival has permanently imported into Scottish life. Only a Scotsman who has suffered all, from the inside, and then despaired, can possibly measure the emptiness of these words.

Robert Nye
59x: A True Tale
1971

The Scotsman *initially published this story in 1974; it was reprinted in* The Hudson Review *in 1975, and most recently in Nye's* The Facts of Life and other fictions *(1983). Robert Nye was born in England in 1939, and has lived in Scotland and Ireland. He is a distinguished poet and critic: his novels* Falstaff *(1976),* Merlin *(1978) and* Faust *(1980) are extraordinary.*

MY FRIEND ARTHUR DODWELL, a man who notices such things, drew my attention a week or so ago to a catalogue of seventeenth, eighteenth, and nineteenth century books in English and French coming up for sale at Dowell's, the auctioneer's, in George Street, Edinburgh. The chief attraction in this catalogue—advertised, indeed, on its front cover—was a Ben Jonson folio containing besides Jonson's translation of Horace's *Ars Poetica* a number of his masques and his superb collections of original poems *Timber* and *Underwoods*. This excited me—but my friend Arthur yawned, and then pointed to Lot 91: *Candide, ou L'Optimisme, traduit de l'allemand de Mr le Docteur Ralph, 1759*.

Now, as every schoolboy knows, there never was a Doctor Ralph who needed translating from the German or anything else. *Candide* is by Voltaire. It was first published early in 1759. It was a clandestine publication but its author's indelible signature of style betrayed his identity on every page, and by February of that year the authorities in Paris and Geneva were already doing their best to supress it. They failed. By the end of 1759 no less than sixteen editions had poured from presses here and there—Amsterdam, Geneva, Paris, Rouen, London—and five English translations had also appeared, plus a sixth, undated, but probably 1759 as well.

So, here, as Arthur pointed out, we had an edition of *Candide*, beautifully bound in calf at the time of publication, with a decorated spine, its text perfect, its general condition excellent.

'Interesting,' I conceded, 'but what's the point of going for just one of sixteen first editions? Voltaire had a tricky mind. You know as well as I do that all of those 1759 books carefully omitted any indication as to the place of publication or even the identity of the printer. You could buy any of the sixteen and think you had a first—and in a way you would have.'

Arthur considered me with that specific pity he reserves for reviewers. 'Down on Dowell's shelf is *the* first edition,' he said. 'It was set up in type at the end of December 1758, by Marc-Michel Rey, and published either by him in Amsterdam, or by Robin in Paris, or through distributors in Rouen or Lyons, or even—and I favour this myself—by Nourse in London, who certainly worked from it in preparing the first English translation and so had the privilege of introducing *Candide* to these islands in two languages.'

We were strolling down the Mound. The sun shone on the statue of John Knox in the courtyard of New College. Knox, however, was holding up his hand as if he expected rain.

'I will allow,' I said,'that in the British Museum catalogue of printed books there is a lovely square bracket against their very first copy of *Candide*, and that in the bracket there is a question-mark followed by the word London and the date 1759. But how can you be so sure that our *Candide* in George Street is the first of the firsts?'

'A sneer ago,' said Arthur, 'you were telling me of Voltaire's tricky mind. Right?'

'Tricky like a fox,' I said.

'And you'll know he had a passion for revisions?'

'He was a stylist.'

'Very well,' said Arthur, producing a fat book from an inner pocket of his voluminous black coat. 'Put up your umbrella and consider this.'

'This' was a volume which I saw was intitled *Voltaire and 'Candide', a Study in the Fusion of History, Art, and Philosophy; with the text of the La Vallière manuscript of 'Candide'*, by Ira O. Wade, published by Princeton University Press, in 1959. As for the umbrella—Knox had been right. We sat down on the steps of the National Gallery and propped the umbrella between us as I turned the pages.

'Professor Wade,' Arthur said, lighting his pipe with an old ten shilling note (one of his eccentricities, he loves the new fifty pence pieces so much, because as he says it is always such a pleasure when you put your hand in your pocket and your fingers find the sharp edges mean that you are five times richer than you had thought), 'Professor Wade, a diligent American gentleman, had access to all the sixteen editions, and to the La Vallière manuscript of *Candide* in the Arsenal Library in Paris, where it had lain unnoticed since the eighteenth century, and—'

281

'Up the Arsenal,' I cried irrelevantly, as some Rangers supporters passed. 'What are these things here—fleurons?'

'You're improving,' said Arthur. 'Pretty, aren't they?' He shifted the umbrella to shield the vignettes of flowers and fruit reproduced in fine facsimile in the tome I now held across my knees. 'Now, listen. Our American agent took the trouble to go to the Institut at Geneva also, and confirm that there *are* minute differences between the sixteen editions.'

I was beginning to lose interest in the rain.'Go on,' I said.

'To cut a long story short,'Arthur said, with that severity which I have sometimes noticed in his own critical remarks upon new books, 'sit up tonight and burn the midnight oil and to hell with the energy crisis. Read first the facsimile of the La Vallière manuscript which Professor Wade includes. Then, if your eyes are no worse than usual, read from page 195 to page 238. That's chapter 4 of part 3,' he explained generously, 'and in it, by collating the evidence of all sixteen editions, the various cancellations, transpositions, and especially the variations within those fleurons, Professor Wade comes up with proof positive that Voltaire had a small trial edition made—an edition Wade calls 59x.'

'Reviewers get too much to read,' I said.

'I thought you liked your work?'

'I love it.'

'And you'd love it even more if I told you that Dowell's has 59x?'

I couldn't think of anything much to say so I blew my nose and smiled at a pigeon.

'Forget reading for a minute,' Arthur invited. 'Look at the pictures. In the vignettes between pages 238 and 239 in Wade you'll find a reproduction of the title page of the first edition of *Candide*—our friend 59x. Observe the extreme right-hand side of the middle of the fleuron.'

My companion took off his deer-stalker hat and handed me the magnifying glass which he keeps in it. Now, my own face has always been the true index of my mind and I must admit that I blushed at the sheer Sherlock Holmesery of this. It seemed to me speecially to be deplored since we were in public view and the statue of Allan Ramsey might even have seen us if he'd turned his head away from that steady contemplation of Australia House which is such a feature of his pastoral work in Princes Street. In any case, what Arthur now went on to point out could be seen readily enough with the naked eye.

'Extreme right middle. What do you notice?'

'A leaf. Much like the other leaves.'

'A leaf attached to the leaf below it?'

'Exactly.'

'What is so obliging about that leaf,' said Arthur, sucking at his pipe, 'is that in all subsequent editions it has turned into a butterfly.'

'You printer's devil,' I said.

'I mean that after edition 59x it is no longer attached to the leaf below it. It flies. It flutters. It is separated from the rest.'

'Arthur,' I said, 'no one will ever describe you as having eyes level with your head and ears not prominent, nor of being of a middling size, and a round, flesh-coloured visage. No one will ever describe you as being five feet five inches high and having a most sweet disposition.'

'I understand,' said Arthur, 'that you are pretty well acquainted with Dr Johnson's admirable translation of the book we are pursuing, and that you mean to intimate that I am not to be identified with the innocent Candide.'

'You remind me more of Deacon Brodie, Dracula, or Mr Hyde,' I said.

Arthur shrugged modestly. 'Cast your eyes now over the rod which runs through the centre of the fleuron on that title page,' he instructed. 'Do you see its extreme right-hand end?'

'A sort of squiggle?'

'In other editions it is a perfect knob,' said Arthur. 'Move your gaze across to the extreme left. You will perhaps perceive a slight fracture in the lower left leaf on that side.'

'Yes, I see it.'

'Later editions of 1759 mend that fracture.'

Arthur was knocking out his pipe on the step. I shut the Wade volume and handed it back to him reverently; then watched, fascinated, as it disappeared into his cavernous pocket. Arthur told me once that the black coat had been specially designed for him in his youth. His Foyle's Book-Stealing Coat, he called it.

I pointed my umbrella in the direction of Hanover Street.

'Let us arise and go now,' I suggested, 'and go to Dowell's fast.'

Arthur favoured me with a grimace.

'The trouble with you,' he said, 'is that your mind was raped by Yeats at an age when it should have been studying the small print in bibliographies.'

*

Arrived in the upper room where the 269 lots of books for auction were displayed upon the shelves, my friend Arthur reached down Lot 91 for me, and directed my attention to page 43. 'I will not burden you with the textual variants,' he promised, 'but do you see that wee island in the white space at the bottom of the emblem on that page?'

'It could be Innisfree,' I said. 'Or Cramond.'

'My boy,' murmured Arthur, 'the same thought may have occurred to Voltaire. For that or a better reason, he had it changed by the time of the second edition, where you will find *no island at all*, but two little boat-like blades of grass instead.'

I had a swift glance round to see if there were other book-fanciers in earshot. There were. But fortunately they seemed busy with the Ben Jonson folio, and with several volumes of prints, plates, and engravings which looked as though they might be suitable for flint-hearted antique dealers to tear apart with their fair bare hands, have framed, and sell to American tourists in the Grassmarket.

'Arthur,' I hissed, 'if what you're saying has even half a dram of truth in it, then this is definitely—I mean, here in Edinburgh we've found—'

'Count the dots round the shield in the centre of that fleuron,' commanded Arthur.

I counted them. 'Fifteen.'

'Voltaire had it changed to twelve for the second run,' my friend said. 'Now turn to page 213. Bit of a clincher, this.'

'But it's the same old island and the shield with fifteen dots,' I protested.

'In all subsequent editions,' explained Arthur patiently, 'you will find *another fleuron altogether* on that page. The fleuron, in fact, which appears on pages 146 and 193 in this edition, where again all the later fifteen have something else. Your myopic little eyes may also miss noticing that the trumpet on both 146 and 193 is a bit squashed-looking. Voltaire had the printer straighten it up before the second edition.'

Blinking, I took this precious *Candide* to the window and considered George Street. The pavements below were suddenly thronged with ghosts. There was Thomas De Quincey—a bottle of ruby-coloured laudanum in one pocket, a half-finished essay on Wordsworth in the other—dodging his creditors as he flitted towards Holyrood Palace and its sanctuary for those in debt. There was Robert Louis Stevenson staring at his own reflection and dreaming about doppelgangers as he stood before the window of Brunton's bookshop. Wilfred Owen and Siegfried Sassoon marched past, in perfect step, eyes ahead, each of them trying not to let the other notice him wince when a taxi back-fired. Lockhart came sauntering along with a little bearded woman on his arm: Maria Edgeworth. Burns was hurrying towards Milne's Bar in company with Dunbar and a bandaged Hugh MacDiarmid. Walter Scott and Byron were engaged in witty conversation with two policemen who had taken objection to the parking of their carriage. Sir Walter drew a writ. Byron drew a pistol.

Thin rain started to fall, half-snow in the late winter light of Edinburgh. The ghosts all vanished. Only the Bank of Scotland looked real. And the spires of St Mary's Episcopalian Cathedral—Barbara and Mary, called after the two spinster sisters who had paid for their building nearly a hundred years ago.

I turned back from the past and looked at Arthur, who was pretending to be interested in Lot 240; *US Fish Commission, Propagation of Food Fishes of the United States, a Report and Enquiry, Washington, 1886.*

'Mr Dodwell,' I said, 'trumpets and fleurons are all very fine. But it's the words that count.'

'Precisely,' whispered my friend, running his fingers appreciatively over a set of *The Boy's Own Paper, 1880–81* (Lot 197), and looking anywhere in fact except in the direction of that edition of *Candide* which now appeared to me to be glowing in my hands like a red-hot poker or a gift from the Angry Brigade. 'It's the words that count. And you have to count the words. Or, let's put it this way: you careless writer fellows don't, but the real hard workers, your printing friends, they'll tell you that they have a devil of a job of it when one of your crowd changes his mind or his adjectives just to the extent of a few words in his text. They have to stitch and patch and run on and the Lord knows what. And it's because of the counting of the words that you have those variations in the fleurons.'

'Eh?'

I must have looked blank. But Arthur was taking no notice of me, anyway. 'Voltaire liked to revise,' he murmured out of the side of his mouth, for all the world absorbed in close perusal of a *Boy's Own Paper.* 'He wasn't quite as bad as that bog Irishman you're always on about, James Joyce, but he certainly wanted his *mots* to be as *juste* as he could make them, and with a brain like his that was pretty *juste*. You follow? The revisions he made to the first edition necessitated the moving of typeface. Those fleurons weren't swapped for fun. The printer had to come to terms with the fact that he now had sometimes more, sometimes less space on a given page.'

'An example?' I said.

Arthur nodded, shutting his eyes. 'Only our first edition, only that 59x you are holding, has a paragraph beginning '*Mais il y a une raison*' six lines from the top of page 31. The La Vallière manuscript has it paragraphed thus. But for the second edition, Voltaire ran the sentence into the preceding one, with a semicolon before '*mais*' and no paragraphing at all.'

'Fascinating,' I said. 'Let me just check that. Page 31, was it?'

'Similarly,' droned Arthur, 'on page 41 you will find '*C'est une necessité que si un Univers existe, ce soit le meilleur des Univers.*' That corresponds with the manuscript as well. Later editions change it to the now proverbial "*Tout ceci ce qu'il y a de mieux.*"' He grinned, returning the wad of *Boy's Own Papers* to their place on the shelf. ' I say, am I boring you?' he enquired hopefully.

I had studied page 31. It was as Arthur said: a paragraph near the top beginning *Mais il y a une raison*. Now I turned to page 41. .

'Pages 84, 103, 125 and 242 will give you further evidence that this is Wade's 59x, the first edition of *Candide*,' hissed my friend.

'Because of verbal changes?'

'Changes and deletions,' Arthur said. '242 is my favourite. It has this paragraph about Homer and Milton, which Voltaire took out because—'

I snapped the book shut. 'OK,' I said. 'I understand revisions. It's the dots that stick in my throat.'

'What?'

'Those damned dots,' I complained. 'I can see the need to straighten out a squashed trumpet. But why change the number of dots round a stupid bloody shield?'

'The shield's all right,' Arthur said.

'So's Innisfree,' I said. 'So why remove it?'

'Innisfree?'

'Cramond. The little island. You told me he took that out and replaced it with blades of grass.'

'Correct,' said Arthur.

'OK,' I said. 'I suppose that could just about make sense for reasons of space. But twelve dots instead of fifteen! Around a shield! That makes no sense at all. Voltaire didn't help any printer by doing that, did he?'

Arthur shrugged.

'So why did he do it!' I demanded.

My voice had risen. I asked the question so loudly, I admit, that I almost caused a dedicated book-vandal to drop his collection of rippable plates of old Edinburth.

Arthur didn't answer me immediately. Instead, he winked, and then went and looked out of the window. Arthur never sees ghosts. He is not a troubled man. His mind is as clear as mine is cloudy. 'Traffic wardens,' he said. 'There's a *mot* there. An illegally parked Austin 1300. A carcase for vultures.'

When my friend turned from the window the sun spilled abruptly over his shoulder and his eyes were filled with good humour.

'Dots,' he murmured.

'Dots,' I said.

'Well,' he said, 'I don't know. I don't know why Voltaire changed the number of dots. But he did.'

'Perhaps,' I suggested, 'it was so that you could notice it?'

'Perhaps it was,' said Arthur.

He took the little leather-bound book from me and put it back on the shelf.

*

We attended the auction at Dowell's on the Monday. I got the Ben Jonson. Arthur got the *Candide*. My Jonson has twenty pages missing. I expect they will turn up soon in Glasgow's Barrowland or somewhere. Arthur thinks not. But then he is no optimist.

Donald Campbell
Betrayal in Morninside
1971

Donald Campbell was born in Wick in 1940, and educated in Edinburgh and London. He published his Poems in 1971, from which this is taken, and it has been followed by several other volumes. He has recently won celebrity as a playwright of remarkable insight and imagination, notably in his historical play The Jesuit, *concerning St John Ogilvie, martyred in 1615, and* The Widows of Clyth, *on the social consequences of a boating tragedy in his native Caithness.*

Embro my ain, ye are aye meant
tae be a city o middle-class douceness
    blue-nosed mediocrity
    bourgeois obtuseness
but
    (listen tae what I'm tellin ye!)
    The ither nicht
in the *Morninside* chippie
I was confrontit by nae fewer than ten
o the reuchest and the teuchest
o yer haurdest-haurd haurd men
    — and (O Gode!) hou I wished I was in Glasgow!